Meister Eckhart and the

Meister Eckhart and the Beguine Mystics

Hadewijch of Brabant, Mechthild of Magdeburg, and Marguerite Porete

Edited by
Bernard McGinn

Continuum • New York

1994
The Continuum Publishing Company
370 Lexington Avenue, New York, NY 10017

Printed in the United States of America

Library of Congress Cataloging-in-Publication Data

Meister Eckhart and the Beguine mystics : Hadewijch of Brabant,
   Mechthild of Magdeburg, and Marguerite Porete / edited by Bernard
   McGinn.
      p.   cm.
   Includes bibliographical references.
   ISBN 0-8264-0681-5 (alk. paper)
      1. Mysticism—History—Middle Ages, 600-1500.   2. Mysticism—
   Catholic Church—History.   3. Beguines.   4. Hadewijch, 13th cent.—
   Influence.   5. Mechthild, of Magdeburg, ca. 1212-ca. 1282—
   Influence.   6. Porete, Marguerite, ca. 1250-1310—Influence.
   7. Eckhart, Meister, d. 1327.   8. Catholic Church—Doctrines—
   History.   I. McGinn, Bernard, 1937- .
   BV5075.M45 1994
   248.2'2'09409022—dc20   94-13185
                                                            CIP

Contents

List of Abbreviations

DW and LW   *Meister Eckhart. Die deutschen und lateinischen Werke* (Stuttgart and Berlin: W. Kohlhammer, 1936–). This standard edition will be cited by volume and page. Individual abbreviations for the German works include:

> Pr.—*Predigt* (German Sermon)
> RdU.—*Die rede der underscheidunge* (*Counsels on Discernment*)
> Va.—*Von abegescheidenheit* (*On Detachment*)

Mirouer   *Marguerite Porete. Le Mirouer des simples ames.* Edited by Romana Guarnieri and Paul Verdeyen (Turnhoult: Brepols, 1986. *Corpus Christianorum. Continuatio Mediaevalis* LXIX).

List of Contributors

Paul A. Dietrich
University of Montana

Amy Hollywood
Dartmouth College

Maria Lichtmann
Berea College

Bernard McGinn
University of Chicago

Saskia Murk-Jansen
University of Cambridge

Michael Sells
Haverford College

Frank Tobin
University of Nevada, Reno

Richard Woods, O.P.
Loyola University, Chicago

Preface

This book grew from the converging lines of scholarly interest represented by the participants and shared by many others, inside and outside academic halls. Though the great Dominican theologian and mystic Meister Eckhart has long had a devoted readership, it is only within the past generation that renewed interest in the women writers of the Medieval Period has begun to uncover to a wide audience the riches to be found in the Beguine women studied in this volume—primarily Hadewijch, Mechthild, and Marguerite Porete.

Several years ago, Paul A. Dietrich of the University of Montana approached me with the idea of trying to collect a volume of essays dealing with Meister Eckhart and medieval women mystics. Given the extensive possibilities offered by such a project, we decided that it would be best to proceed by holding a conference of some sort devoted to the theme in order to see if the materials presented would be sufficiently original and interrelated to give promise of a coherent and useful volume. As an American representative and patron of The Eckhart Society, headquartered in England, I agreed to make such a proposal to the Center for Medieval Studies of Western Michigan University for possible inclusion at its annual International Conference on Medieval Studies. With the Center's approval and the encouragement of the Eckhart Society, we were able to sponsor two sessions devoted to "Eckhart and the Women Mystics" at the 28th International Medieval Conference held at Kalamazoo, Michigan, in May of 1993.

The essays contained in this volume are the revised forms of the papers given at these meetings. The introduction is a much-expanded version of remarks I gave at the first of the sessions, while the conclusion has been developed from a response made by Richard Woods to the second. The opportunity to hear each other's papers, to engage in ongoing discussion, and to revise and expand the essays in light of this experience has greatly aided the process of shaping the volume into an organized, if still necessarily exploratory, presentation of one of the most important new frontiers of medieval studies, the conversation between male and female theologians on the mystical goal of human living.

I would like to express my gratitude to the Continuum Publishing Company, especially to my friend and long-time editor Frank Oveis, for encouraging us to proceed with the task of making our research available to a wider audience. I also wish to thank all those whose support and efforts made the volume a reality—the contributors for their many efforts, as well as their patience; The Medieval Center at Kalamazoo for giving us an initial venue; and finally, The Eckhart Society for its support of contemporary efforts to spread Eckhart's message.

Bernard McGinn

Introduction

Meister Eckhart and the Beguines in the Context of Vernacular Theology

Bernard McGinn
University of Chicago, Divinity School

S ometime not long before 1290 the noted Paris scholastic theologian Henry of Ghent disputed the question: "Whether a woman can be a doctor of theology?"[1] After setting up a few typical arguments for and against, Henry's resolution, in good scholastic fashion, used a distinction to settle the issue. Women cannot officially (*ex officio*) serve as doctors of theology, because they cannot possess the four public marks of doctoral status (constancy, efficacy, authority, and effect). But Henry was too good a theologian to put a limit on the action of divine grace, so he continued: "Speaking about teaching from divine favor (*ex beneficio*) and the fervor of charity, it is well allowed for a woman to teach just like anyone else, if she possesses sound doctrine. But this should be done privately and in silence, not in public and before the church." He also restricted women's teaching "to other women and girls, not to men, both because their address might incite the men to lust (as they say), and also would be shameful and dishonorable to the men, as Jerome told Paulina."[2]

Henry's remarks may seem like patronizing patriarchalism to many today, but they do indicate an important shift taking place in the thirteenth century: the earliest large-scale emergence of women's voices in the history of Christian thought. Henry's comments prove that the Paris theologians were aware of the new role that women were taking in the intellectual life of Christianity. Some two decades after he wrote, on June 1, 1310, a woman named Marguerite Porete was publically burned to death as a relapsed heretic because she not only did not observe the limitations set

---

[1] Henry of Ghent, *Summae Quaestionum Ordinarium*, vol. 1 (Paris: Badius Ascensius, 1520: reprint, St. Bonaventure: The Franciscan Institute, 1953), Art. XI, quaest. 11, ff. 77v–78r.

[2] Ibid., fol. 78r: "Loquendo autem de docere ex beneficio et charitatis fervore, bene licet mulierem docere sicut & quemlibet alium si sanam doctrinam habeat: & privatim: & in silentio: & non in publico & in facie ecclesiae. . . . & hoc maxime mulieres alias & puellulas: viros autem non, tum quia sermo earum viros ad libidinem inflammaret, ut dictum est, tum quia est turpe & inhonestum viris, secundum quod Hieronymus ad Paulinam."

on women's teaching that Henry set down, but also because she was accused of departures from "sound doctrine." Paradoxically, this female teacher's book, *The Mirror of Simple Souls*, appears to have had a profound effect on one of the most noted scholastics of the day, the Dominican master of theology known as Meister Eckhart. The book continued to be read in French, Latin, English, and Italian versions in the later Middle Ages. Today it is being increasingly hailed as one of the most profound, if still controversial, works of speculative mysticism in the Christian tradition.[3]

Marguerite Porete was a Beguine, a woman who had adopted a free style of religious life that had grown in popularity in many areas in Europe from the end of the twelfth century.[4] Beguines (the exact meaning of the name is still in dispute) did not follow any of the traditional rules for the religious life—a fact which automatically made them suspect to many. Rather, women, and to a lesser extent men (called Beghards), came together in small groups, mostly in urban environments, to attempt to live lives of poverty, celibacy, prayer, and service, after the model of the Gospel. This is how Matthew Paris, an English Benedictine historian, reports on them in the early 1240s:

> At this time, especially in Germany, people of both sexes, but chiefly women, have called themselves "religious" and have adopted a religious profession, though a light one. They take private vows of celibacy and simplicity of life, though they don't follow the rule of any saint, nor submit to enclosure. Their number has increased so much in a brief time that two thousand or more are found in Cologne and the neighboring area.[5]

The Beguines were just one form, though arguably the most creative, of the important new styles of religious life adopted by women in the twelfth and thirteenth

---

[3] The first full translation of the *Mirror* into Modern English has only recently become available. See *Marguerite Porete, The Mirror of Simple Souls*, The Classics of Western Spirituality Series (New York-Mahwah: Paulist Press, 1993).

[4] For a brief account of the Beguines, see R. W. Southern, *Western Society and the Church in the Middle Ages* (Baltimore: Penguin Books, 1970), 319–31. In English, see also E. W. McDonnell, *The Beguines and Beghards in Medieval Culture, with Special Emphasis on the Belgian Scene* (New Brunswick: Rutgers University Press, 1954); and Robert E. Lerner, *The Heresy of the Free Spirit in the Later Middle Ages* (Berkeley: University of California Press, 1972), especially chaps. 2–3.

[5] Matthew Paris, *Chronica Majora*, ed. by Henry Richards Luard, vol. 4, Rolls Series (London: Longman, 1877), 278. "Eisdemque temporibus, quidam, in Alemannia praecipue, se asserentes religiosos, in utroque sexu, sed maxime in muliebre, habitum religionis, sed levem, susceperunt, continentiam et vitae simplicitatem privato voto profitentes, sub nullius tamen sancti regula coarctatae, nec adhuc ullo claustro contenti. Earumque numerus in brevi adeo multiplicabatur, ut in civitate Coloniae et partibus adjacentibus duo milia invenirentur."

centuries, the movement that German medievalists have referred to as the
Frauenbewegung (i.e., women's movement).[6] All the new religious orders of the time
came to have female branches closely associated with them—Cistercian and
Carthusian nuns among the monks; Premonstratensian canonesses in the canonical
reform; female "second orders" for both major mendicant groups, the Franciscans
and Dominicans. The Beguines were the only new form of "apostolic life" (*vita
apostolica*) in which women took the leadership role. The *Frauenbewegung* has often
been treated only as a movement of the heart, that is, an outpouring of religious
fervor and dedication. Marguerite Porete's *Mirror*, and the writings of other
Beguines, show that it was also a movement of the head.

Marguerite Porete was not the first Beguine to have taken upon herself a teaching role, nor even the first Beguine to have left us theological writings. Though
much has doubtless perished, there are other precious witnesses to the teaching of
the thirteenth-century Beguines. Notable among these are the works of Hadewijch,
a Beguine from Flanders active in the first half of the century, and the German
Mechthild of Magdeburg, who lived as a Beguine for many years before she retired
in extreme old age to the Cistercian nunnery of Helfta where she died probably in
the 1280s. Hadewijch's corpus is fairly large and varied, consisting of letters, visions,
and two forms of poetry (poems in strophes and poems in couplets, or
Mengeldichten). Mechthild's is restricted to a single substantial work containing
seven books of visions—*The Flowing Light of Godhead*. Like Marguerite's *Mirror*,
these works enjoyed a considerable public in the later Middle Ages. After centuries
of neglect, they have been rediscovered in the past hundred years and especially
today enjoy a growing readership as important documents in the history of
Christian mysticism.

The purpose of this volume is not to give a full account of the Beguine movement, or even of all the women writers of the thirteenth century—a task of monu-
mental proportions given the extensive literature that has been devoted to these
issues.[7] It is rather to try to open up something of the vitality of the mystical theology of the thirteenth century by a series of explorations of the relations of these
Beguine authors to Meister Eckhart, the great Dominican mystic. Recent research
has made it clear that Eckhart very probably had read Marguerite Porete's *Mirror of
Simple Souls*. While the case for direct influence of Hadewijch and Mechthild on

---

[6] The classic work remains that of Herbert Grundmann, *Religiöse Bewegungen im Mittelalter*,
2nd ed. (Hildesheim: Georg Olms, 1961).

[7] Some idea of the extent of this literature, for the Germanic realm alone, can be found in the
*Bibliographie zur deutschen Frauenmystik des Mittelalters. Mit einem Anhang zu Beatrijs van
Nazareth und Hadewijch*, ed. Gertrude Jaron Lewis, Frank Willaert, and Marie-José Govers
(Berlin: Erich Schmidt, 1989).

Eckhart remains questionable (though certainly possible), this is really irrelevant to the essential issues taken up by the essays in this volume. Determination of sources (German *Quellenforschung*) is the beginning, not the end, of the task of theological understanding. These papers are not really interested in what Meister Eckhart may have *learned* from the Beguine authors, but rather seek to grasp what Eckhart *shared* with them, that is, the community of discourse and joint concerns in which his thought and theirs developed and enriched each other. For us, the study of Eckhart together with these Beguines will provide new insight into one of the most creative periods in the history of Christian thought.

This introduction does not intend to summarize these six explorations into so rich a field of study. Nor does it try to raise critical questions for debate and further study, as do the valuable concluding remarks that Richard Woods has developed from his role as commentator. Rather, I wish to put the conversation into context by locating it within the broad history of the development of medieval theology. My purpose is to show how Meister Eckhart and the Beguines were able to become involved in a form of unprecedented theological conversation—a real mutual interchange between male and female theological voices carried on in the vernacular.

The Three Forms of Medieval Theology

Anyone who pursued the history of medieval theology between about 1850 and 1950 knew exactly what the object of study was. Medieval theology was scholasticism, primarily the scholasticism of Thomas Aquinas. The Thomist revival, begun in Germany and Rome about the middle of the nineteenth century, guaranteed Thomas such a dominant position among medieval thinkers that one could argue that in the long run it was as bad for the proper appreciation of his thought as it was unfair for assaying the significance of the other masters of the schools.[8]

Some may bewail what may seem like an eclipse of Thomas Aquinas in post-Vatican II Catholic theology, but I would argue that it has provided us with the opportunity to begin to appreciate the Angelic Doctor as he really was and as he thought himself to be—one theologian in the long tradition of those who have sought to make Christian faith intelligible for their age, not some timeless seer with all the answers for all the questions of all the ages. Thomas believed that truth was timeless and eternal, not theologians. The ill effects on the history of medieval

---

[8] For an account of the intellectual and political agenda behind the Thomist revival, see James Hennessey, S.J., "Leo XIII's Thomistic Revival: A Political and Philosophical Event," in *Celebrating the Medieval Heritage: A Colloquy on the Thought of Aquinas and Bonaventure*, ed. David Tracy (Chicago: University of Chicago, 1978; *The Journal of Religion. Supplement* 58 [1978]), S185–S197.

theology of the a-temporal and triumphalist view of Thomas Aquinas are too evident to require extensive review. One has only to look at the generations of scholars who labored to make the great Franciscan theologian Bonaventure into a Thomist to be convinced that something was wrong. The recent work that demonstrates the important theological differences between the Franciscan and the Dominican, for all they shared in belief and scholastic formation, makes this abundantly clear. These older views of medieval theology were even more at fault in contending that it was only thinkers like Bonaventure and Aquinas who were really theologians in the proper sense, that is, that the *only* form of medieval theology was the scholastic one created primarily in the twelfth century and flourishing in the universities of the thirteenth century.

The idea that scholastic theology was the only kind of medieval theology first began to be questioned between 1940 and 1950. This is a somewhat artificial date, to be sure. More than sixty years ago, Étienne Gilson, the great historian of medieval scholasticism, in a series of lectures given in 1933 (later published as *The Mystical Theology of St. Bernard*) defended Bernard's position as a profound dogmatic and mystical theologian, not just a pious preacher. It was the same Gilson who in 1940 convinced a young Benedictine monk named Jean Leclercq to direct his attentions to the riches of the theology of the medieval monastics rather than the schoolmen. The rest is history, as they say. In a series of programmatic essays of the 1950s, in his memorable book *The Love of Learning and the Desire for God* (1957), and later revisions and qualifications of his original theses,[9] Jean Leclercq, along with a number of other scholars of medieval monasticism, demonstrated the importance of a monastic theology that was different from, but also, at least in some ways, complementary to the scholasticism that was for so long thought to be the only game in town.[10] This is scarcely the place to enter into the debates surrounding the nature of the monastic theology that flourished especially between the time of Gregory the Great (c. 600) and Bernard of Clairvaux (d. 1153). My point is a simple one—every competent historian of theology today would agree that the story of theology between 500 and 1500 cannot be responsibly told by giving

---

[9] See especially Leclercq's final major statement of the relation between monastic and scholastic theology in the twelfth century, "The Renewal of Theology," *Renaissance and Renewal in the Twelfth Century*, ed. Robert L. Benson and Giles Constable with Carol D. Lanham (Cambridge: Harvard University Press, 1982), 68–87. For a summary of Leclercq's notion of monastic theology, see Bernard McGinn, "Jean Leclercq's Contribution to Monastic Spirituality and Theology," *Monastic Studies* 16(1985):7–23.

[10] The "discovery" of monastic theology went hand-in-hand with the return to patristic theology led by Jean Daniélou and others and evident in the foundation of the *Sources chrétiennes* series in 1942.

attention only to scholastic authors. A half century of research proves that anyone who would dismiss monastic thinkers as not being "real" theologians has done nothing more than prove the narrowness and insufficiency of his or her understanding of theology.

I would argue that the research of the past generation is also making it increasingly clear that we can no longer think of medieval theology just in terms of these two main intellectual and sociological strands—the monastic and the scholastic— but that we must now also recognize a third dimension or tradition of theology beginning in the thirteenth century, one that I think can be best described as the vernacular theological tradition. It is in this tradition that women, for the first time in the history of Christianity, took on an important, perhaps even a preponderant, role.

Vernacular theology is, of course, a more diffuse and ambiguous term than even the monastic theology that has been the subject of so many disputes. Indeed, it may well be more correct to speak of vernacular theologies given how these writings and systems of thought were shaped in varying ways by their expression in the developing vernacular languages of western Europe. But insofar as we can speak of theology broadly as a reflective presentation of Christian belief presented in a public way, that is, through teaching and writing, it is difficult to see how we can deny at least some of the vernacular religious literature of the later Middle Ages the title of theology, though of course, not that of technical scholastic theology. Even a scholastic like Henry of Ghent seems to have recognized this in his willingness to allow women, for whom access to the university teaching of theology was impossible, a restricted role as "doctors" of theology *ex beneficio*. (It has also been accepted by contemporary Roman Catholicism in a more official way, as witnessed by the declaration of Teresa of Avila and Catherine of Siena as "Doctors of the Church" in 1970.)

I call the third strand of medieval theology "vernacular" to indicate its primary distinguishing mark—linguistic expression in the medieval vernacular tongues.[11] The modern hermeneutical movement has taught us how great a role language plays in all thinking, and we need not be strict proponents of any particular form of hermeneutical theory to recognize that the language in which any form of

[11] Though the term "vernacular theology" may be fairly new, the reality it points to has been noticed before. In his Gifford Lectures of 1948–49, published as *Religion and the Rise of Western Culture* (Garden City: Doubleday, 1957), Christopher Dawson made the following statement about William Langland's "Piers Plowman": "And his poem seems to prove that the fundamental principles of the creative period of medieval religion had been more completely assimilated and incorporated by the new vernacular culture of the common people than it had been by the higher and more literary culture of the ruling elements of Church and state" (219).

theological reflection comes to birth is an essential part of its being. New "language-fields" offered new theological possibilities, especially in an era when the still-forming vernacular tongues of Europe were in many cases finding their earliest written expression. Some of the aspects of this interaction will be studied below.

We must underline the fact, emphasized by a number of scholars of German mysticism such as Herbert Grundmann, Josef Quint, and Kurt Ruh,[12] that the explosion of religious writing in the vernacular was not just a case of simple translation, but was a complex and still inadequately studied creation of new theological and linguistic possibilities. Even in the case of some authors (think of Francis of Assisi, the Italian mystic Angela of Foligno, or the fourteenth-century Swedish visionary, Birgitta) who survive to us largely in Latin form, we get the sense of a new style of religious, and I would argue, theological expression dependent, in large part, on the vernacular linguistic matrix in which it took form.

One of the most significant aspects of the new linguistic fields in which theology came to speech in the thirteenth century was the potential challenge it offered to medieval understanding of the roles of men and women. The Latin language, as the learned second language of the clerical and educational male hierarchy, was not totally closed to women, but it was difficult for all but a very few women to gain access to it in any substantial fashion. To be sure, we can admire the good sense of the ninth-century noblewoman Dhuoda as expressed in the moral handbook she wrote for her son, and we can be in awe at the mastery of Latin displayed in the plays of the tenth-century nun, Hrotswitha. The famous names of Heloise and Hildegard of Bingen show that some twelfth-century women could attain a knowledge of Latin that allowed them a significant teaching role.[13] But these were notable exceptions. In the case of the vernacular languages, however, men and women began on the same footing, and it is instuctive to note how often female writers, including the vernacular theologians, appear at the very beginnings of the written forms of many of the European languages. The new conversation between men and women in the vernacular mystical texts facilitated reexaminations of the gender roles that long tradition, both cultural and ecclesiastical, had made to seem inviolable to many. Modern gender studies have enabled us to be more sensitive to the remarkable ways

[12] See, for example, Herbert Grundmann, *Religiöse Bewegungen*, Chap. VIII; Josef Quint, "Mystik und Sprache: Ihr verhältnis zueinander, insbesondere in der spekulativen Mystik Meister Eckharts," *Altdeutsche und Altniederländische Mystik* (Darmstadt: Wissenschaftliche Buchgesellschaft, 1964), 113–51; and Kurt Ruh, *Scholastik und Mystik im Spätmittelalter*, Band II, *Kleine Schriften* (Berlin and New York: Walter De Gruyter, 1984).

[13] For an introduction to these women authors, see Peter Dronke, *Women Writers of the Middle Ages. A Critical Study of Texts from Perpetua (d. 203) to Marguerite Porete (d. 1310)* (Cambridge: Cambridge University Press, 1984).

in which medieval mystical texts challenge or subvert stereotypes about men and women both of the past and the present, as will be evident from all the essays in this volume, but most especially from those dealing with Porete and Eckhart. Meister Eckhart's "conversation" with the Beguines (understood in the Latin sense of *conversatio*, that is, a living with, a familiarity that includes but is not limited to verbal discussion) provides a particularly instructive example. Michael Sells puts it well in the final essay: "Eckhart, as a Dominican 'Meister,' was placed in a position of administrative and theological control over nuns and other women, but rather than controlling the powerful currents of late thirteenth-century women's spirituality, he joined them."[14]

Not only the language but also the audience was new. The movement into the vernacular implied a different and wider audience than that addressed by traditional monastic and scholastic theology. The presence of such an audience already existed in the twelfth century, as shown by texts like the Old French version of Bernard of Clairvaux's sermons on the Song of Songs, or the Middle High German poetic commentary on the Song known as the "St. Trudpert Song of Songs." Increasing lay literacy and new forms of social diversification form an important part of the background to the new vernacular theology, as do cheaper and more effective means of communication. (For example, it has been suggested that the thirteenth-century transition from expensive vellum to cheaper paper for books was almost as important for the diffusion of knowledge as the shift to print technology in the fifteenth century.) The movement into the vernacular had its fitful beginnings in the twelfth century, but became a flood in the thirteenth.

But in what sense were the new religious writings in the vernacular *theology*? Jean Leclercq once noted that if the scholastic theologians took as their own, in a special way, the Augustinian program of "I believe that I may understand" (*Credo ut intelligam*), the emphasis of monastic theologians like Bernard of Clairvaux on personal experience of God could be captured in the phrase "I believe that I may experience" (*Credo ut experiar*).[15] However, it was a monk himself, Anselm of Canterbury, who did more than anyone to put the program of "faith seeking understanding" (*fides quaerens intellectum*) at the center of scholastic theology, and other monks did not neglect the speculative understanding of the appropriation of belief, as a glance at such a powerful and original mind as William of St. Thierry shows. The great scholastic masters, such as Bonaventure and Thomas Aquinas, would have been horrified at the thought that the scientific scholastic mode of theological

[14] M. Sells, "The Pseudo-Woman and the Meister," 143.

[15] Leclercq, *The Love of Learning and the Desire for God* (New York: Fordham University Press, 1961), 213.

appropriation was not finally intended to increase love for God. All medieval theology involved both the *intellectus fidei* and the *experientia amoris*, though in different configurations. The vernacular theological tradition was a true theology, like the scholastic and the monastic, insofar as it was a serious attempt to foster greater love of God and neighbor through a deeper understanding of the faith. Naturally, the ways in which the teaching of the vernacular theologians related *intellectus* and *amor*, understanding and love, were expressed in forms that were somewhat different from those used by the monks and the schoolmen.

Vernacular theology differed from both its monastic and scholastic cousins not only in audience, but also in how it organized and presented its teaching. Scholastic theology, with its scientific and academic concerns, achieved its formal structure through the articulation of the methodological difference between *lectio* (commentary on text), *quaestio/disputatio* (the search for scientific intelligibility), and *praedicatio* (the communication of the intelligibility attained). All three forms of teaching and writing contributed to the concern for the systematic and scientific presentation of Christian teaching found in the great textbooks often called *summae*. Monastic theology, as Leclercq and others have shown,[16] had its own distinctive genres, the most important of which was biblical commentary that mingled many levels of presentation from literal reading, through doctrinal teaching, to moral and mystical appropriation. Monks also wrote letters that were often really theological treatises on particular problems, and they composed highly developed rhetorical sermons and meditations, such as those of Bernard and William of St. Thierry, that rank among the great theological writings of Christian history.

The characteristic genres of vernacular theology are less easy to describe. Given the practical and synthetic nature of much vernacular theology, there is some overlap with monastic genres, though vernacular theology has less room for explicit biblical commentary, especially because technical biblical study was inaccessible to most laymen and to all women. Much vernacular theology was expressed in sermonic form, though of many different kinds. A wide variety of treatises and "little books" were employed, as well as hagiography and letters. Poetry was also of significance. The three Beguines studied in these essays were gifted poets and presented important parts of their message in verse. Eckhart, of course, was perhaps the most distinctive preacher of the Middle Ages, in the sense that his sermons are like no one else's, though they were often imitated by his followers. Eckhart appears to have been a poet as well, if the mystical sequence known as the "Mustard Seed" (*Granum Sinapis*) can be ascribed to

[16] Leclercq, *The Love of Learning*, chap. VIII.

him.[17] Of special importance in vernacular theology was the visionary account.[18] Both Hadewijch and Mechthild composed accounts of their visions, and the great fourteenth-century English vernacular theologian, Julian of Norwich, created a new genre in her *Shewings*, a combination of visionary narrative and extensive theological meditation.

Late medieval vernacular theology not only created distinctive theological models, it also produced new, and sometimes challenging, insights into the mysteries of the faith. Much of the originality of vernacular theology concerns what was later called mysticism, though the ways in which vernacular theology began a new era in moral theology have not yet really been explored. For example, the *ars moriendi* treatises of the late Middle Ages were often theological documents, though not mystical ones, and much of the theology of the "Devotio Moderna" movement is not mystical in the proper sense, but is concerned with the theological bases of moral reform. Nevertheless, it is fair to say that the greatest contribution of medieval vernacular theology came in the area of mysticism.

This is not the place to try to describe the major characteristics of the many and varied figures who contributed to late medieval mystical teaching in the vernacular, nor to try to relate their doctrine to earlier forms of mysticism and to the ongoing Latin mystical literature of the time.[19] However, Meister Eckhart and the Beguine authors considered in the essays in this volume do share a number of concerns that were distinctive of some of the most original currents of late medieval mysticism.

Both Eckhart and the Beguines spoke to a new and potentially wider audience than the monastic mystics of the early Middle Ages. The Dominican's preaching in the vernacular is one of the most significant witnesses to the new "democratizing" trend in mystical teaching evident in the thirteenth century. Eckhart preached the possibility of a radical new awareness of God, in rich and often difficult terms, not to the clerical elite of the schools, but to women and men of every walk of life. Finding one's ground in the depths of the Godhead did

---

[17] For a text and discussion, see Alois Haas, "Granum Sinapis: An den grenzen der Sprache," *Sermo mysticus: Studien zu Theologie und Sprache der deutschen Mystik* (Freiburg, Schweiz: Universitätsverlag, 1979), 301–29.

[18] On the important shift in medieval visionary accounts from an early medieval type characterized by a unique transport to heaven or hell designed to effect a conversion to a late medieval type that is repeatable, generally more mystical, and also confirmatory of individual sanctity, see Peter Dinzelbacher, *Vision und Visionsliteratur im Mittelalter* (Stuttgart: Hiersemann, 1981), esp. chaps. 12 and 16.

[19] I intend to treat these issues more fully in the third volume of my ongoing history of Christian mysticism. See *The Flowering of Mysticism*, vol. 3 of *The Presence of God* (forthcoming).

not require adopting a traditional religious way of life, especially not one that involved fleeing from the world. As Eckhart once put it:

> When people think they are acquiring more of God in inwardness, in devotion, in sweetness, and in various approaches than they do by the fireside or in the stable, you are acting just as if you took God and muffled his head up in a cloak and pushed him under a bench. Whoever is seeking God by ways is finding ways and losing God, who in ways is hidden.[20]

Eckhart's public preaching of this radical message that perfection was possible within the "secular" realm did not please everyone. In this connection it is noteworthy that the Bull of Condemnation issued by Pope John XXII in 1329 against selected excerpts from Eckhart's writings specifically mentions that he "presented many things as dogma that were designed to cloud the true faith in the hearts of many, things which he put forth *especially before the uneducated crowd in his sermons* and that he also admitted into his writings" (my emphasis).[21]

The Beguine authors discussed here demonstrate a variety of attitudes towards this democratizing and "secularizing" trend evident in Eckhart and in much late medieval mystical teaching. Their writing in the vernacular made their message accessible to the lay audience, and none of these Beguine authors places any stress on the importance of belonging to a religious order in the institutional sense. But while the mystical message of Hadewijch and Mechthild appears potentially universal, that is, accessible to any Christian who truly seeks to love God in the highest possible way, Marguerite Porete's teaching in the *Mirror* involves a complex form of esotericism based on the conflict between Reason and *Dame Amour*. Her emphasis on the special position of a spiritual elite of annihilated souls was a root element in the difficulties she encountered with the institutional church.[22]

There are other interesting variations that detailed study of the mystics examined in this volume could uncover, such as that on the role of love. Meister Eckhart certainly had an important place for love of God within his teaching,[23] but his

---

[20] Meister Eckhart, Pr. 5b (DW 1: 91.3–8). I use the translation in *Meister Eckhart: The Essential Sermons, Commentaries, Treatises and Defense*, trans. and intro. by Edmund Colledge, O.S.A., and Bernard McGinn (New York: Paulist Press, 1981), 183.

[21] For a translation of the papal bull "In agro dominico," see *Meister Eckhart: The Essential Sermons*, 77–81.

[22] On this question, see Bernard McGinn, "Donne mistiche ed autorità esoterica nel XIV secolo," *Poteri carismatici et informali: chiesa e società medioevali*, ed. Agostino Paravicini Bagliani and André Vauchez (Palermo: Sellerio, 1992), 153–74.

23. I have tried to sketch elements of Eckhart's understanding of love in my paper, "St. Bernard and Meister Eckhart," *Cîteaux* 31(1980):373–86.

conception of love is quite different from the bridal and courtly motifs found in the Beguines, and especially from their powerful evocations of the madness or insanity of love found in the encounter between God and the human lover. Another important difference concerns the role of visionary experience, which is central to Hadewijch and Mechthild of Magdeburg, but is unimportant, perhaps even misleading, for Marguerite and Eckhart.

Despite these variations and even disagreements, the new form of mysticism found in Meister Eckhart and Beguines exhibits many shared approaches, or at least common expressions, about major themes of Christian mystical theology. Some of these are treated in detail in the essays found in this volume. I would like to close this brief introduction by highlighting one crucial area of communality in which these essays allow us to eavesedrop on the conversation between the Beguines and Eckhart—the question of what kind of union with God is possible in this life.

I have elsewhere suggested that two broad ways of conceiving of what came to be called mystical union (*unio mystica*) can be found in the Medieval Period.[24] The first of these, formed in the Latin patristic period and reaching a level of explicit thematization in the twelfth century, held that the soul could attain a loving union of wills with God, an *unitas spiritus* whose basic human analogue was to be found in the marriage embrace of the lovers portrayed in the Song of Songs. But in the thirteenth century, first among some of the women vernacular theologians, a second form of understanding mystical union began to emerge, a potentially more radical and possibly more questionable understanding which emphasized a goal of "union without difference," or what in Eckhartian terms we can describe as an *unitas indistinctionis*—the insistence that in the ground of reality there is absolute identity between God and the soul. Aspects of this teaching can be found in all the authors studied in this volume, though it is especially strong in Marguerite Porete and Eckhart.

The new understanding of mystical union was given a theoretical scholastic presentation in the Latin works of Eckhart, through language adapted from the Neo-Platonic tradition. But its creation cannot be envisaged as merely some form of revival of Neo-Platonic ideas. *Unitas indistinctionis* was born not in books but in the depths of the experience of the mystics of the thirteenth century, in their attempts to live the annihilation (*anéantissement*) of Marguerite Porete, or the perfect detachment (*abegescheidenheit*) of Meister Eckhart. The ramifications of this understanding of

[24] See Bernard McGinn, "Love, Knowledge, and *Unio mystica* in the Western Christian Tradition," *Mystical Union and Monotheistic Faith: An Ecumenical Dialogue*, ed. Moshe Idel and Bernard McGinn (New York: Macmillan, 1989), 59–86. Though some Greek patristic writers, such as Pseudo-Macarius and Pseudo-Dionysius, occasionally used expressions equivalent to "mystical union," the term did not become a technical one in the West until the seventeenth century and does not seem to have been popularized until modern times.

mystical union, the different images and conceptualizations which sought to bring it to expression, were manifold. It is instructive to see how Eckhart and the Beguines studied here attempted to express this deepest mystery of the Christian life.

For example, the necessity for the total destruction or annihilation of the created will appears in Hadewijch and later becomes central to the conversation between Marguerite Porete and Eckhart. This annihilation of the will implied a return to primordial existence in God, the life "in the principle" (*in principio*) that Eckhart analyzed with scholastic rigor in his Latin works, but which he expressed in his famous *Predigt* 52 with the words: "If a person really wants to have poverty, he ought to be as free of his own created will as he was when he did not exist."[25] Or, as Marguerite Porete puts it: "I cannot be in Him unless he places me there of Himself without myself, just as when He made me by Himself without myself."[26] This insistence on radical poverty was among the most significant corollaries of the *unitas indistinctionis* understanding of mystical union, especially since the debate over the true meaning of poverty was one of the central religious concerns of the time.[27] The equation of poverty and true freedom reminds us that suspicions that too much "freedom" was being claimed by the mystics gave birth to the ecclesiastical attack on the *secta libertatis*, the so-called heresy of the Free Spirit.[28] Absolute metaphysical poverty, annihilation of the whole created will, true freedom, all have a theoretical ring. On the practical level of concrete expression in the vernacular, these mystical authors created a new and more potent way of saying the same thing—"To live without a why." One could argue (though I will not attempt it here) that a consideration of the meaning of "living without a why" encapsulates the most profound insights of these vernacular theologians, nothing more nor less than a new way of understanding the ancient relation between theory and practice.[29]

On the more theoretical level, the importance of attaining, or returning, to one's preexistent state in God invited new ways of formulating the Neo-Platonic

[25] Meister Eckhart, Pr. 52 (DW 2: 491.8–9). Translation from *Meister Eckhart: The Essential Sermons*, 200.

[26] Marguerite Porete, *Mirouer*, chap. 111 (302.15–17). I use the translation of Babinsky, *The Mirror of Simple Souls*, 183.

[27] For reflections on the role of poverty in the Beguines and Eckhart, see Herbert Grundmann, "Die geschichtlichen Grundlagen der deutschen Mystik," in *Altdeutsche und altniederländische Mystik*, 72–99.

[28] For the debate surrounding the heresy of the Free Spirit, see Lerner, *The Heresy of the Free Spirit*.

[29] For reflections on this issue in Meister Eckhart, see Dietmar Mieth, *Die Einheit von vita activa und vita contemplativa in den deutschen Predigten und Traktaten Meister Eckharts und bei Johannes Tauler* (Regensburg: Pustet, 1969).

categories for expressing the God-world relation in terms of emanation and return, flowing out and flowing back. All of the authors studied here have rich treatments of the langage of emanation and return. Finally, we should also note that the ineffable character of union without difference often made it more profitable to suggest aspects of its mysterious realization in symbolic form rather than to try to fix it in conceptualizable, essentialist language, which could only utltimately betray the very thing it attempted to serve. The vernacular theologians of the thirteenth century were at their most creative in the ways in which they used the barrenness of the wilderness or desert as a potent symbol for mystical annihilation, as shown by Paul Dietrich's essay. Similar studies could be made of other symbols of *unitas indistinctionis*, such as the ocean and the abyss, especially the mutual abyss through which God and the soul realize their final indistinction.[30]

These suggestions are meant only to frame the discussion that will be carried out in more detail in the essays in this volume. Even these essays themselves, as well as the concluding comments made by Richard Woods, are more a beginning than a conclusion. They are presented to invite the modern seeker after God to reenter the conversation that took place seven centuries ago between some of the most remarkable men and women in the history of Christian theology.

---

[30] For an overview of the symbols, see Bernard McGinn, "Ocean and Desert as Symbols of Mystical Absorption in the Christian Tradition," *The Journal of Religion* 74(1994):155–81; and "The Abyss of Love" (to appear in the memorial volume for Jean Leclercq to be published by Cistercian Publications).

Part I

Hadewijch, Mechthild, and Meister Eckhart

1

Hadewijch and Eckhart

Amor intellegere est

Saskia Murk-Jansen

Academics today may be forgiven for wondering why so little attention has been paid to the question of influence between Hadewijch and Eckhart, or at least to the possibility of common themes in their work. Hadewijch, after all, was writing around the middle of the thirteenth century in an area that was geographically and linguistically not very far removed from Eckhart's own, half a century or so later. The manuscripts of her works were known to ecclesiastic scholars in the fourteenth century although not very widely disseminated, certainly not compared for example to those of Marguerite Porete. Like Marguerite Porete, Hadewijch is thought to have been a Beguine, and the Beguines had particularly close links with the Dominicans, so there exists at least the possibility that Eckhart could have heard of her work from others within his order. Nevertheless, this whole field of inquiry has been left lying fallow. Why? Is this lack of attention by eminent Hadewijch scholars earlier this century because the evidence against is so overwhelming that there is no point in pursuing this line of inquiry? In what follows I shall argue that it may in fact be due more to twentieth-century politics than to medieval history or theology. By divorcing the question from the thorny problem of influence, bound up as that is with twentieth-century values such as originality which have little or no significance in the medieval context, another field of inquiry is opened up: namely the existence and distinctive characteristics of theological writing in the vernacular during the thirteenth century. I will argue that Hadewijch and Eckhart were drawing on such a tradition, and that the ideas and expressions which they share formed part of a common heritage of theological thought which they helped both to shape and to define.

It has been said that there is no possibility that Eckhart could have been influenced by the work attributed to Hadewijch because he would have been quite unable to read it. With great respect (as they say in the British House of Commons), and leaving aside the fact that there are more ways of learning of something than by reading alone, that is unlikely to be true. Certainly Eckhart was born in a village in Thuringia, in northern Germany, and probably grew up speaking that dialect. However, in much the same way as dialect speakers today also learn the standard form of the language, Eckhart is almost certain to have been familiar with the Middle High German of northern Germany. Later in his life he traveled widely through Germany as well as to Paris where, of course, he obtained his formal training in theology. He may have communicated with his fellow Dominicans in Latin, but he can scarcely have spoken to the nuns and Beguines in Strasbourg and Cologne in Latin. Nor, if his native Thuringian dialect was unintelligible to German speakers in the south, would he have done so in his dialect. For the purposes of everyday life as he traveled through his province, it is inconceivable that Eckhart would not have been able to understand and to communicate in a form of High German, and very probably also in the dialect of Cologne.

All this is of course rather hypothetical. What is not hypothetical is the extent to which German and Dutch were mutually intelligible in this period. The relationship of Modern German to Modern Dutch is deceptive, although even today the language of the area of Cologne is very close to that on the Dutch side of the border. Modern German developed from the High German of southern Germany and is quite far removed from the Middle High German which was spoken in the north. Dutch, on the other hand, is very much closer to the Middle High German spoken north of the Rhine than to the High German of the south. As a result, Modern Dutch is in many ways closer to much Medieval German than is Modern German.[1] Modern Dutch has developed directly from the Medieval Dutch preserved in the majority of the manuscripts. The language of Eckhart, a native of northern Germany, would therefore have been closer to that of Hadewijch, and indeed even to Modern Dutch, than it would have been to Modern German.

An example of the ease with which literature crossed what are today linguistic barriers is that of one of the great Dutch courtly-love poets, Hendrick van Veldeke. Veldeke, who was active in the late twelfth century, is claimed by both Dutch and German literary historians. Two of his inarguably German contemporaries, Wolfram von Eschenbach and Gottfried von Strassburg, highly praise Veldeke and his contribution to German poetics. Veldeke wrote much of his work for his major patron, Agnes van Loon. The lands of the Van Loons were in what is now Belgium and the Netherlands, but Agnes came originally from the court in Thuringia and Veldeke traveled a great deal between the court in Belgium and those in Cleves and Thuringia. This single example could be expanded by a number of others, notably the significant collections of secular poetry in a German/Dutch language mix.[2]

---

[1] I experienced one effect of this while teaching at the University of Aachen where German students wishing to take a course in Medieval German Literature were recommended to learn Modern Dutch first.

[2] For a study of the language mixtures in the principal manuscripts during this period, see B. Schludermann, "A Comparison of German/Dutch Language Mixtures in Texts From the Gruuthuse-Ms, the Hague MS 128 E2, and the Berlin MS mgf 922. A Quantitative Analysis" (Ph.D. diss., University of Cambridge, 1980).

Another question to be addressed is that of opportunity: how might Eckhart have been exposed to the thought of Hadewijch and other Dutch mystics? We know that a complete manuscript of Hadewijch's work was in a monastery in the vicinity of Diest in modern Belgium, and it may be of interest to note that even today the local dialect of the area around Diest is quite heavily colored with German. Dominicans, however, traveled widely and had close ties with Beguines throughout the Rhineland; indeed there is evidence in Hadewijch's work that she knew and respected the Order.[3] It could be argued that Dominican thought developed such a rich vein of speculative theology precisely as a result of the dialogue over many years between the Dominicans and the Beguines and nuns in their care. It is not out of the question that Eckhart could have become acquainted with Hadewijch's thought through discussion with those who had traveled in the areas where she was known. As one whose interest in mystic thought and in women's spirituality must have been as well known to his contemporaries as it is to us, Eckhart would have been a natural recipient of such information and participant in discussions. What more natural way for him to become acquainted with the thought world of vernacular feminine spirituality than from discussions with his brother Dominicans who were so closely involved with the spiritual welfare of the Beguines?

The silence in the Netherlands and Belgium concerning the possible influence of Eckhart's thought on thirteenth-century mystic writing in Dutch and vice versa has been, as they say, deafening. The reasons for this may have less to do with Eckhart than with twentieth-century European history. In 1923 J. Van Mierlo published, in reply to an article by A. C. Bouman which had appeared earlier that same year, an article entitled "Hadewijch en Eckhart" in which he vehemently argues the case against the possible influence of Eckhart on Hadewijch.[4] In view of the relative dates of Eckhart (1268–1329) and Hadewijch (c. 1240), the controversy now seems somewhat empty, but there was far less unanimity concerning Hadewijch's dates in the first quarter of this century than there is now. This article by Van Mierlo was practically the last time any serious work was done on the question of the possible relationship between the thought of Hadewijch and that of Eckhart.[5] Attentive readers may recall Van Mierlo's oblique reference to the fact that Bouman's article had appeared in German, but the

[3] In *Mengeldicht* 3: 50–56 Hadewijch describes Mary Magdalene, already a favorite and later to become the Patron Saint of the Order of Preachers, as the great example. There are several interesting aspects to this choice of Hadewijch's, not least that she uses the example of Mary, instructed by the risen Christ to go and tell what she had seen, to validate her own teaching activity and those of her circle.

[4] A. C. Bouman, "Die literarische Stellung der Dichterin Hadewijch," *Neophilologus* 8 (1923): 270–79; and J. Van Mierlo, "Hadewijch en Eckhart," *Dietse Warande en Belfort* (1923): 1138–55.

[5] Those articles which have appeared concentrate on the later influence of Eckhart in the Netherlands, and the antipathy of Jan Ruusbroec and of his pupil Jan van Leeuwen to Eckhart's thought. For a definitive bibliography of work on Eckhart including an appendix of

significance of this remark may have escaped all except those who have a detailed understanding of Belgian history in the first half of this century.

The discovery of the Hadewijch manuscripts in the nineteenth century coincided with the gradual emancipation of the Dutch language in Belgium.[6] Dutch was traditionally the language of the poorer, agricultural parts of Belgium, while French was spoken in the, until relatively recently, wealthier industrial and coal-mining areas, and was the language of government and officialdom. The discovery, therefore, of a figure of the stature of Hadewijch writing in Middle Dutch was seen as a substantial boost to the morale of Dutch-speaking Belgian academics, many of whom were at the forefront of the movement to get the Dutch language established and recognized as an official language.

The emancipation of the Dutch language made slow progress. Then, in the First World War, Belgium was invaded by Germany and the invaders exploited the linguistic and political conflict to strengthen their own hold on the country by giving greater rights and privileges to the Dutch-speaking community. The establishment of the University of Ghent as a Dutch-speaking university dates from this time. The end of the First World War meant that those who had collaborated with the Germans were seen as traitors, and that almost all Dutch speakers were under suspicion of, at best, passive treason. To distance oneself from the German enemy and from German culture became a first priority for Dutch speakers, and particularly for Dutch-speaking academics. Another factor in Van Mierlo's attack on the German article in which Bouman suggested that Hadewijch had been influenced by Eckhart is that of heresy. In 1329, twenty-eight propositions taken from Eckhart's work were condemned as heretical. In the light of the Jesuit mission against heresy and their suspicion of mysticism, it is scarcely surprising that the Dutch-speaking Belgian Jesuit scholar Van Mierlo should have found explanations which preempted the possibility of any similarity between the theology of Hadewijch and that of Eckhart sufficiently compelling to look no further. The polemical arguments seeking to prove Hadewijch completely orthodox, not only in thirteenth-century terms but also in terms of nineteenth- and twentieth-century Catholic theology, have been a significant strand in Hadewijch criticism this century.

By the second half of the 1920s the case against Eckhart, or rather the reasons that any connection between Hadewijch and Eckhart was unacceptable, had

selected works by National Socialist writers, see N. Largier, *Bibliographie zu Meister Eckhart* (Freiburg: Universitätsverlag, 1989).

[6] I use the word Dutch in preference to Flemish because the term Flemish has been used by the French-speaking Belgians to imply that the language spoken by the Dutch speakers is a dialect form and therefore inferior to the French spoken in Belgium. In fact, the languages on either side of the Dutch-Belgian border are more similar to each other than are British and North American English.

developed even further. In the period shortly after Bouman and Van Mierlo published their articles, Eckhart was "adopted" by the National Socialists as a symbol of German superiority; as the father of the German language, he was held also to have been the spiritual father of the German race. While the Nazis claimed Eckhart for their own, however spuriously, it could never be acceptable for Belgian or Dutch academics even to consider whether there might have been some common elements in his thinking and that of Hadewijch, let alone influence. It is really only now as the study of these great figures is being undertaken by scholars less influenced by the events of the two world wars, that the question is becoming academically acceptable once more. The question, possibly, but perhaps not the answer.

In his article Bouman discusses a number of close similarities he perceived between the Hadewijch manuscripts and the work of Eckhart. He dismisses Van Mierlo's opinion that the *Mengeldichten* 17–29 are not by Hadewijch, and draws much of his Hadewijch material precisely from these poems.[7] This enabled Van Mierlo in turn to dismiss Bouman's evidence, and closed for many years the question of the authorship of these texts. In his article Van Mierlo does not engage with the substantive points of similarity raised by Bouman, concentrating rather on the question of authorship. This emphasis has tended to divert attention from the main interest of Bouman's observations. The similarities to which he drew attention derserve serious consideration. Analysis shows that they are not confined to texts which can be dismissed as by another author than Hadewijch. Close reading of Hadewijch and of the German sermons (*Predigten*) of Eckhart confirms Bouman's impression that the two authors had much in common, although this may have been a common tradition of vernacular theology rather than the effect of direct influence.

In his article Bouman discusses in some detail two texts from the Hadewijch manuscripts, *Mengeldicht* 27 and *Mengeldicht* 19. He also suggests a possible connection between Veldeke and Hadewijch, posited on her probable familiarity with his work.[8] In his discussion of *Mengeldicht* 27, Bouman suggests that it is a paraphrase

[7] For a detailed description of the Hadewijch manuscripts and a discussion of the evidence for and against Hadewijch's authorship of the *Mengeldichten*, see S. Murk Jansen, *The Measure of Mystic Thought: A Study of Hadewijch's Mengeldichten* (Göppingen: Kümmerle Verlag, 1991).

[8] Bouman suggests that the similarities between Hadewijch's *Strofische Gedichten*, and the courtly lyrics of Veldeke in particular, may be an indication of direct influence. This suggestion is predicated on the fact that Veldeke's work would have been intelligible to Dutch as well as German audiences. That this was so is a further indication of the mutual intelligibility of Dutch and German in this period. The importance of the influence of secular love lyrics on Hadewijch's poetics has subsequently been examined at length in N. de Paepe's *Hadewijch's Strofische Gedichten in het kader van de twalfde en dertiende eeuwse Minnelyriek* (Ghent: Koninklijke Vlaamse Academie voor Taal en Letterkunde, 1967); and F. Willaert's *De Poëtica van Hadewijch in de Strofische Gedichten* (Utrecht: n.p., 1984).

of the pseudo-Eckhartian piece "*von dem überschalle*." In support of this assessment, he reprints *Mengeldicht* 27 showing in italics all the words which that poem has in common with the Eckhartian text. It is certainly the case that most if not all the significant words in the poem are in italics, as well as a number of less significant ones. However, not all the evidence which he brings forward to argue for the direct dependence of the poem on the text by Eckhart is equally convincing. To show that the similarity between these texts is not merely a matter of vocabulary, but that it extends to the interpretation and presentation of concepts, Bouman presents some quotations from pseudo-Eckhart. One of these quotations, though using similar words, in fact implies the contrary to what is said in the poem. Bouman quotes pseudo-Eckhart as saying: "Daz ist diu dunster stilheit, die nieman kan verstan dan der, in den ez liuchtet" (that is the dark stillness which none can understand save him in whom the light shines). The light of God shining in the darkness is, according to this text, the only means whereby the dark stillness can be comprehended. In the third stanza of *Mengeldicht* 27 the poet uses the same passage from John differently:

> The accident of multiplicity
> takes from us our singleness;
> as Saint John the Evangelist said:
> the light shines in the darkness
> and the dark darkness does not understand
> the clarity of the light shining in her.[9]

The poet is here doing little more than paraphrasing the passage from John 1:5 "And the light shineth in darkness; and the darkness comprehended it not." Both use the familiar passage from John to speak of the light of God shining into his creature, man. However, the interpretations are different even in terms of grammar, the darkness being subject in one and object in the other. The Eckhartian text implies, drawing perhaps on the Dionysian concept of the "divine dark," that both the dark stillness and knowledge of it are desirable. The poet of the *Mengeldicht*, on the other hand, uses the passage to indicate that the darkness is that of our *menichfuldicheit* (multiplicity) which is not able to comprehend the clarity of the light shining in it. She goes on to say that only by attaining the simplicity or unity of being, empty of all things, will we be able to see that light in the light. For the poet of the *Mengeldicht*, the darkness is very different from the "divine dark"—it is not something to be understood, but rather an impediment to an understanding of the light.

---

[9] The only edition of these *Mengeldichten* is: J. Van Mierlo, *Hadewijch Mengeldichten*, Leuvense Studiën en Tekstuitgaven (Antwerp: N.V. Standaard Boekhandel, 1952). The translations are mine. A new edition and English translation is currently in preparation.

Bouman then goes on to discuss the possibility that *Mengeldicht* 19 may have been directly influenced by Eckhart's *Predigt* 30. There are marked similarities between the two texts, but I would suggest that the evidence, when examined in detail, does not support the thesis of direct influence. There are, for example, salient features of each which are absent in the other. I would therefore suggest that the similarities are more easily explained as evidence for a tradition common to both the texts found in the Hadewijch manuscripts and the vernacular sermons of Eckhart, rather than by positing direct influence. The similarities between the two texts can be reduced to three main points: the concept that reason is a superior way to approach God; the necessity of seeing without intermediary; and the notion derived from Gregory the Great that it is needful to love as one who is dead, without the help of the senses or of the intellect. These three points are all characteristic of Eckhart's thought though not necessarily uniquely his.

In the first lines of the *Mengeldicht* the poet observes:

Above scripture
and created beings
reason can teach
and clearly perceive
and narrowly spy out
the way of our Lord. [19: 1–6]

Elsewhere in the *Mengeldichten*, and in other texts attributed to Hadewijch, love is consistently presented as the best and the highest way to approach God, but here reason is being compared with written authorities and the words of man. The sentiment of this stanza has an almost modern ring to it and could be an indication that the author was familiar with the debate in the universities concerning the application of Aristotelian logic to matters of theology. Eckhart, on the other hand, who most certainly was familiar with the debate, places intellect in relation to the will in a more traditional dichotomy. He writes: "The masters ask whether the kernel of eternal life lies more in the intellect or in the will. Will has two operations: desire and love. The intellect's work is onefold, and therefore it is better."[10] This consideration of the relative merits of intellect and will in the approach to God was an area of debate between the Franciscans and the Dominicans, and here Eckhart gives a good Dominican point of view. The author of the *Mengeldicht* addresses not the relationship between reason and love but between reason and recognized

---

[10] The quotations and numeration of Eckhart's sermons are taken from *Meister Eckhart: Sermons and Treatises*, 3 vols., ed. and trans. by M. O'C. Walshe (Rockport, Mass.: Element, 1991). This example is taken from vol. 1: 224. Hereafter the volume and page number will be given in the text.

"authorities." As in the case of the passage from John, I would suggest that the differences between the Eckhart text and the *Mengeldicht* may be more significant than the apparent similarities. It should also be noted that the rest of the *Mengeldichten* as well as the other texts in the Hadewijch manuscripts are more sympathetic to the Franciscan than to the Dominican point of view, regarding the will as the ultimate way to approach God precisely because it is comprised of desire and love. According to these texts, man's love for God is increased by his constantly unfulfilled and unfulfillable desire for him, and this desire is the *locus* of union with the love that is God.

The similarity between Eckhart's sermon and *Mengeldicht* 19 is most marked on the subject of seeing without intermediary. The poet of *Mengeldicht* 19 writes:

> To see [be] simply [naked], without means [intermediary]
> that is great
> well for him who can do it. [19: 13–15]

Line 13 is a good example of the way in which the poet capitalizes on the ambiguity of language to create additional levels of meaning in the text. I have argued elsewhere that the use of the same kinds of puns, paradoxes, and ambiguities in texts traditionally ascribed to Hadewijch and in the *Mengeldichten* 17–24 is an indication of how closely they are related.[11] In his sermon Eckhart writes: "If the soul were without means [intermediary], she would see God naked" [vol. 1: 225]. The similarity between these passages could be attributable to direct influence, if not from this specific text at least from Eckhart's other writings. The concept is not unique to Eckhart's thirtieth sermon and occurs in a number of earlier texts as well, although not in this vivid form.

The third marked similarity is that in both texts the authors emphasize the need to be "dead" in order to be able to see God or to approach him. The poet writes:

> To desire and to love
> without the help of senses/intellect
> this is necessary;
> and then inwardly and outwardly to be
> without knowledge
> like a dead man. [19: 43–48]

In *Predigt* 30 Eckhart attributes this idea to Gregory: "How should a man be who is to see God? He must be dead . . . Now St. Gregory says he is dead who is dead to the world . . . This is the first point: that one must be dead if one would see God"

---

[11] Murk-Jansen, *The Measure of Mystic Thought*, 71–76.

[vol. 1: 224]. It is clear that both authors have a shared perception of the nature of the relationship between God and man, but it is not evident that this is best explained by positing direct influence. The demand to withdraw from sense perceptions and the activity of the intellect as a preparation for drawing close to God is referred to in numerous texts by Bernard of Clairvaux, William of St. Thierry, and others. The idea cannot therefore be said even to be unique to the vernacular spirituality of the thirteenth century, although the articulation of it by the extreme image of death may be.

The evidence for the similarity of thought between *Mengeldicht* 19 and Eckhart's *Predigt* 30 is very strong, but there remain differences which do not accord with the theory of immediate influence. For example, Eckhart's sermon revolves around the significance of the three names of Peter, but the apostle is not even mentioned in the *Mengeldicht*. Similarly, the *Mengeldicht* refers to the need to look within, to the soul as a mirror of God, in order to gain knowledge. This concept can, of course, be found elsewhere in Eckhart, but it does not occur in *Predigt* 30. Although the evidence is not sufficient to prove Bouman's suggestion of the direct or indirect influence of Eckhart's *Predigt* 30 on *Mengeldicht* 19, he has drawn attention to the notable similarities in thought between the text in the Hadewijch manuscript and Eckhart's *Predigten*.

In his article Bouman also notes the similarity between *Mengeldicht* 26 and Eckhart's *Predigt* 87 on the poor in spirit. For the benefit of his argument with Van Mierlo, it is a shame that Bouman restricted himself to a consideration of the parallels between Eckhart's sermon on poverty and *Mengeldicht* 26, as this enabled Van Mierlo to dismiss the evidence as referring only to texts which he did not attribute to Hadewijch. Parallels to the salient elements of Eckhart's thought in this sermon are, however, also to be found in numerous texts Van Mierlo did ascribe to Hadewijch. Indeed the correspondence between *Mengeldicht* 26 and Eckhart's sermon is less striking than that with other Hadewijch texts when the texts are compared in detail.

Mengeldicht 26 is a description of the life and condition of those who are poor in spirit. Divested of similitudes and of all creaturely wisdom, they are simple and live in an eternal expanse of singleness of being, in contrast to the *menichfuldicheit* which was equated with darkness in *Mengeldicht* 27. The poem is particularly concerned with defining and describing the place where the poor in spirit are. Eckhart's sermon, on the other hand, concentrates rather on the place (or absence of place) where God is in the poor in spirit. For the author of the *Mengeldicht* the poor in spirit dwell in God, whereas for Eckhart, in this sermon, the salient point is that God dwells in the poor in spirit. The nature of the mystic experience appears to be such that these two positions are not mutually exclusive.[12] However, it does make it less likely that the one text was written under the direct influence of the other.

Many of the concepts and themes in Eckhart's sermon on poverty, which are perceived as so typical of Eckhart's thought, can also be found within texts that were ascribed to Hadewijch by Van Mierlo. The following will examine one or two in more detail. Both mystics associate union with a total absence of will, indeed an absence of a self to have a will. The advocation of such an absence of personal will and of a self which could have individual desires causes both to advocate an apparent impassivity and indifference to personal fate. Both Hadewijch and Eckhart, however, insist that the mystic continue to do good, simply relinquishing any sense of personal involvement in the outcome. One aspect of union, which both Hadewijch and Eckhart clearly consider potentially and ideally a permanent state rather than a fleeting experience, is that the mystic also loses the awareness of God—being so closely united involves the loss of a consciousness of the other and even of the sweetness of union. To argue for direct influence from Hadewijch to Eckhart would be inappropriate, but the extent of the similarity does suggest that Eckhart was writing in a tradition of spirituality and vernacular theology that had its roots earlier in the thirteenth century.

In his sermon on poverty, and elsewhere, Eckhart was misunderstood by the Inquisitors and by many later scholars to mean that the perfected soul should shun the doing of good works. A more dispassionate reading of Eckhart than the Inquisitors were able to make suggests that he was in fact urging his auditors to avoid personal involvement in the good works they perform, but to do them impersonally and impartially. In this he was following in the tradition of thirteenth-century lay piety. In Hadewijch's tenth *Letter* is a passage which echoes the prayer of St. Francis, "Let us labor, not seeking for any reward save that of knowing that we do thy will." Speaking of the wise who always seek to do good she writes: "They ask love for no other sweetness than that she grants them that in all things they may recognise her dearest will."[13] Hadewijch develops this thought and argues for an impassivity, almost an indifference which was to become such a feature of later spirituality, such as that of Marguerite Porete and Eckhart. In her second *Letter* she

---

[12] Speaking of the experience of mystic union as described by Teresa of Avila, Pike observes: "This is to say that [the soul] has been absorbed into God and that God has also been absorbed into [the soul]." Nelson Pike, *Mystic Union: An Essay in the Phenomenology of Mysticism* (Ithaca: Cornell, 1992), 10.

[13] A recent edition of the letters of Hadewijch is that of M. Ortmanns-Cornet, *Hadewijch Brieven* (Bruges: Uitgeverij Tabor, 1986). The translations are mine. In this edition the passage quoted occurs on p. 66. Hereafter, the page on which the quoted text appears will be given in the text.

writes: "Do good in all things. But do not care about success, neither about blessing nor about cursing, nor about salvation, nor about torment, but do and leave undone all things for the sake of love's honor" [18]. Here she articulates clearly what is largely implicit in Eckhart's work, namely that good must be done, but that it should be done only for the sake of God, without any sense of personal individual involvement. Concerning this indifference to personal fate, Hadewijch writes in her third *Mengeldicht*:

> For the finest life that I know
> Although I know myself unprepared for it
> That were that one let God ordain
> In taking, in giving, in storm, in peace,
> were it in loving, were it in hating;
> That should all be equal, sufficient,
> Whether God wished to come or to go. [3: 83–89]

Hadewijch here commends not only indifference to one's fate, but even to the presence or absence of God. Whatever is the will of God should be equally acceptable. This impassivity, or total abandonment of personal desire, which Hadewijch commends so highly, is not dissimilar to that condemned in the Papal bull *In agro dominico*, article 8: "Those who seek nothing, neither honor nor profit nor inwardness nor holiness nor reward nor heaven but who have renounced all this, including what is their own—in such men is God glorified" [Walshe, vol. 1: xlviii]. In *Letter* 19 Hadewijch uses the term *ongherijnlec* to describe this attitude. *Ongherijnlec* can be translated as unmoved, unmoveable, unaffected, or impassive. Hadewijch writes: "The soul which is most impassive, is most like God. Hold yourself unmoved by all people in heaven and on earth until the day that God is lifted up from the earth and that he draws you (and) all things to him" [126].[14] To be like God the soul must be impassive, without desires, and this state is the means to union with God. This impassivity to earthly events and personal fate does not contradict the emphasis laid elsewhere in these texts on the need for a passionate desire for God. Rather it is comparable with that discussed above in relation to *Mengeldicht* 19 that only one who is as though dead to the world is able to concentrate his love and desire sufficiently on God to see him.

Eckhart's definition of poverty is similarly radical. In his *Predigt* 87 Eckhart describes true poverty as having not even a will with which to want to do God's

---

[14] The biblical source for this concept is John 12:32. "And I, if I be lifted up from the earth, will draw all men unto me."

will. He writes: "As long as a man is so disposed that it is his will with which he would do the most beloved will of God, that man has not the poverty we are speaking about: for that man has a will to serve God's will—and that is not true poverty!" [vol. 2: 270]. The absolute loss of individual will as both a necessary condition and a consequence of union is a corollary to the need to be impassive to personal fate in Hadewijch's work also. To quote once more from her nineteenth *Letter*: "For if nothing exists for her [the impassive soul] but God, and she retains no will but lives only his will, and the soul has come to naught and wills with his will all that he wills, and is swallowed up in him and come to naught, then is he fully raised up from the earth and thus draws all things to himself" [126]. In such union the soul swallowed up in God has returned to her origins, to where and how she was before she was created—without distinction in God, the source of all creation. The soul has become nothing and is conscious of nothing except God whose will is her life. This reference to God being "raised up from the earth" recalls Eckhart's description of the Godhead, of God being raised up to what he was before he had creatures—to God as he was in himself—drawing all things back to their being within him before he spoke and they were created.[15]

Not only must one be indifferent to the presence or absence of God as Hadewijch points out in *Mengeldicht* 3, but being without God is also directly associated with union for both Hadewijch and Eckhart. Eckhart unambiguously recommends that his audience pray to be free of God: "Therefore let us pray to God that we may be free of God that we may gain the truth and enjoy it eternally" [vol. 2: 271]. Hadewijch also speaks of the need to be free of love (God), and of love's satisfaction when this is achieved. Unlike Eckhart, she also speaks of the sense of loss involved in giving up the sweetness of the consciousness of close association. She writes:

> That pleases love most of all, that one should be wholly robbed [devoid] of all pleasure of strangers and of friends and of herself. And that is a fearful life that love demands, that one must do without her fulfilment in order to fulfil her. They who are thus drawn into love and removed [received], and whom she binds, they owe so overly much to love to fulfil her on account of the great power of her strong nature. [86, 88]

For Hadewijch as for Eckhart, the need to do without the consciousness of the presence of love (God) is associated with union, with being drawn into love. It is

---

[15] For example, the following excerpt from his Pr. 22: "The Father always speaks to the Son in unity and pours forth all creatures in him. They all have a call to return whence they flowed forth. All their life and being is a calling and a hurrying back to what they came out of" [vol. 1: 179].

precisely those received by love, drawn into her, who owe it to love wholly to fulfill her by doing without the fulfillment of union with her. For Hadewijch that union which she is dedicated to achieving and towards which she is urging her audience involves no cloying sweetness. Rather it is a terrifying paradox of experiencing fulfillment only when embracing, welcoming, the reality of eternal lack of fulfillment. Moments such as this enable the modern reader to peer into the abyss and to feel something of the awe described by Hadewijch as she looks at the vortex which is the reality of her experience of union with God: "And in the middle under the disc [the seat of God] was a whirlpool turning so fearfully that heaven and earth might wonder at it and be afraid; . . . the deep whirlpool that is so fearfully dark that is divine union in its hidden storms."[16]

In conclusion, I hope that this reappraisal of Bouman's article has shown that the similarity which Bouman perceived between the work of Hadewijch and that of Eckhart should not be summarily dismissed. That the explanation which Bouman put forward for this similarity, namely Eckhart's direct influence on Hadewijch, appears flawed does not diminish the value of his observations. There are fashions in scholarship, and currently the fashion is less to identify major individual authors and to measure their greatness in terms of the number of others they influenced, than to see them as the peaks in more general currents of thought, thereby reevaluating the many unnamed voices in the chorus. Following the current fashion, therefore, I am not looking to show direct influence from Hadewijch to Eckhart, although to do so would satisfy another currently fashionable trend, which is to draw attention to the contribution of women. Unless some further evidence should come to light, direct influence will be impossible to prove. Rather, I am interested to establish that many of the themes and ideas which have traditionally been conceived of as typically Eckhartian are also to be found in texts which predate him by at least fifty years and which are evidence for the kind of mystic theology current in the groups of laywomen during the thirteenth century. The similarity is sufficiently great to suggest that both authors, if not influenced directly the one by the other, were at least drawing on common material.

Clearly, one short essay cannot hope to do justice to such a complex subject as the relationship between the theology of Eckhart and that of Hadewijch. It is time the silence imposed by the events of the two world wars was broken and that the question of the relationship between them should be posed once again. On

---

[16] Vision 1. A good recent edition is that of Paul Mommaers, *De Visioenen van Hadewijch*, 2 vols. (Nijmegen: Uitgeverij B. Gottmer, 1979). The translation is mine. In that edition the lines quoted are: 204–7, 214–16.

reexamination, the evidence in Bouman's article shows that there are substantial similarities between the theology of Hadewijch and that of Eckhart. The discussion of these similarities may however still arouse hostility, even though they have argued that it should be seen as evidence for the existence of a tradition of vernacular spirituality and theology during the thirteenth century, and not as evidence for direct influence.

2

The Wilderness of God in Hadewijch II and Meister Eckhart and His Circle

Paul A. Dietrich

(T)he grotto was . . . secluded in the midst of this wild solitude (*wüsten wilde*) . . . (Love) is hidden away in the wilds (*wilde*), the country that leads to her refuge makes hard and arduous going—mountains are strewn about the way in many a massive curve. The tracks up and down are so obstructed with rocks for us poor sufferers that, unless we keep well to the path, if we make one false step we shall never get back alive. But whoever is so blessed as to reach and enter that solitude (*wilde*) will have used his efforts to most excellent purpose, for he will find his heart's delight there. Whatever the ear yearns to hear, whatever gratifies the eye, this wilderness (*wilde*) is full of it. *Tristan*, chap. 26[1]

Gottfried von Strassburg's description of the *Minnegrotte* suggests the metaphorical potential of wilderness imagery in medieval poetry. Within the world of late medieval Rhineland mystical texts, references to wildness (*wilde*), wilderness (*wüste*), and desert (*einöde*) are part of an apophatic discourse linked to theological claims about the nature of God and the soul. In addition to these more formal, metaphysical (or anti-metaphysical) assertions, wilderness language also describes a process of personal transformation, a phenomenology of mystical experience. The topography of wilderness and desert provide the imagery for the twin discourses of ontology (or disontology) and psycho-spirituality; the same set of terms may illuminate the territory of the divine nature as well as the landscape of the soul.

---

[1] Gottfried von Strassburg, *Tristan*, trans. A. T. Hatto (Baltimore: Penguin, 1969), 265–66. Cf. Karl Marold, ed. (Berlin: Walter de Gruyter, 1977; reprint of 1906 edition), 17075–102: 238.

In three poems attributed to Hadewijch, Meister Eckhart, and Tauler, a vocabulary of wilderness and solitude is typically part of a cluster of topics including: (1) the simplicity or purity of the divine nature and the soul often expressed in terms of their essential nakedness or bareness; (2) the mystery of God's simultaneous total transcendence and absolute immanence; (3) the self's abandonment and detachment from all contingent reality (the self's inner asceticism); (4) the soul's reversion to its source and the union of God and the soul understood as *unitas indistinctionis*; and finally, (5) the identity of God's ground and the soul's ground, often expressed in the correlative terms of abyss, nothingness, and darkness. The poems enact a fundamental shift in perspective and bear witness to the transformative function of mystical language.

A relationship of reciprocal assimilation can be discerned between the religious literature of Germany and the Low Countries during the late Medieval Period. There are no linguistic borders, rather linguistic zones; medieval Dutch works were not so much translated as "Germanized" and vice versa.[2] Parallels and affinities in language and doctrine between the works of Hadewijch and her circle and the German mystics are striking; however, the question of influence, direct or indirect, is more problematic. The difficulties of establishing chronologies and possible influence are exacerbated by the issue of pseudonymity. When both authorship and date are uncertain, discussion of influence becomes extremely tentative. The following observations will be largely confined to a discussion of similarities, a comparison of the poems suggesting underlying unities of thought.

Hadewijch and Hadewijch II

The *Mengeldichten* are a collection of twenty-nine poems found in the manuscripts of the poems, visions, and letters of the thirteenth-century mystic Hadewijch. The editor of the first critical edition of the poems distinguished between the first sixteen *Mengeldichten* and the last thirteen, claiming that the earlier poems alone were by Hadewijch, reflecting her affective mysticism and Augustinian spirituality.[3] According to this view, *Mengeldichten* 17–29 were by a later hand, dating from the late thirteenth or early fourteenth century and exhibited a quite different sensibility, an apophatic mysticism and Dionysian spirituality. Recently, following the lead of several Dutch scholars, S. M. Murk-Jansen has argued for a further distinction

[2] Kurt Ruh, cited by Alois M. Haas, "Rhénane (Mystique)" *Dictionnaire de spiritualité* 13: 511–12.

[3] Jozef Van Mierlo, *Hadewijch Mengeldichten* (Brussels: n.p., 1912), xxviii.

between *Mengeldichten* 17–24 and 25–29.[4] Generally speaking, *Mengeldichten* 17–24 share a common vocabulary and spiritual perspective with *Mengeldichten* 1–16 and the *Strofische Gedichten*, *Letters*, and *Visions* of Hadewijch, though offering perhaps a more sophisticated understanding of mystical union. These poems may have been written by someone in Hadewijch's immediate circle, a person thoroughly familiar with her works, or perhaps by Hadewijch herself. The language and teaching of *Mengeldichten* 25–29, however, are more explicitly apophatic and closer to the thought of Marguerite Porete and Meister Eckhart.

One of the consequences of locating *Mengeldichten* 17–24 in close proximity to Hadewijch is the increasing recognition of the apophatic dimension of her thought. There is a solitude at the heart of this most affective of love mystics; she speaks of abyss, bareness, detachment, liberty, nothingness, and wilderness. Consider *Letter* 18 on the greatness of the soul:

> Now understand the deepest essence of your soul, what "soul" is. Soul is a being that can be beheld by God and by which again, God can be beheld . . . the soul is a bottomless abyss in which God suffices to himself; and his own self-sufficiency ever finds fruition to the full in this soul, as the soul, for its part, ever does in him. Soul is a way for the passage of God from his depths into his liberty; and God is a way for the passage of the soul into its liberty, that is, into his inmost depths, which cannot be touched except by the soul's abyss.[5]

Alois Hass has described this passage as a mystical commentary on Psalm 41:8, "*abyssus abyssum invocat*";[6] it might also be a commentary on the identity of the ground of the soul and the ground of the Godhead in Eckhart. A consideration of the similarities between Hadewijch and Eckhart is outside the scope of this paper; however, by simply indicating the apophatic element in Hadewijch's work, we arrive at a second consequence of the investigation of *Mengeldichten* 17–29. *Mengeldichten* 17–24 are clearly of a piece with the fabric of Hadewijch's spirituality. What about *Mengeldichten* 25–29? I believe that it is possible to accept literary analysis which shows the linguistic distinctiveness of the last poems, and still argue for a thematic continuity with the teaching of Hadewijch. If the spirituality of wilderness does

---

[4] Saskia M. Murk-Jansen, *The Measure of Mystic Thought: A Study of Hadewijch's Mengeldichten* (Göppingen: Kümmerle Verlag, 1991), 6–7, 31–33, 101–2, 163–66, et passim.

[5] Hadewijch, *The Complete Works*, trans. Columba Hart, O. S. B., Classics of Western Spirituality Series (New York: Paulist Press, 1980), 86. Cf. *Strofisch Gedicht* 36, "Wilderness of Love," and *Vision* 11, "The Abyss of Omnipotence."

[6] Alois M. Haas, "Hadewijch," *Geistliches Mittelalter* (Freiburg, Switzerland: Universitätsverlag, 1984), 404.

indeed form a significant component in her writings, then some of the radical vocabulary of *Mengeldichten* 25–29 may simply be later formulations of themes already adumbrated in the earlier poems, letters, and visions.

I would like to turn to the most striking of the later poems, *Mengeldicht* 26. The author of this poem, often referred to as Hadewijch II, shares with Hadewijch a strong sense of responsibility for the spiritual progress of others; the poet is a self-proclaimed spiritual guide. There is a consciousness of the solitude of the soul with God (reminiscent of *Letter* 18 cited above), of the nobility and intangible liberty of the soul, and of the absolute primacy of spiritual freedom and an immediate relation to God.[7] The poem's description of the true nature of spiritual poverty reflects contemporaneous debates among the mendicant orders and Beguines such as Marguerite Porete.

Mengeldicht 26

I will approach love gladly
If I have the power to reach the heart.
But no one will sing there with me
Who mingles with creatures.

Naked love (*blote minne*) who spares nothing
In her wild death (*welde oueruaert*)
Stripped of all accident (*toeuals*)
Recovers her simple unity.

In Love's pure abandon
No created good can subsist:
For Love strips of all form
Those she receives in her simplicity.

Free from all modes (*wisen*),
Strangers to every image,
This is the true life
Of the poor in spirit.

True poverty is not simply
Exile and begging for bread.
The poor in spirit must live
Without notions in a vast simplicity.

---

[7] Jean-Baptiste Porion, *Hadewijch d'Anvers* (Paris: Éditions du Seuil, 1954), 11.

Without end or beginning,
Without form, modality, reason or sense,
Neither opinion, thought, attention, nor knowing,
One that is boundless and without limit.

In this wild wide simplicity
Live the poor in spirit in unity (*enecheit*);
Nothing is there except silent emptiness (*ledecheit*)
Ever answering to eternity.

I've had my say in a short poem,
But the way is long as I well know,
And those who want to finish the course
Endure much suffering.[8]

The poem opens and closes with a formulaic assertion of the poet's authority and long-suffering, a sort of reverse modesty formula. The experience of love authorizes the poet to speak. Pure love (*blote minne*) in her wild "overcoming" or "crossing over" (*welde oueruaert*), an example of *mors mystica*, is stripped of all images and recovers her simple unity. Nudity, purity, simplicity, and unity are synonyms indicating the telos of the soul's process of self-annihilation. True poverty of spirit is distinguished from physical poverty and the outward life of the mendicant. The poor in spirit live in unity (*enecheit*) and emptiness (*ledecheit*) in a vast wild simplicity (*welde wide eenvuldecheit*) without end or beginning, beyond form, modality, reason, or sense, beyond the mental operations of imagination, thought, contemplation, indeed beyond knowledge—a boundless desert.

This vast wilderness is simultaneously the soul's own recovered primal nature, a condition of unmanifest openness and emptiness beyond space and time, without a "why" (*sonder waeromme*, cf. *Mengeldicht* 18), *and* the *locus* of an unmediated union with the abyss, the desert, the ocean of the Godhead in its primal nature. There are striking parallels with Eckhart's *Predigt* 52 (in the Quint edition) on spiritual poverty, and also in his teachings on *abegescheidenheit* in the vernacular treatises and other sermons.

Wilderness or desert, understood as metaphors for both the essential nature of the soul and the meeting place between God and the soul, can also be seen in the work of Jan Ruusbroec who was deeply indebted to both Hadewijch and Hadewijch II. In a passage which echoes *Mengeldicht* 26, Ruusbroec writes: "(b)ut

---

[8] I am indebted to Dr. S. M. Murk-Jansen for permission to consult her forthcoming edition of the *Mengeldichten* and for her advice on Medieval Dutch terminology.

we must regard our created essence as a wild, waste desert, where God, who rules us, lives. And in this desert we must wander, stripped of our own modes and manners."[9]

Meister Eckhart and the *Granum Sinapis*

Meister Eckhart has been described as the mystic of the "inner desert" (e.g., Pr. 81, "einoede in sich selber").[10] We might paraphrase Bernard Mojsisch and find in Eckhart's thought a metaphysics of wilderness.[11] Theologically, wilderness is a statement about the divine nature; in a vernacular treatise from Eckhart's circle, "Dionysius" is quoted: "God's desert is God's simple nature" (*gotes wüestenunge ist gotes einvaltigiu nâture*).[12] Although the use of desert imagery is not part of the authentic Dionysian corpus, the medieval association of desert and the divine nature reflects the kataphatic dialectic concerned with the purity and unity of the divine nature articulated in *The Divine Names* 13, and an apophatic dialectic of divine obscurity in the *Mystical Theology* 1.[13] This Platonic inheritance is retained in John the Scot: "In a higher understanding the desert is understood as the ineffable height of the divine nature, separate from all things" (*altiori vero theoria desertum intelligitur divinae naturae, ab omnibus remotae, ineffabilis altitudo*).[14]

In Eckhart's vernacular sermons God is described as a "still desert (*stille wüste*) . . . in his oneness and in his solitary wilderness, in his vast wasteland, and in his own ground."[15] Wilderness is also the meeting ground for God and the soul. In the *Liber Benedictus*, and elsewhere, Eckhart quotes Hosea 2:14: "I will lead her into solitude and speak to her heart" (*Et ducam eam in solitudinem, et loquar ad cor eius*), adding

---

[9] Jan Ruusbroec, *Werken* (Tielt: Ruusbroecgenootschap, 1944–48) III, 217, cited in *Boecsken der verclaringhe* (Leiden: E. J. Brill, 1981), 30.

[10] Hans Bayer, "*Vita in deserto*. Kassians Askese der Einöde und die mittelalterliche Frauenmystik," *Zeitschrift für Kirchengeschichte* 98 (1987): 5.

[11] Bernard Mojsisch, *Meister Eckhart-Analogie, Univozität und Einheit*, (Hamburg: Felix Meiner Verlang, 1983), 141, on Eckhart's "Metaphysik des Grundes."

[12] Tractate XI "Von der übervart der gotheit" in *Meister Eckhart*, ed. Franz Pfeiffer (Göttingen: Vandenhoeck and Ruprecht, 1924; reprint of 1857 edition), 502-3.

[13] Pseudo-Dionysius the Areopagite, *The Mystical Theology* 1 and *The Divine Names* 13, in *The Complete Works*, Classics of Western Spirituality Series, trans. C. Luibheid (New York: Paulist Press, 1987), 135–37; 127–31.

[14] Jean Scot, *Commentaire sur l'Évangile de Jean* (*In Johannis Evangelium*), ed. E. Jeauneau (Paris: Cerf, 1972, Sources chrétiennes 180) I, 27:140.

[15] Meister Eckhart, Pr. 10 (DW 1: 171, 12–15): "got in sîner wüestunge und in sînem eigenun grunde." Trans. by Bernard McGinn, *Meister Eckhart Teacher and Preacher*, Classics of Western Spirituality Series (New York: Paulist, 1986), 265. Cf. also Pr. 12, 28, 29, 48, 60, 81, 86.

"one with One, one from One, one in One, and in One, one everlastingly."[16] Wilderness betokens one of the poles of Meister Eckhart's discourse. In the words of Michael Sells, "the unnameable, unknowable transcendent that continuously recedes beyond reference."[17]

Wilderness is the domain of God, the between, and the inside of all things. As in Hadewijch II, wilderness is also a metaphor for the ground of the soul: "The creature's wilderness is its simple nature" (*der creaturen wüstenunge ist ir einveltigiu nâture*).[18] What is initially an apophatic statement about the divine nature closely linked with related symbols of abyss, ground, darkness, nakedness, as well as themes of divine purity/simplicity/unity and otherness, is interwoven with anthropological claims about the nature of the soul and its mimesis of the divine nature. Wilderness then becomes transformed into a metaphor for the psycho-spiritual process of mystical union, the *unitas indistinctionis* of God and the soul—an interior transformation characterized by abandonment, detachment, emptiness, and liberty.

The most important poetic expression of these Eckhartian concepts is the Middle High German poem, *Granum Sinapis*. Written in Eckhart's Thuringian dialect, the poem is a virtual summary of the master's themes. Kurt Ruh has argued that the work is an early one by Eckhart, a conclusion gradually gaining acceptance by other scholars.[19] Regardless of authorship, the *Granum Sinapis* certainly breathes the spirit of Eckhart and is from his sphere.[20]

The poem is in the form of a sequence set to the standard melody of Adam of St. Victor. The first line echoes the prologue of the Gospel of John: "In the Beginning, High above understanding Is ever the Word." The first three strophes establish the liturgical style and invoke the Trinity, thus the traditional name of the sequence, the *Dreifaltigkeitslied*. The treatment of the *perichoresis* of the Three Persons, the inner-trinitarian movement, is strongly Augustinian and reminiscent of the trinitarian spirituality of Hadewijch or Ruusbroec. In the third strophe the

---

[16] *Liber Benedictus* 2 (DW 5: 119.6-7): " . . . ein mit einem, ein von einem, ein in einem und in einem ein êwelîche." Trans. in *Meister Eckhart: The Essential Writings*, ed. and trans. Bernard McGinn and Edmund College, Classics of Western Spirituality Series (New York: Paulist Press, 1981), 247.

[17] Michael Sells, *Mystical Languages of Unsaying* (Chicago: University of Chicago Press, 1994).

[18] Cf. references in Grete Lüers, *Die Sprache der deutschen Mystik des Mittelalters im Werke der Mechthild von Magdeburg* (Munich: Verlag Ernst Reinhardt, 1926), 295.

[19] Kurt Ruh, *Meister Eckhart. Theologe. Prediger. Mystiker* (Munich: C. H. Beck, 1985), 49–50; Alain de Libera, *Poème. Granum Sinapis suivi d'un commentaire latin anonyme* (Paris: Arfuyen, 1988), 55.

[20] Alois M. Haas, "*Granum Sinapis*. An den Grenzen der Sprache," *Sermo mysticus. Studien zu Theologie und Sprache der deutschen Mystik*, ed. A. M. Haas (Freiburg, Switzerland: Universitätsverlag, 1979), 301–29.

imagery of ground and abyss is introduced: "Here is a depth without ground" (*sunder grunt*). God is likened to a circle and a point, recalling the famous definition from the twelfth-century *Book of XXIV Philosophers* and Alan of Lille.

There is a clear distinction between the first three sections of the poem and the following five. We move from an Augustinian theology of the Trinity to a Dionysian spirituality of the mystical path.

> IV.
> The mountain of this point
> Ascend without activity,
> (O) intellect!
> The road leads you
> Into a marvelous desert, (wûste wûnderlich)
> So broad, so wide,
> It stretches out immeasurably.
> The desert has
> Neither time nor place,
> Its mode of being is unique.[21]

The ascent of the mountain leads to an immense wilderness in a juxtaposition of imagery of ascension and introversion. The shift from the mountain to the desert is pursued in the next two sections of the poem which further describe the wilderness of the Godhead in apophatic terms.

The poem has survived accompanied by an anonymous Latin commentary, perhaps written by one of Eckhart's disciples. At this point in the commentary the author echoes "Dionysius" and Eriugena, "de mistico deserto, quod est esse divinum ipsum."[22] The desert is once again a metaphor for the Godhead, emphasizing the simplicity and unity of the divine nature. This "good desert" (*wûste gût*) is beyond the created order, ineffable, and characterized by paradoxical claims—here and there, far and near, deep and high, "neither this nor that" (*weder diz noch daz*) (Section V). The desert is light and dark, free of beginning or end—unnamed (*unbenant*), unknown (*unbekant*), pure and naked (*blôs âne wât*) (Section VI). This description of the wilderness of the Godhead constitutes an apophatic litany.

The final two sections of the sequence shift the focus from the wilderness of the Godhead to the means of entering the wilderness:

---

[21] I am indebted to Bernard McGinn for permission to quote from his unpublished translation of the *Granum Sinapis*.

[22] Maria Bindschedler, ed., *Der lateinischen Kommentar zum Granum Sinapis* (Basel: Schwabe, 1949), 86ff.

VII.
Become like a child,
Become deaf, become blind,
Your own something
Must become nothing; (*dîn selbes icht/muz werden nicht*)
Drive away all something, all nothing!
Leave place, leave time,
Avoid even image!
Go without a way
On the narrow path,
Then you will find the desert's track (*der wûste spôr*).

VIII.
O my soul,
Go out, (let) God in!
Sink all my something
In God's nothing (*sink al mîn icht/in gotis nicht*),
Sink in the bottomless flood!
If I flee from You,
You come to me.
If I lose myself,
Then I find You,
O Goodness above being (*uberweselîches gût*)!

These last sections recount the familiar Eckhartian processes of *abegescheidenheit* and *gelassenheit*, detachment and self-emptying.

In this lyrical gloss on the parable of the mustard seed we see, in the words of Alain de Libera, the transformation of the injunctions and concepts of Dionysian theology into authentic and repeatable experience.[23] The intellectual culture of Eckhart the *lesemeister* comes together with the simple wisdom, the sapiential perspective, of Eckhart the *lebemeister*.

Tauler and the *Song of Bareness*

The conventional portrait of Eckhart's disciple Johannes Tauler is that of a dynamic preacher uninterested in the speculative abstractions of his mentor, that is, a *lebemeister* concerned to guard against the doctrinal excesses of the *valsche ledecheit* of the "free spirits." Recent scholars have placed Tauler more securely within the

---

[23] Alain de Libera, *Poème*, 56.

context of the Rhineland Dominicans from Albert the Great to Dietrich of Freiburg; Tauler emerges as a mystic deeply grounded in the culture of Dionysian and Proclean Platonism, one whose differences with Eckhart are a matter of rhetorical strategy rather than doctrinal content.[24] Indeed Tauler cites Proclus in his sermons and seems to be aware of the radical implications of Proclus' description of the One beyond being and existence.

Along with typically Eckhartian discourse on mystical union (*ein einig ein, einecheit*), releasement (*gelazenheit*), breaking-through (*durchbruch*), bareness (*blozheit*), ground (*grunt*), and wilderness (*wüste, wüstenunge*), Tauler surpassed the Meister in his exploration of the groundless ground (*grundelos grunt*) or the abyss (*abgrunde/abgrunt*). He was especially fond of glossing Psalm 41:8, *abyssus abyssum invocat*. Tauler was also partial, as we shall see, to the language of "unbecoming" (*entwerden*).

For Tauler wildness is that which is inaccessible to the intellect, beyond means and modalities. In Sermon 11 he describes the individual led into a "wild wilderness" (*wüste wilde*), indescribable, beyond the soul's faculties, beyond distinctions, ways, modes, and manners, an "unfathomable darkness." The soul is led into "the oneness of God's simple unity" (*der simpelen wiselosen einikeit*) . . . "in this unity all mutiplicity is lost; it is the unity which unifies multiplicity (in) an incomprehensible, wild wilderness" (*unbegriffenliche wilde wüste*).[25] This is the desert of the divine nature, the "simple hidden wilderness beyond being" (*einveltig überwesenliche verborgene wüste*), "the still solitary divine wilderness" of Sermon 60 (*der götlich wüstenunge in der stillen einsamkeit*). Wilderness has several dimensions: (1) the locus of the soul's encounter with God; (2) the primal nature of God; and (3) the self's own primordial condition, the individual's *inre wüstenunge*. Commenting on the Hosea passage, Tauler describes the meeting of the soul's inner wilderness with the "quiet empty wilderness of the Godhead" (Sermon 60: *die wüsten stillen lidigen gotheit*).[26]

---

[24] Loris Sturlese, "Tauler im Context. Die philosophischen Voraussetzungen des 'Seelengrundes' in der Lehre des deutschen Neuplatonikers Berthold von Moosburg," *Beiträge zur Geschichte der Deutschen Sprache und Literatur* 109/3 (1987): 390–426; Alain de Libera, *Introduction à la Mystique Rhénane* (Paris: O. E. I. L., 1984). Cf. also Stephen Ozment, *Homo Spiritualis* (Leiden: E. J. Brill, 1969); Paul Wyser, O. P., "Taulers Terminologie vom Seelengrund" (1958), reprinted in Werner Beierwaltes, ed. *Platonismus in der Philosophie des Mittelalters* (Darmstadt: Wissenschaftliche Buchgesellschaft, Wege der Forschung 197, 1969), 381–409; and Claire Champollion, "La place des termes 'gemuete' et 'grunt' dans la vocabulaire de Tauler," *La Mystique Rhénane* (Paris: Presses Universitaires de France, 1963), 179–92.

[25] *Predigt* 11, in *Die Predigten Taulers*, Ferdinand Vetter, ed., (Berlin: Deutsche Text des Mittelalters XI, 1910), 54–55 (hereafter "V").

[26] *Predigt* 60, V, 277–78.

The so-called "Tauler Canticles" provide a lyrical formulation of many of the themes in the Dominican's sermons. The canticles have received little scholarly attention. They were published in early printed editions of Tauler's works (e.g., the 1548 Latin edition of Surius), and again in the nineteenth century.[27] Whether or not the canticles can be attributed directly to Tauler, they certainly reflect his language and concerns. The *Song of Bareness* richly embodies the apophatic language of the soul's kenosis is the dark abyss of the Godhead.

Song of Bareness

I will sing of bareness (*blozheit*) a new song,
for true purity (*luterheit*) is without thought.
Thoughts may not be there,
so I have lost the "mine":
I am decreated (*entworden*).
He who is unminded (*entgeistet*) has no cares.

My unlikeness (*ungelich*) no longer causes me to err:
I am as gladly poor as rich.
I want nothing to do with images (*bilden*),
I must stand free (*ledig*) of myself:
I am decreated.
He who is unminded has no cares.

Would you know how I escaped the images?
I perceived the right unity (*einicheit*) in myself.
That is right unity
when neither weal nor woe displaced (*entsetzt*) me:
I am decreated.
He who is unminded has no cares.

Would you know how I escaped the mind?
When I perceived neither this nor that in myself,
save the bare Godhead unfounded (*bloze gotheit ungegrundet*).
Then I could no longer keep silent, I had to tell it:
I am decreated.
He who is unminded has no cares.

---

[27] Laurentio Surius, ed. *Institutiones Taulerianae*, (Cologne: 1548). Cf. A. Ampe, S. J., "Een kritish onderzoek van de 'Institutiones Taulerianae,'" *Ons Geestlijk Erf* 40, II (1966). Ph. Wackernagel, ed., *Das deutsche Kirchenlied*, vol. 2 (Leipzig: 1867), 305–6.

Since I am thus lost in the abyss (*abgrunde*)
I no longer wish to speak, I am mute.
The Godhead clear has swallowed me into itself.
I am displaced.
Therefore the darkness delighted me greatly.

Since I have thus come through to the origin (*ursprunge*),
I may no longer age, but grow young,
So all my powers have disappeared
and have died.
He who is unminded has no cares.

Then whosoever has disappeared
and has found a darkness
is so rich without sorrow.
Thus the dear fire has consumed me,
and I have died.
He who is thus unminded has no cares.

Whosoever has died and is decreated,
To him the Father is revealed,
And the Son and Holy Spirit also,
In Christ Jesus is every good bliss and delight,
It is above all measure,
Who is not unreleased, he shall suffer.[28]

In this poem we find echoes of both Hadewijch and Eckhart, especially a further
development of Hadewijch II's discourse on spiritual poverty. The now familiar
apophatic vocabulary presents itself: nakedness/bareness (*blozheit*), right unity (*rechte
einicheit*), and the abyss of the Godhead. Following Michael Sells' translation of
apophasis as "unsaying" or "saying away" we can discern a radical unsaying, here the
purposive transgression of linguistic boundaries. The poetic voice speaks of having
escaped, of being lost, swallowed, mute, disappeared, consumed, dead. The self is
displaced (*entsetzt*), unminded (*entgeistet*), decreated/unbecome (*entworden*).

For Eckhart (in Pfeiffer, *Predigt* 56) "God becomes and unbecomes (*entwirt*)";
for Tauler, the individual must "unbecome" by releasing works, ways, and one's own

---

[28] Slightly modified text in Wackernagel, *Das deutsche Kirchenlied*. Translation based, in part,
on text in Martin Buber, ed. *Ecstatic Confessions* (New York: Harper and Row, 1985), 76–77.
E. T. of *Ekstatische Konfessionen* (Eugen Diederichs Verlag, 1909).

nature, and sinking into the deep, bottomless sea of God—*solt du in Got gewerden, so must du din selbes entwerden*.[29] In the *Song of Bareness* a condition is sought beyond thought and images, free (*ledig*) of self and distinctions (neither this nor that), breaking through to the naked abyss of the Godhead. In the first four stanzas the poet announces his decreation; in the next, he is displaced; in the final three, "I have died." This "death" following decreation resembles Eckhart's *duchbruch* to one's own source.[30] It also echoes the ecstatic wild death or crossing over in Hadewijch's *Mengeldicht* 26 (*welde ouervaert*).

I have been attending to the overlap between poetic and mystical discourse—that intersection which invites consideration of the performative and transformative functions of language. The goal in each of the poems considered here is to effect a shift of perspective within the reader or listener. Each articulates a vision of radical spiritual freedom following from the soul's unmediated union in the wilderness of the Godhead.

These three poetic renditions of the *via negativa* also invite questions concerning provenance, chronology, and possible influence. Hadewijch II may or may not be the "missing link" between Eckhart and Ruusbroec, as Jean-Baptiste Porion once suggested.[31] The author may have exercised a considerable influence on Eckhart's notion of *abegescheidenheit*, as Alois Haas has claimed.[32] But the vocabulary, imagery, and teachings of Hadewijch II show undeniable affinity with Meister Eckhart and his circle of disciples. Perhaps it is enough to observe the similarities and to take a further step toward placing Meister Eckhart in historical context by describing the remarkable worlds of mystical thought and expression of women who lived a generation or two earlier.

---

[29] *Predigt* 60, V, 277–78; 41, 175.

[30] See e.g., Quint edition, Pr. 48 and 52.

[31] Jean-Baptiste Porion, *Hadewijch d'Anvers*, 47.

[32] Alois M. Haas, "Hadewijch," 401. Cf. Emilie Zum Brunn, "Une source méconnue de l'ontologie eckhartienne," *Métaphysique, Histoire de la Philosophie* (Neuchâtel, 1981), 111–18.

I am grateful to Bernard McGinn for allowing me to consult his essay "Ocean and Desert as Symbols of Mystical Absorption in the Christian Tradition" as I completed the final draft of my essay.

3

Mechthild of Magdeburg and Meister Eckhart

Points of Coincidence

Frank Tobin

Though Mechthild of Magdeburg and Meister Eckhart are both recognized as medieval Christian mystics who left us remarkable evidence of their intensely vital interior lives, it is their differences within this shared context that are most immediately apparent. Mechthild, vividly imaginative, relates her not infrequent confrontations with the devil and starkly describes her Dante-esque visions of purgatory and hell. Eckhart so ignores these staples of medieval religious culture that he could easily be mistaken for a post-Enlightenment Unitarian. Mechthild clothes her descriptions of the soul's commerce with God in erotic images, and bases much of her work squarely on the tradition of bride mysticism. Eckhart uses this tradition sparingly, so much so that it calls attention to itself when it does occur. Mechthild draws heavily on the traditions of the prophets, both in her attempts to call her less spiritually minded contemporaries—especially among the clergy—back to the path of divinely ordained morality, and in her apocalyptic depictions of the end of time. Eckhart seems, rather, to assume basic moral goodness in his audiences and is much more concerned with conveying the timelessness of the God-soul relationship than anything about the end of time.

Although both pursued their goals with equal intensity and persistence, their temperaments and talents caused them to embark on quite separate paths to reach those goals. Mechthild craved immediate personal experience. Today we would say that she had a hunger for life. In line with the traditions of Augustine, both she and her contemporaries would interpret this hunger as a desire to possess God. Certainly, as a term to express Mechthild's longing, hunger is an appropriate expression, as are other metaphors of the body and its needs. She had to *see, hear, taste,* and *touch* God. Eckhart, with a restlessness no less intense, craved to *know* God, the only object that could satisfy his intellect. Then there is the disparity of their schooling. Eckhart achieved the highest academic honors of his time and used his professional vocabulary and authority to further his mystical message. Mechthild, an enthusiastic admirer of the Dominicans, was, as she herself admitted, an *ungelerter munt* (uneducated voice). Given the personality that emanates from her writings, one can be quite sure that she would not have been unduly intimidated by learning such as Eckhart's. Nor, given her own talents, should she have been. Nevertheless, she had to rely on more general cultural means for self-expression; and an urgent side issue, as she composed her book, was the constant need to establish and legitimize her authority.

One difference between the Beguine and the Dominican *lese- und lebemeister* that is critical to understanding them and to establishing a possible relationship between them is the wide divergence in the kind of mysticism each represents. Mechthild is an ecstatic and visionary mystic. One searches Eckhart's works in vain for clear evidence that he had like experiences. Because he makes few references to personal experiences of any kind, assertions by scholars that Eckhart was privileged with mystical favors are generally based on indirect evidence, namely, that such experiences are the only explanation for the profundity and brilliance of his mystical thought. The fact that the mysticism Eckhart preaches in his vernacular sermons is so utterly devoid of evidence of supernatural favors received by him and so completely grounded in mainstream scholastic philosophy and theology, it has been suggested, is not merely a result of his spiritual and intellectual bent, but is also an indication of a conscious effort to counteract the dangers of a mysticism based on singular private experiences. Winfried Trusen argues plausibly the case that Eckhart's activity in Strasbourg immediately after the Council of Vienne (1311–12), which condemned heretical teachings attributed to Beghards and Beguines and pronounced severe strictures on their way of life, represented an attempt on the part of the Dominicans to minister to the needs of the spiritually sophisticated nuns and Beguines of the area while at the same time leading them away from exotic forms of mysticism sometimes prevalent in such communities. Often the teachings and behavior of these women that church authorities found dangerous or threatening seemed to derive from "experiential" mysticism.[1] Eckhart nowhere condemns visions and ecstasies; rather, he pays them scant attention while, at the same time, emphasizing the astonishing union with God possible to souls based simply on their nature as his creatures.

[1] Winfried Trusen, *Der Prozess gegen Meister Eckhart: Vorgeschichte, Verlauf und Folgen* (Paderborn: Schönigh, 1988), especially 19–61.

Certainly, Eckhart was aware of the kind of mysticism Mechthild experienced and described. Was he also aware of Mechthild herself? Did he know and was he influenced by her book *The Flowing Light of the Godhead*? Oliver Davies has addressed these questions and gives credible arguments for Eckhart's being familiar with Mechthild and her book.[2] Dietrich of Apolda, the author of the most extensive biography of St. Dominic at the time, was a member of the Dominican community at Erfurt, when Eckhart was prior there, and was writing or had recently completed his biography of the order's founder. Dietrich incorporates passages from the Latin translation of Mechthild's book into his work and praises its author, saying that the Lord has revealed many things to her and that the parts of his biography based on her book are taken "from very intimate and true revelations."[3] It seems likely that the intellectually inclined prior would be familiar with Dietrich's work and thus with the sources he was using. Dominicans of the previous generation at Halle, sixty miles from Erfurt, had thought very highly of Mechthild. She had been dead less than twenty years at the time of Dietrich's writing and, because he sees fit to use her as an authority, she must have had a good local reputation, at least among Dominicans. The Cistercian convent at Helfta, where she spent her last years, lay about fifty miles from Erfurt.

While familiarity seems likely, the presence of any palpable influence by the Beguine on Eckhart is more difficult to demonstrate. Here Davies is more guarded and speaks simply of similarities or, at most, "more specific areas of congruence."[4] Indeed, the material they have in common can readily be accounted for by the fact that they shared in a common tradition. Certainly, they were kindred spirits in many ways. They shared a love of paradox. Both were driven by a sense of mission and a need to leave their mark on others. And both advertized that their writings contained things that were new, strange, and never heard before.[5] In juxtaposing them, however, one must bear in mind the striking differences between them. The comparisons which follow are intended to bring the specific characteristics of the

---

[2] Oliver Davies, *Meister Eckhart: Mystical Theologian* (London: SPCK, 1991), 59–60.

[3] "Ex secretis et verissimis revelationibus sumpta sunt quae sequuntur." *Acta sanctorum Aug.* I, 251.

[4] Davies, *Meister Eckhart: Mystical Theologian*, 60–65.

[5] For example, Eckhart promises "nova et rara" in his *Prologus generalis in opus tripartitum* (LW 1: 149). Mechthild, after her great vision of heaven, feels obliged to justify her unusual descriptions: "Nu mag etliche lúte wundern des, wie ich súndig mensche das mag erliden, das ich sogtan rede schribe." Quotations are taken from *Text*, vol. I of *Mechthild von Magdeburg: Das fließende Licht der Gottheit*, ed. Hans Neumann (Munich and Zurich; Artemis, 1990), References are given according to book, line, and page number of the Neumann (N) edition. Here: III 1, 162–63; N 78.

mysticism of each more sharply into focus rather than to demonstrate a cause-effect relationship. We shall pursue three points of comparison: first, how each uses the language of desert barrenness and desolation to express mystical concerns; second, how the idea of the Trinity functions in each's mysticism; and finally, how both seek by different means to provide universal scope and validity for their mystical world, so that it speaks to all Christians.

Language

In addressing the question of similarities in language, we can use the statements of three important scholars both to give us direction and to define the limits beyond which the evidence does not let us safely go. The first statement is that of Wilhelm Preger, made well over a hundred years ago. Despite his misguided attempts to turn both Mechthild and Eckhart into card-carrying Lutherans and despite his obvious ignorance of the scholastic origins of much of Eckhart's terminology, Preger showed healthy academic instincts in the question of language. He asserted that one finds echoes of Mechthild's language in Eckhart, but that she is not the creator of this language. Rather, he insists, there existed in German prior to both of them a linguistic tradition that they both exploited and, especially in the case of Eckhart, enriched.[6] Second, there is the thesis of Herbert Grundmann that many of the ideas found in Eckhart—for example, poverty of spirit or leaving God—were already present in religious communities of women, and that these communities provided both the sociological and the spiritual underpinnings that turned the speculative mysticism of an Eckhart into much more than just an academic concern of the schools.[7] Finally, Kurt Ruh, in writing of the connection between Marguerite Porete and Meister Eckhart, provides a third operative principle, though it is in need of modification if we are to apply it here, because evidence that Eckhart consciously exploited Mechthild's *Flowing Light of the Godhead* is very thin. However, Eckhart's relationship to Marguerite's ideas is fundamentally his relationship to the whole

[6] "Mechthild berührt vielfach die Tiefen, welche das Element der speculativen Mystik bilden, und ihr Einfluss ist selbst bei ihrem tiefsinnigen Landsmanne, bei Meister Eckhart erkennbar, in dessen Schriften ihre Sprache nachtönt." And: "Mechthild ist nicht die Schöpferin dieser speculativen Ausdrucksweise. . . . Es sind vielmehr vor Mechthild und Eckhart einzelne charakteristische Theoreme der speculativen Mystik zumeist in gebundener Rede in's Deutsche ungesetzt [*sic*] und stereotyp geworden." Wilhelm Preger, *Geschichte der deutschen Mystik im Mittelalter* vol. I, 97, and 108 (Munich, n.p., 1874–93).

[7] Herbert Grundmann, "Die geschichtlichen Grundlagen der deutschen Mystik," *Deutsche Vierteljahrsschrift für Literaturwissenschaft und Geistesgeschichte* 12, (1934): 424–29. Also in *Altdeutsche und altniederländische Mystik*, ed. Kurt Ruh (Darmstadt: Wissenschaftliche Buchgesellschaft, 1964), 94–99.

mystical tradition preceding him: Cognizant of its ultimate source or not, Eckhart will take up an already existing term or phrase and give it a more precise and more theologically grounded meaning.[8]

Besides these three guiding principles, one would do well to add a fourth, which is closely linked to the point Ruh makes and which is an important factor in any attempt to establish Eckhart's connection to traditional sources. Most obvious in his interpretation of Scripture, but evident in other areas as well, is his penchant for taking a traditional reading or idea and giving it startling new dimensions. So, for example, in *Predigt* 86 (DW 3: 481–92) he dramatically reevaluates the relationship of Mary to Martha, of the contemplative to the active life, claiming against tradition that Martha had actually chosen the better part, a part Mary had yet to grow into. Or, again, he takes Christ's straightforward question to the cunning Pharisees (Mt. 22:20)—about whose image and name is on the Roman coin they use to pay taxes—and invests it with a wealth of metaphysical implications (*Sermo* XLIX; LW 4: 421–28). As often as not, Eckhart changes the material he has received, giving it a strange new twist that jolts his listeners out of their complacency and forces them to look at the material with new eyes. The effect these creative subversions of tradition must have on attempts to establish sources for his thoughts is clear. Since his relationship to tradition is not simply one of passive receptivity, one must often be satisfied with establishing the tradition he chooses to subvert rather than any specific source. At times the novelty of his thought obscures even this relationship to his sources.

Both mystics employ to their particular advantage the image of *wüstenunge* or *einöde*. Both terms denote an empty, barren expanse of land—a desert, a wasteland, a desolate solitude. However, in the mystical vocabulary of both Mechthild and Eckhart, these terms are used *positively* to describe an ascetical state of the soul conducive to receiving God. The historical justification for so doing is, of course, Jesus' fasting in the desert and the traditions of the desert fathers, who fled the enticements of the world and sought out bleak surroundings that would starve their senses, thus eliminating those forces that might impede a spiritual union with God.

Mechthild clearly alludes to this history of the term when, in a prayer, she addresses Mary Magdalene and draws on the tradition that Magdalene spent her later years as an ascetic in the desert. She prays: "Mary, I live with you in the *wüstenunge* (desert), for all things are foreign to me but God alone" (II 24, 63–64; N 61). She goes on to complain that she is too fragile a vessel to profit from God's least spark (*vunke*) and that the senses, the dwelling place of undisciplined love, are enmeshed in earthly things.

---

[8] Kurt Ruh, *Meister Eckhart: Theologe, Prediger, Mystiker* (Munich: Beck, 1985),104.

Consequently, for Mechthild, the desert (*wüstenunge* or *einöde*) is that state of emptiness in the soul that permits God to enter. Thus, in a vision concerning divine approbation of the rule governing canons, she has God tell a worried canon to remain under the rule—that he will give the canon divine sweetness in the desert (*einöde*) of his heart (VI 2, 14–15; N 207). In another chapter, she counsels that God whispers (*rûnet*) to his beloved within the confines of the desert (*einöde*) of her soul (II 23, 35–36; N 57). Or again, in Book VII, written after her entrance into the convent of Helfta in her declining years, when dreamy, less intense night visions predominate, Mechthild speaks to the Lord at night in the *einöde* of her heart (VII 53, 2–3; N 299). Referring to the convent, she asks the Lord how he likes this "prison," and he replies that he, too, is imprisoned in it and elaborates by declaring that in all aspects of his suffering on earth he was united with the good sisters, among other things fasting with them in the *wüstenunge* (desert). Thus, for Mechthild, the desert is the soul made ready to receive God through the absence of competing forces. It is a personal place of great intimacy and tranquility where the soul and God can commune without distraction.

Once, early in her book, Mechthild makes the desert the subject of a short chapter, and it is here that similarities with the thought of Eckhart are most apparent. One lives in the "true desert," she affirms, if one loves *das niht* and flees *das iht*. One should stand alone, go to no one, keep busy, be free of all things, console others but have no consolation oneself. Rather, one should drink the water of suffering and fuel the fire of love with the wood of virtue (I 35, 2–15; N 24–25). Her naming God *niht* (nothingness), the opposite of *iht* (somethingness), certainly points ahead to Eckhart and confirms the presence of these terms in the German vernacular tradition before him. In the context of her own writing, however, as she turns geographical space into the landscape of the soul, terms of negation, such as *niht*, *alleine*, and *vri* reinforce the empty barrenness of the desert and contribute to a stark picture of lonely wastes that characterize the "true" desert of the soul. Her refusal to accept consolation and her preference, rather, to drink from the cup of suffering will occupy us later.

If, then, we assume from the case of Mechthild, that, in using *einöde* and *wüstenunge*, Eckhart relies on images already familiar to his mystically inclined listeners, one can note that he modifies them or their context in at least two important ways. First: the desert in which God and the soul commune is no longer the soul; rather, it is the vast empty expanse of the divinity, or the divine spark in the creature. Perhaps he was not original in this, but his usage is a clear departure from Mechthild's practice. Second: here, as with many other staples of mystical imagery, he turns mysticism into metaphysics by implying what seems to be a more than accidental change in the creature that can result, when the creature grasps the potentialities of his being and acts accordingly. Some examples should clarify these points.

In Eckhart, it is most frequently the *vunke*, or highest power of the soul, that enters the desert: "God leads this spirit into the desert and into the oneness of himself" (Pr. 29; DW 2: 77). This power strives to penetrate to the "ground and silent solitude (*stille wüste*) of God where there are no more differences of divine persons" (Pr. 48; DW 2: 420). Once, however, when Eckhart is speaking of this wonderful highest power of the soul, its metaphysical location becomes open to question. This power, he asserts, is above the created nature of the soul. Not even the pure being of an angel has it. Like God, it is more unnamed or unnameable than named. It has kinship with God and is one in itself. In this context, stressing its divineness, Eckhart calls this power an *elende* (foreign thing, foreignness) and a *wüstenunge* (Pr. 28; DW 2: 66). In other words, this power itself is that vast expanse which in other contexts Eckhart has used to describe God.

To reach this desert—or to become this desert—we must fulfill the preacher's very radical demands. What keeps us from the desert? Corporality, multiplicity, and temporality. If we could overcome these seemingly necessary conditions of our natures, we would live in oneness and in the desert (*wüstenunge*), where we would hearken to the eternal Word (Pr. 12; DW 1: 193). Reaching this desert would seem to depend on changes more fundamental than those usually thought possible through practical asceticism.

In keeping with his sometimes playful use of language, the preacher exploits an aspect of the desert which the Beguine overlooks. One of the Middle High German words for desert or desolation, namely, *einöde*—containing *ein* or one, as it does— lends itself to word play (once the preacher has called attention to it) because it expresses simultaneously the paradox of God's oneness and vastness. Thus, in a barrage of epithets, he can state that this power of the soul seeks God not as he is good or true, but in his *einunge* (oneness), in his *einöde* (one vast emptiness), in his *wüstunge*, and in his own ground (Pr. 10; DW 1: 171). Or, in a tour de force with which he concludes his sermon on *The Nobleman*, he improves on a verse quoted from the prophet Hosea (2:14 or 16), saying that the Lord will lead the noble soul into a wilderness (*ein einöde*) and will speak to her "one with one, one of one, one in one, and in one one forever" (*ein mit einem, ein von einem, ein in einem und in einem ein êwiclîche*; DW 5: 119).

If Eckhart seems to have found more and richer applications for the vernacular terms for desert solitude, it is Mechthild who is able to invest with a wealth of meaning the kindred terms *vremd* (foreign, strange), and *vrömedunge* (estrangement, alienation). For Eckhart, *entvremden* is a process of making things strange to oneself, of freeing oneself from things (RdU; DW 5: 287), though with characteristic radicalism he requires that one free oneself from all images or image making (*bildicheit*) if one is to see God (Pr. 23; DW 1: 404). Mechthild applies *vremd* and *vrömedunge* to what appears at first to be an entirely different situation—estrangement or alienation from God. *Vrömedunge* is the equivalent of the dark night—a terrible loneliness and separation. Early in Book II, in a lyric passage relying in part on images from courtly poetry where the lady laments the absence of her lover, Mechthild begs God to inflame her with love and relieve her aridity. A day of his absence is like a thousand years. Should it last eight days, she would rather be in hell, for that is the state she is in with God absent. Just as the nightingale would die if it could not sing, so is God's absence affecting her (II 2, 16–31; N 38).

How different her attitude is sometime later, as she is composing Book IV. Anxious fear has been replaced by acceptance, but not a resigned and acquiescent acceptance wrung from her by circumstance. We find her, rather, eagerly welcoming this condition that had earlier filled her with dread. She begins by saying that she is strangely dead—that she has a taste only for God. Thus, by implication she has achieved *entvremden* or estrangement from creatures as defined by Eckhart. In this state of being completely focused on God, whom she describes as an insatiable lover, she vows to give him up if it will add to his praise. A great darkness then overwhelms her and the constant alienation from God (*die stete vrömedunge*) envelops her, but she responds to the situation thus: "Welcome, very blessed alienation! You bring me unusual joy, incomprehensible marvels, and unbearable sweetness" (IV 12, 65–68; N 125). She renounces this sweetness, and she is willing when God wishes to cool his ardor with her, but only in such a way that he is satisfied and not she. Darkness again descends upon her and she again addresses blessed *gotzvrömedunge* (alienation from God), this time with the paradoxical assertion that the more she binds herself to it and takes it on as her companion, the more strongly and marvelously does God descend upon her.

How are we to understand this paradox? Embracing alienation from God results in an intensification of God's presence in her life. Indications are that it can best be explained as the ultimate alienation that Eckhart, too, demands: that one leave God for the sake of God (*got durch got lâzen*). But by accepting alienation from the God she knows—the God of consolation, the God she has, in a sense, created, imposing upon him the limitations of her own mind—by giving up this God, she opens the way for God to give himself to her as he is. She finds she does not sink away from God as she accepts this alienation. On the contrary, *Mere ie ich tieffer sinke, ie ich süsser trinke* (IV 12, 107; N 127). The more deeply she sinks, the more sweetly she drinks. Eckhart similarly warns us (with his own play on *iht* and *niht*): "Whoever sees anything of God, sees nothing of God" (Pr. 62; DW 3: 66). And he urges us, in his famous sermon on poverty of spirit, to "become rid of God" and thus perceive and enjoy truth forever (Pr. 52; DW 2: 493).

Characteristically, Eckhart couches his admonition to leave God for God in terms that describe the experience as something largely intellectual, and he, the preacher, seems certain of the outcome—that, in the end, the soul will be the winner and will be richer upon reaching the other side. Mechthild describes this passage from God to God as being accompanied by existential uncertainty. She is not in control. Something mysterious and incomprehensible is happening to her, and her actions are reactions. She, too, emerges the winner, but there was no guarantee that she would do so.

The Trinity

For both Mechthild and Eckhart, the mystery of the Trinity is very real and plays an essential role in their religious thought. As in the case of the image of the desert, so too, in addressing the thought of the two mystics on the Trinity and how they express it, we shall stress common elements without claiming dependency. Because Mechthild was not a trained theologian, but a poet and visionary, images are her principal means of expression. Eckhart's thought on the Trinity is more complex, detailed, and abstract, as one would expect from a professor of theology.[9] And although he ran afoul of church authorities for stressing God's oneness and for seeming to exclude his threeness, we find the Trinity occurring frequently in his works as an essential element in his doctrine.[10] He, too, employs images when treating the Trinity, some of which one also finds in Mechthild's book. Both also derive much of their thought from traditional sources.

One tradition both draw upon in their elaborations is the conception of the Trinity, deriving from Abelard, according to which the Father is power (*potentia*), the Son wisdom (*sapientia*), and the Holy Spirit goodness (*bonitas*). Mechthild, describing an ecstatic vision, tells us that the Father was adorned with power (*almehtikeit*), that the Son equaled him in infinite wisdom (*wisheit*), and that the Holy Spirit was equal to both in goodness or overflowing richness (*miltekeit*). She then describes how the Holy Spirit strikes a chord on the Trinity (functioning as a

[9] For a clear and concise treatment of Eckhart's teaching on the Trinity as it would interest his colleagues in theology in the scholastic tradition, see Bernard McGinn, "Theological Summary" in *Meister Eckhart: The Essential Sermons, Commentaries, Treatises, and Defense*, trans. and intro. Edmund Colledge, O.S.A., and McGinn, Classics of Western Spirituality Series (New York, Ramsey, Toronto: Paulist Press, 1981), 30–57; and McGinn, "The God Beyond God: Theology and Mysticism in the Thought of Meister Eckhart," *Journal of Religion* 61 (1981): 1–19.

[10] Articles 23 and 24 of the papal bull, *In agro dominico*, state theses from Eckhart's works that are judged to be "evil sounding" and "suspect of heresy" because they seem to exclude the possibility of a Trinity in God. For a translation of the bull, see Colledge and McGinn, *Meister Eckhart*, 77–81.

stringed instrument), whose characteristic virtues provide sweet harmonizing tones, and intones a song that calls upon God to begin the work of Creation (III 9, 8–17; N 86). Eckhart translates two of Abelard's terms differently but obviously has the same tradition in mind. In explaining how Jesus speaks in the soul—and Jesus speaks the same Word that the Father speaks and in the Word the Father speaks—Eckhart says that God reveals himself there in his fatherly *herschaft*, in his boundless *wisheit*, and in his infinite *süzikeit* and *richeit* from the power of the Holy Spirit.[11]

In Mechthild's book, references to the Trinity are proportionately more frequent than in Eckhart's works, and the Beguine avails herself of a variety of images to describe its activity, both internal and in creatures.[12] In one instance, she depicts the Trinity as an apple tree which bends down to the beloved so that she might pick its green, white, and red fruits, which are its humanity (II 25, 120–25; N 67). In another, she describes how the Father is the innkeeper, the Son the cup, the Holy Spirit the pure wine, and the Trinity the full cup—with love being the serving girl (II 24, 19–23; N 59). More frequent are images of fire. In one example, she speaks of those who truly know God as being consumed (*verbrant*) in the fire of the Trinity (II 16, 5–7; N 130). The bride wishing to enter into the Trinity is warned that she will go blind, so fiery hot, glowing, shining, and burning is that which flows from God's divine breath out of his human mouth through the counsel of the Holy Spirit (I 44, 64–68; N 30).

More frequent still are images of light. In activity internal to the Godhead, the Persons shine together in such a way that each is illuminated by the others; yet they remain one (III 9, 6–8; N 86). In her grand vision of heaven, Mechthild sees the Trinity upon its throne as a dynamic mirror. The Father in his divinity is the mirror itself; the Son is the image within; the Holy Spirit is the light which allows the heavenly assembly to understand how three can be one.[13] Activity emanating from the Trinity towards creatures is also represented by light. Beams of light shoot forth from the crossbow of the Trinity through the nine choirs of heaven, striking all present with love (II 3, 13–15; N 39).

---

[11] Pr. 1; DW 1: 18–19. Clearly both authors find it difficult to come up with a vernacular equivalent for *bonitas*.

[12] For a more extensive treatment of the Trinity in Mechthild's writings, see Margot Schmidt, "'die spilende minnevluot.' Der Eros als Sein und Wirkkraft in der Trinität bei Mechthild von Magdeburg," *Eine Höhe über die nichts geht: Spezielle Glaubenserfahrung in der Frauenmystik?* ed. Schmidt and Dieter R. Bauer (Stuttgart-Bad Cannstatt: Fromann-Holzboog, 1986), 71–133.

[13] III 1, 68–71; N 75. Petrus Tax, "Die große Himmelsschau Mechthilds von Magdeburg und ihre Höllenvision," *Zeitschrift für deutsches Altertum und deutsche Literatur* 108 (1979): 19, calls attention to these lines and rightly emphasizes the artistry of their simplicity.

In her most daring use of the Trinity, Mechthild identifies her book with the triune God. Feeling the sting of the criticism of her book, she sees God appear before her holding her book in his right hand. This book, he declares, is threefold. The parchment indicates his humanity (Son), the words his divinity (Father), and the voice of the words his dynamic (*lebendig*) Spirit who guarantees the book's truth and proclaims God's intimate secrets (*heimlichkeit*. II 26, 7–17; N 68). Her equation of the book with the Trinity was not lost on the Latin translator(s). The prologue to the Latin version states simply that the author is the Father, Son, and Holy Spirit.[14]

By far the most frequent image Mechthild employs in connection with the Trinity, particularly when the life of the Trinity is described as affecting the soul, is that of water richly flowing. Early in Book I, she gives a poetically charged description of the way in which the mystic experiences rapture. The *gruos* or greeting, as she terms it, comes "from the heavenly flood of the spring of the flowing Trinity." The *gruos* is so powerful that it drains all strength from the body and reveals the soul to itself clothed in the divine splendor that the saints enjoy (I 2, 2–5; N 7). In the final book, she again speaks of how the divine power has come over her—the experience renders her speechless, and is one that she has never heard spoken of on earth. It is the *spilende minne-vluot*, or playful outpouring of love, that in a mysterious way (*heimlich*) flows from God into the soul (VII 45, 12–19; N 291).

Though Eckhart, too, uses images of light and heat to describe activity within the Godhead and the effect of this activity on creatures, it is his use of flowing that most particularly recalls Mechthild's imagery to mind. Both are indebted to Neo-Platonic sources for the idea of divine energy overflowing and descending into the world of creatures. While Mechthild was, no doubt, unaware of these sources, Eckhart was quite conscious of them. Bernard McGinn considers *ebullitio* (bubbling or boiling over) along with *bullitio* (the same activity, immanent and confined to the Godhead) to be a central tenet, if not the central tenet, of Eckhart's mystical theology.[15] Certainly, images of overflowing and boiling over (heat and flowing combined) are frequent in both his German and his Latin works. In the passage mentioned above, where the preacher, drawing on Abelard, describes *bonitas* emanating from the Holy Spirit, he invests this outflowing with astonishing poetic

---

[14] Sanctae Mechtildis, *Liber specialis gratiae*, Accedit Sororis Mechtildis *Lux divinitatis*, vol. II of *Revelationes Gertrudianae ac Mechtildianae*, ed. Louis Paquelin (Poitiers and Paris: Oudin, 1875 and 1877), 436.

[15] McGinn, "Theological Summary" in Colledge and McGinn, *Meister Eckhart*, especially 39–42.

intensity. This sweetness (*süzikeit*) and abundance (*richeit*) is pouring forth (*uzquellende*) from the resources of the Holy Spirit, spilling over (*überquellende*) and flowing into (*invliezende*) all receptive hearts with overflowing full abundance and sweetness (*mit übervlüzziger voller richeit und süzikeit*: Pr. 1; DW 1: 19, 3–5).

The remarks offered thus far regarding the Trinity in the thought and language of the two mystics should be considered preliminary, connecting the two merely accidentally, and explained by the fact that they shared a common tradition. What follows, though not offered as evidence of Eckhart's dependence on Mechthild, is an observation concerning a striking similarity between the two that touches the substance of their spirituality. Far more arresting than shared images and traditions is the fact that both describe the life of the soul as being subsumed into the immanent activity of the Trinity.

Mechthild addresses this vital union of the soul with the Trinity in two ways: as a visionary and ecstatic personal experience, and as a spiritual doctrine. The experience she describes is one in which she is taken up into the Trinity before time. Here she sees and hears the triune God plan the creation and redemption of the human race (III 9; N 86–89). As doctrine, she states that souls who know true divine love are consumed in the fire of the Trinity, are pervaded by the flowing being of God (*mit gotte durvlossen und umbevangen*), and do not live in themselves (IV 16, 2–14). "What are you made of," she asks the soul, "that you blend into the Trinity yet remain completely in yourself?" (*mengest dich in die heiligen drivaltekeit und blibest doch gantz in dir selber*: I 22, 37–39; N 18). She has the bride say, as she rests in the locked treasury of the Trinity, that it is the playful flood (*die spilenden vluot*) flowing in the Trinity that alone sustains the soul (IV 12, 15–18; N 123). In introducing her most elaborate variation on this theme, she avows that she saw this truth (*ware rede*) in the Trinity while at prayer. The achievement of true detachment, she says, makes one a divine god (*ein götlich got*) with the heavenly Father. Acting out of love of God, and not for earthly reward, makes one a human god with Christ. And performing acts of charity makes one a spiritual god with the Holy Spirit. Someone who accomplishes all this is one complete person with the Trinity (VI 1, 78–98; N 203–4).

Eckhart conceives the union of the soul with the Trinity to be an integral part of his teaching on the birth of the Son, although he also gives a detailed analysis of how all creation, especially creatures endowed with intellect, is one with the Trinity without a clear reference to the birth.[16] In *Predigt* 6, however, he explicitly identifies the birth of the Son in eternity with the birth of the Son in the soul. The key passage shows Eckhart's oratorical skills at their best:

---

[16] See, for example, the concluding section of *Predigt* 1 (DW 1: 15, 10–20, 8).

The Father gives birth to his Son in eternity, equal to himself. "The Word was with God, and God was the Word" (Jn. 1:1); it was the same in the same nature. Yet I say more: He has given birth to him in my soul. Not only is the soul with him, and he equal with it, but he is in it, and the Father gives his Son birth in the soul in the same way as he gives him birth in eternity, and not otherwise. He must do it whether he likes it or not. The Father gives birth to his Son without ceasing; and I say more: He gives me birth, me, his Son and the same Son. I say more: He gives birth not only to me, his Son, but he gives birth to me (as) himself and himself (as) me and to me (as) his being and nature. In the innermost source, there I spring out in the Holy Spirit, where there is one life and one being and one work.[17]

One can hardly imagine the union of Trinity and soul being put more starkly or more eloquently.

Universality

In addition to similarities in language and their common assertion of a vital relationship to the Trinity, the Beguine and the preacher-professor both intend that their mysticism have universal application. Eckhart achieves universality by basing his mystical thought squarely on the thought of the schools. He has at his disposal a fully developed body of knowledge that is common currency in his intellectual environment. With few exceptions, the chief terms of his vernacular works are rooted in the professional Latin vocabulary of scholastic theology. His mysticism is concerned with the metaphysical composition of creatures, especially of the human person as such—so much so that metaphysical mysticism rather than speculative mysticism seems a more appropriate term for describing his thought. Rather than considering this body of thought as the *means* by which he expresses his mysticism, it is more accurate to say that his mysticism is indistinguishable from it or is, at most, an extension of it. The coming to be of the just man and the birth of the Son are events we are all capable of experiencing because they are made possible by our very nature, a nature common to us all. Eckhart's mysticism is, in McGinn's terms, an *exoteric* mysticism, one open to all; and not *esoteric*, or limited to a special group of "elect."[18]

---

[17] Colledge and McGinn, *Meister Eckhart*, 187. The original is in DW 1: 109, 2–11. I have added parentheses around words in Colledge's translation that are *not* in the original German. This is not to criticize Colledge's translation, but to show how stark Eckhart's actual formulation is.

[18] Bernard McGinn, *The Foundations of Mysticism*, vol. I of *The Presence of God: A History of Western Christian Mysticism* (New York: Crossroad, 1991), 98–99, 155–57, and passim.

Mechthild achieves universality in a different way. One cannot say that her mysticism is exoteric in the same sense as is Eckhart's. It is experiential mysticism accompanied by divine favors not granted to all. However, the spiritual teachings she derives from her esoteric experiences do apply to everyone, and she considers divine favors special only in that they show God's power and goodness. They are no more valuable in helping one attain one's final end than any other human activity. She says: "One should do everything in equal measure to honor God. My most commonplace taking care of a natural need I would rank as high in God's sight as though I were in the highest state of contemplation that a person can attain. Why? If I do it out of love to honor God, it is all the same" (I 27, 8–11; N 21). Thus her mysticism, though based in part on esoteric experiences, directs its message to *all* the faithful.

There is yet another sense in which Mechthild's mysticism is universal. In contrast to the majority of spiritual writings that focus on the personal experience of the author, Mechthild's concerns range far beyond the special intimacies she enjoys. But because she is unlearned, Eckhart's means of achieving a universal perspective are not at her disposal. Forced to attain universality in other ways, she does so by showing a global concern and by offering us cosmic visions.

Already in the prologue to her book, concern for all of Christianity—the whole of the real world for her—is the explicit justification for the book's existence. God says that he is sending this book to all the clergy, both the good and the evil, because they are the pillars of the whole church and must not crumble (I, 3–4; N 4). She repeatedly prays for all Christians, and her efforts are successful. As a result of her reception of the Eucharist and her entreaties, Christ ransoms seventy-thousand souls from purgatory, releasing them ten years early (III 15, 29–67; N 95–57). She prays for all those who suffer because of wars and for those who have wronged her. She joins with *all* creation in praising God. Thus she takes an active role in the ongoing history of salvation as globally conceived.

In many other cosmic visions, she is simply the seer, the passive viewer of momentous events. Such visions function as a magical time machine that carries her to periods before time began and after its end, to the ends of the earth and into supernatural space. We have seen her wafted away into the Trinity as it existed before time, to witness and vividly describe for us the deliberations among Father, Son, and Holy Spirit as they plan creation and foresee the often sad fortunes of the creatures whom they resolve to redeem in spite of everything. The Son even offers to spill his blood for them (III 9; N 86–89). Another crucial event in salvation history unfolds before her eyes when she sees Mary in Nazareth. Gabriel comes down suffused with celestial light that frightens the young maiden. We are allowed to be present and follow the events, like members of an audience viewing *Welttheater*, from the Nativity, to the visit of the magi, and the flight into Egypt. We are even privy to the troubled conversations of Lucifer and Satan about this strange child. Anticipating a practice of Henry Suso in his *Little Book of Eternal Wisdom*, she interjects herself into the scene, asking Mary after the birth of Jesus where Joseph has gone off to. To get some fish and bread, Mary replies (V 23; N 174–81). By combining such homely intimacy with a dramatic visual presentation, Mechthild is able to give the events an immediacy and intensity seldom equalled in religious literature.

Often, her cosmic role can be likened to that of the Hebrew prophets who castigate, warn, and foresee cataclysmic events. As a hidden observer she is present at Rome watching the pope in prayer, as he is told by the Lord that the spiritual shepherds have become murderers and wolves. The Lord warns the pope that he will suffer an early death, as did his two predecessors, if he does not hearken to God's hidden commands (VI 21; N 231–32). With evident dependence on the apocalyptic thought originating in Joachim of Fiore, she vividly depicts for her readers the events at the end of time, when a new religious order is constituted, when the Antichrist appears and inflicts great suffering on the faithful, and when Enoch and Elias return to earth (IV 27 and VI 15; N 142–48 and 222–25). By means of such visions she is intimately involved in and involves her readers in cosmic events and the drama of salvation. She shows us heaven and the heavenly orders, hell in all its ghastliness, and purgatory in its ambivalence as a place of punishment and suffering, but where there is hope because one knows that it will end. She transports us to the lush garden of paradise, a region between heaven and earth, the home of Enoch and Elias until the end of time (VII 57; 302–4).

Finally, to achieve a view embracing all of history as seen from the point of Christ's salvific act as it is celebrated after the Last Judgment, Mechthild describes the crown that the Son in triumph shall then receive from his Father. Reminiscent of the façade of a medieval cathedral, where the whole drama of salvation history is portrayed, the crown, as Mechthild describes it, includes the whole church triumphant: patriarchs, prophets, martyrs, apostles, popes, Mary, and John the Baptist next to the Lamb with his converts present holding flowers in their hands. Created by the Father and fashioned in the fiery love of the Holy Spirit, the crown will be honored in the song of the angels, who alone, because they are not human and thus not redeemed by the Son, are not represented on it (VII 1; N 254–58). In depicting the crown and its glorification, Mechthild joins her own private spiritual vision to events of importance for all Christians and compels her readers likewise to see themselves as integral parts of a divine order.

One could point to further congruences between Mechthild and Eckhart. For example, the orthodoxy of both was called into question and both reacted in a spirited manner, averring their loyalty and adherence to the church and its teachings. Both felt misunderstood by their critics. Perhaps more striking than these similarities, however, is that each was faced late in life with relinquishing something each held very dear. Both were forced to put into practice the mystical renunciation they valued so highly, not in some grand and heroic fashion—as when overwhelmed by the force of some sudden spiritual insight or emotion—but in a powerless manner, compelled to do so by external circumstance. To explain and give what evidence there is for this assertion may take us beyond the bounds of usual academic inquiry and, at least in the case of Eckhart, involve speculation that one might judge excessive. In spite of this, it will be worthwhile to elaborate on the proposition that both found themselves faced with one final act of renunciation, one that forced them to overcome the last vestiges of egotism peculiar to them.

In Eckhart's case, the crisis confronting him struck at the very core of the way of life he had chosen and followed with distinction for some five decades. The Dominican order had been called into being to protect the faithful against the threat of heresy and to deepen their understanding of the faith by subjecting the truths of Christian doctrine to the penetrating light of the intellect. Eckhart, who had served these goals as a professor, preacher, spiritual guide, and religious superior, suddenly found himself charged with spreading heretical teachings. How abhorrent the charge must have been to him. Did this happen, as has been suggested, because Eckhart sided with the beleaguered Beguines and because he tried in his sermons to give an orthodox foundation to some of the startling formulations current in the heady religious atmosphere in Strasbourg and Cologne?[19] Perhaps we shall never know for sure, and it is too pat an explanation to cover all of the shocking formulations and radical thought one finds in his works. In any case, the whole dismal business of defending himself in court—first at Cologne and then at Avignon—as is the case with anyone facing legal charges, must have cast its pall over him. We know he protested his innocence vigorously. However, the final months in Avignon, where he probably died, brought no vindication. The papal bull, composed after his death, implies, rather, that he "sowed tares over the seeds of truth" and states that "he turned his ear from the truth and followed fables." It condemns several of his formulations outright and calls others seriously into question.[20] There are indications some fight was still left in him. Though the bull reports that he recanted and "deplored" the articles judged heretical or dangerous, he did so only "insofar as they could generate in the minds of the faithful a heretical opinion, or one erroneous and hostile to the true

[19] See Trusen, especially 33 and 41.

[20] See Colledge and McGinn, *Meister Eckhart*, 77–81. The quotations here are from page 77.

faith."[21] He seems not to have admitted that the formulations themselves were contrary to the faith, although the papal bull declares at least seventeen articles heretical.

Perhaps this was a small private victory, but the larger fact is that Eckhart's last recorded act is his recantation. This final act of renunciation was demanded of him, and it must have pained him deeply to be made to confess publicly that his life and high-minded striving on behalf of his fellow human beings had been, in effect, misguided and even injurious to them. He had wrought evil. This was no lofty otherworldly event in which he emptied himself because, in the overwhelming presence of God, he recognized his nothingness. Eckhart's final act of renunciation was public and demeaning, playing itself out in the petty and often vicious world of church politics. It must have been deeply humiliating to depart the stage in this manner. Was he able to "let go" in such circumstances? Henry Suso's vision of Eckhart contains perhaps the closest thing we have to an answer to this question. In his *Life*, Suso relates how Eckhart appears to him and advises him to "withdraw from himself in deep detachment" and to "receive all things from God and not from creatures," and to "adopt an attitude of calm patience toward all wolfish men."[22]

Mechthild's final years, though spent in the protective environment of the flourishing convent at Helfta, bear resemblance to those of Eckhart in that Mechthild, too, was forced to "let go" of *real* things, personal rather than mystical, and in ways that must have been difficult. Her writings, as is true of Eckhart's as well, hardly present the author, in spite of her genuine humility, as someone suffering, as one might say today, from low self-esteem. She is a proud person, fiercely independent, a strong personality with a sense of her own dignity; willing, certainly, to compare herself to a worm or a dog in her relation to God, but hardly meek and self-effacing in her dealings with her fellow creatures. Age forces her to give up her independence and seek refuge in a convent with women who, judging from her reactions, seem to have regarded her as a living legend or relic rather than as a member of their community. She feels alienated by all the book learning among them.[23] As she grows more infirm and her sight fails, she becomes even more dependent. Her talents as a gifted lyricist diminish, and she is conscious of the fact. Yet this loss is also a gain. Her voice as author changes. In the early books one can detect a certain role-playing on the part of the author-narrator. She is conscious of being literary in her creation. She is able to turn her mysticism into an aesthetic

---

[21] Colledge and McGinn, *Meister Eckhart*, 81.

[22] Henry Suso, *The Exemplar with Two German Sermons*, trans., ed., and intro. Frank Tobin, Classics of Western Spirituality Series (New York and Mahwah: Paulist Press, 1989), 75.

[23] See, for example, VII 21, 2–3; N 273.

experience. She both is and poses as a literary artist. In the final book, the pose is largely gone, replaced by a frankness lacking any literary pretensions.

Having lost control over her life, she is powerless to control her death. In one of the final chapters, she reports that, because of a serious indisposition, she felt her wish to die was about to be fulfilled. After uttering the *de rigeur* "not my will but thine be done," and seeing in the heights how the saints in glory—and devils as well—begin to gather for her death, she recovers and is faced with resigning herself yet awhile to life on earth (VII 63; N 308–9). This, too, she accepts, and the following chapter is a hymn of thanksgiving to God that he has taken everything from her: her own clothes and food, the use of her eyes and hands, and even the power of her heart (*die maht mines herzen*: VII 64, 2–10; N 309). She has nothing more to renounce. She has sunk as low as she can. And yet one perceives no wavering or inconsistency in her. The facile rhyme from Book IV, *Mere ie ich tieffer sinke, ie ich süsser trinke* (The deeper I sink, the sweeter I drink), was no pose. Though enigmatic and impervious to rational inquiry, her sentiment was genuine. As she has told us, the nature of love first flows out in sweetness, then becomes rich in knowledge, and finally becomes *girig in verworfenheit* (passionately yearning in rejection, or, when rejected because of worthlessness: VI 20, 11–13; N 230). The mind strains to follow her and understand. Such depths are as vertiginous as pseudo-Dionysian heights.

In concluding, we might recall the words of Hans Urs von Balthasar, who wrote about Mechthild with great sympathy and insight. He warns us against what he terms the "Neo-Platonic superstition" of blindly accepting the Augustinian hierarchy concerning visions and the concomitant implication that speculative mysticism is by its nature more lofty than other forms.[24] It is sheer presumption for us to attempt to rank Eckhart's and Mechthild's particular mystical achievements. The thought of someone undertaking this would certainly be abhorrent to them. We have much to learn from them both; and if comprehension seems to come easily and we are able to reduce their thoughts to academically generated categories, perhaps we should be suspicious of our success.

---

[24] Hans Urs von Balthasar, "Mechthilds kirchlicher Auftrag," in Mechthild von Magdeburg, *Das fließende Licht der Gottheit*, Modern German trans. Margot Schmidt (Einsiedeln, Zürich, and Cologne: Benziger, 1955), 23.

Part II

Marguerite Porete
and
Meister Eckhart

4

Marguerite Porete
and Meister Eckhart

The Mirror of Simple Souls Mirrored

Maria Lichtmann

M arguerite Porete, burned at the stake in Paris in the early fourteenth century, left to posterity a book which managed to escape complete incineration at the hand of her inquisitors. Disengaged from its author, her mystical treatise, *The Mirror of Simple Souls*, influenced mystics and mystical traditions down the centuries. At one point, it was even mistaken by the Carthusian, Richard Methley, for the work of the Blessed Jan Ruusbroec.[1] Still, its greatest influence, that on the Meister Eckhart himself, went undetected until the last twenty-five years. Now that the treatise has been rejoined to its author by the Italian scholar Romana Guarnieri,[2] we can begin to assess the extraordinary verbal dependence and affinity of thought between Marguerite's work and Meister Eckhart's. Marguerite's and Eckhart's paths into the nothingness of the Godhead both converge and diverge, like parallel lines that meet in infinity. While the divergence of their paths should be noted, it must be viewed in the light of the much greater convergence of mystical destiny.

Sometime between 1296 and 1306, Marguerite's writings were publicly burned in the square of Valenciennes by the local bishop, Guy de Colmieu. Unwilling to let her voice and mystical teaching be silenced, she went on to seek and win the approval of three theological authorities, a Franciscan, a Cistercian, and a scholastic

---

[1] For an overview of the *Mirour*'s fate in orthodox settings, see the informative summary (in Romana Guarnieri, "Frères du Libre Esprit," *Dictionnaire de spiritualité*, V (1964): 1257–59; Also Kurt Ruh, "'Le Miroir des Simples Ames' der Marguerite Porete" Zweiter Band, *Verbum et signum*, (München: n.p., 1975), 365–87.

[2] Ms. Guarnieri first announced her finding in *L'Osservatore Romana*, when she identified the first article extracted from the Paris theologians' list. Her extensive research is published as "Il movimento del Libero Spirito, Testi e documenti" in *Archivio italiano per la storia della pietà* 4 (1965): 353–708.

philosopher.[3] Then in 1309, still not silenced by the bishop's warnings not to spread her teachings, she was brought before the papal general inquisitor of France, William of Paris, who was also confessor to the king, Philip the Fair. After an inquisition process involving twenty-one theologians, Marguerite was accused of being a "relapsed heretic" in the strongest language and sentenced on May 31, 1310. According to the continuation of the chronicle begun by William of Nangis, on the following day she was burned in the Place de Grève in the presence of secular authorities, church dignitaries, and a growing crowd of people who, according to the chronicler, were moved to tears of compassion at the sight of her nobility. On June 1, 1310, she became the first heretic burned to death in the Paris inquisition.

In assessing circumstances surrounding the outcome of her inquisition, we must ask to what extent Marguerite's status in the marginalized group of semireligious called Beguines affected her vulnerability before the Paris authorities. Her lack of protection by an established religious order, a confessor, or other form of institutional sanction gave Marguerite no buffering against the inquisitorial regime. She had no Jacques de Vitry, no Francis of Assisi, no Ubertino da Casale. With Marguerite we therefore have the chance to observe head-to-head combat between a noncredentialed, nonacademic mystic and the scholastic theologians at Paris.

It was Marguerite's fate to bring her vision before the religious authorities at the end of the thirteenth century, a time of increasing suspicion toward extra-canonical groups like the Beguines. Tremendous ambivalence had been building up in ecclesiastical attitudes toward these semireligious who took no vows but lived the *vita apostolica* in the world in the wake of Lateran IV's prohibition of new orders.[4] Beguines sought a way of living the Gospel outside monastic walls in reaction to a church given to growing clericalization and corruption. Some commentators spoke highly of them,[5] and papal bulls gave ambiguous signals about their approval or disapproval. However, by 1274, at the Second Council of Lyons, a tract written by Gilbert of Tournai accused the Beguines of "cultivating

---

[3] These authorites are cited in the Prologue to the Middle English translation, as found in "'The Mirrour of Simple Soules,' A Middle English Translation," Sr. Marilyn Doiron, *Archivio italiano per la storia della pietà* 5 (1968): 249–50.

[4] On the positive side, Jacques de Vitry championed Marie d'Oignies (1177–1213) against ecclesiastical adversaries; his advocacy actually won the Beguines the approval of the Pope Honorius III. *Acta SS. Junii*, t. IV, 637; quoted in J. van Mierlo, S.J., "Béguins, Béguines, Béguinages," *Dictionnaire de Spiritualité* II: 1341–52.

[5] Caesarius Heisterbach (1180–1240) for example said of them, "In the midst of worldly people they were spiritual, in the midst of pleasure seekers they were pure, and the midst of noise and confusion they led a serene, eremitical life." Quoted in *Beguine Spirituality: Mystical Writings of Mechthild of Magdeburg, Beatrice of Nazareth, and Hadewijch of Brabant*, ed. and intro. Fiona Bowie; trans.Oliver Davies (New York: Crossroad, 1990), 14.

novelties in their vernacular exegeses of Scripture."[6] Not only did they use the Gallic idiom, but they read the Scriptures irreverently and audaciously in conventicles, street corners, and public squares.

Gilbert of Tournai perfectly expresses the authorities' anxiety over lay and vernacular readings of Scripture, an anxiety exacerbated by Beguine spirituality. The shift to the vernacular is a shift away from the center and toward the periphery, or in Marguerite's metaphor, from top to bottom. For her, the "Great Church" (*l'église la grande*) of God's true lovers was to teach and nurture the "Lesser Church" (*l'église la petite*). Use of the vernacular is an implicit statement of freedom from the language established by a centralized hierarchical authority. With that implicit freedom goes explicit freedom, the subject of Marguerite's condemned text on the "ame anientie" or liberated soul. For, as religious experience becomes more defiant of boundaries, it becomes less conceptual and systematic and more free to explode the old scholastic categories of thought. It is here that a *Frauenmystik*, a mysticism of women's experience, has its life.[7]

Unlike the three theological authorities Marguerite consulted who had approved the book as a whole, the twenty-one theologians summoned by the inquisitor responded to articles extracted out of context of the book itself, which was never even named throughout the process. Although they recorded only the first and fifteenth articles in the documents of the inquisition, the theologians concluded unanimously that it was "so heretical and erroneous and containing such heresy and error as to be eliminated."[8] The inquisitorial method of abstracting from the book as a whole, with its epistemology of knowledge as discrete propositions, though common among the disputations of the scholastics, would have been foreign to the book's author and its mystical message of intimacy and union rather than abstraction and distance. The Paris theologians and inquisitors who judged

---

[6] "Sunt apud nos mulieres, quae Beghinae vocantur, et quaedam earum subtilitatibus vigent et novitatibus gaudent. Habent interpretata scripturarum mysteria et in communi idiomate gallicata, quae tamen in sacra Scriptura exercitatis vix sunt pervia. Legunt ea communiter, irreverenter, audacter, in conventiculis, in ergastulis, in plateis." In *Collectio de scandalis ecclesiae*; quoted in Paul Verdeyen, S.J., "Le procès d'inquisition contre Marguerite Porete et Guiard de Cressonessart (1309–1310)," *Revue d'Histoire Ecclésiastique* 81 (1986): 47–94.

[7] Kurt Ruh, "Beginenmystik: Hadewijch, Mechthild von Magdeburg, Marguerite de Porete," *Zeitschrift für deutsches Altertum und deutsche Literatur* 106 (1977): 265–77, speaks of the greatest and earliest feminine mysticism as that of the Beguines, and comments, "Vernacular mysticism begins in the 13th century with Frauenmystik" (266).

[8] Records of Marguerite's inquisition have been preserved in the National Archives in Paris. They have been published in P. Fredericq, *Corpus documentorum inquisitionis haereticae pravitatis Neerlandicae*, t. I, Gand (1889), 155–60 and in Verdeyen, "Le procès d'inquisition," 47–94.

and condemned her work with their scholastic disputational method lived in the very world of Reason which Marguerite anticipated would fall far short of comprehending the language of Love spoken by "l'église la grande" to which she belonged. In addition to numerous counsels about the difficulty of reading her book, Marguerite appears to anticipate the response of the learned clergy in her poetic "Explicit":

Vous qui en ce livre lirez,	You who would read this book,
Se bien le voulez entendre	If you indeed wish to grasp it,
Pensez ad ce que vous direz,	Think about what you say,
Car il est fort a comprendre;	For it is very difficult to understand
. . . Theologiens ne aultres clers,	Theologians and other clerks,
Point n'en aurez l'entendement	You will not have the intellect for it,
Tant aiez les engins clers	No matter how brilliant your abilities,
Se n'y procedez humblement	If you do not proceed humbly.
Et que Amour et Foy ensement	And may Love and Faith, together,
Vous facent surmonter Raison,	Cause you to rise above Reason,
Qui dames sont de la maison.[9]	Since they are the ladies of the house.

The book can be understood only in an intuitive grasp of the whole, and the scholastic, disputational method is wholly at odds with its message.

In addition to the already precarious combination of her gender, her social marginality, and her religious idiosyncrasy, none of which had been sufficient to threaten the lives of earlier women Beguines such as Marie d'Oignies, Hadewijch of Antwerp, or Mechthild of Magdeburg, Marguerite appeared in the political arena at an extremely unfavorable time. France's king, Philip the Fair, may well have used Marguerite's case to reestablish favor with the pope after pursuing his personal vendetta toward the too powerful Knights Templar. The chief inquisitor who prosecuted Marguerite's case spent the year and a half of her incarceration engaged in the case against the Templars. As Robert Lerner sees it, by prosecuting the first heretic to appear, the king could demonstrate his "unwavering orthodoxy" to the pope.[10] It would seem, then, that the authorities were so hopelessly prejudiced by political and social considerations that the inquisitorial cards were stacked against her

---

[9] *Marguerite Porete: Le Mirouer des Simples Ames*, ed. Romana Guarnieri; and *Margaretae Porete: Speculum Simplicium Animarum*, ed. Paul Verdeyen, S.J., *Corpus Christianorum*, Continuatio Mediaeualis, 69 (Turnholti: Typographi Brepols Editores Pontificii, 1986), 8. Hereafter cited in text as *Mirour*. The translation used here is that of Ellen L. Babinsky, *Marguerite Porete: The Mirror of Simple Souls*, Classics of Western Spirituality Series (New York-Mahwah: Paulist Press, 1993), 79.

[10] Robert E. Lerner, *The Heresy of the Free Spirit in the Later Middle Ages* (Berkeley: Univ. of California Press, 1972), 77.

from the beginning. Given the propensity of her work to find a place in orthodox settings over the centuries, the patently heretical nature of Marguerite's *Mirror of Simple Souls* has hardly been established. It is a source of wonder that despite her condemnation and branding as a heretic, despite her having been shut out of the academic world by her gender, and despite her inability to garner sufficient ecclesiastical support for protection, Marguerite's work became known to Eckhart.

Marguerite's Beguine spirituality was thus both vernacular and lay, a deliberate move away from the center and toward the margins. Hers became a mysticism of the margins, which yet laid claim to authenticity and spoke with the authority of its own experience. Addressed to a female audience and with a feminine divine, *Dame Amour*, at its center, Marguerite's mysticism is overtly female, entailing a set of values at odds with patriarchal norms. Her *Mirror* catches reflections not only of the interior life of the soul, but, through inversion, of the kind of church and society in which "simple souls" could flourish. Unlike earlier Beguines like Marie d'Oignies, Hadewijch of Antwerp, or Mechthild of Magdeburg, Marguerite saw her simple souls as having a teaching mission toward "sainte église la petite," the Little Church ruled by reason rather than love. She realized that her vision of the mystical relation to God could develop only in the context of an external ecclesiastical order whose present hierarchy was inverted, with the "Great Church" of God's lovers on top, and the present hierarchy of the "Lesser Church" subverted. Out of her mystical vision of a subverted hierarchy arose an inverted moral vision of Love over Reason. In their subversion of ecclesiastical structure and values, her mysticism and morality were boldly gendered, embodying her particularly female perspective. She consequently set herself and the Greater Church of God's true lovers in direct opposition to what she must have judged as the ecclesiastical institution's petty-mindedness.

Where Marguerite probably irked her inquisitor-theologians from the University of Paris was in her polemical dialogue between Reason and Love. Here she joined battle with the prevailing patriarchal rationality of the hierarchical church, and at every opportunity showed it up as inadequate and stupid. This dialogue must have been important to her, for Reason keeps asking its nagging questions until Love complains that Reason has protracted the dialogue. Marguerite's personal struggles with the hierarchical church are hinted at in Love's question, "And why would Holy Church not recognize these royal ones, daughters of the king, sisters of the king and brides of the king? Holy Church could only recognize them perfectly if it could be within their souls. And nothing created, but God alone who created them, can enter into their souls. Therefore only God who is within them can recognize these souls" (*Mirouer*, 76; chap. 19). In her treatise's allegorical dialogue between *Raison* and *Amour*, and implicitly therefore between the Little Church and the Great Church, she anticipates the failure of communication between these language games and theological universes. This failure of communication occurred so totally at her own inquisition process that she answered only with silence. Ironically, it was Marguerite's fate to submit her book to the very court of reason that she knew would not understand it.[11]

Thus, as woman, as Beguine, and as mystic, Marguerite transgressed all the appropriate boundaries. Yet, it is not unimaginable that Eckhart overcame ecclesiastical divisions of gender and rank to recognize in Marguerite a spirit kindred to his own in audacity of expression, and more importantly in authenticity of experience. The influence is most obvious and most verbal in Eckhart's *Predigt* 52, the *Beati pauperes spiritu*, but there seems no compelling reason not to look beyond it to the central Eckhartian themes of *abegescheidenheit* and *durchbrechen* which are in Marguerite *anéantissement* and the fall from love into nothingness.

Two great German scholars, Josef Koch, one of the editors of Eckhart's Latin corpus, and Herbert Grundmann, were convinced that Marguerite's *Mirror* was a source for Eckhart's thought. Yet both these scholars were unable to publish their results before they died. Eckhart, who was in Paris three times, as lecturer on the Sentences in 1293–94, in 1302–03 when he held the non-Franciscan chair of theology, and again in 1311–12, actually shared a house in the Dominican community of Marguerite's inquisitor, William Humbert of Paris. Grundmann speculates that Eckhart may have seen copies of Marguerite's treatise confiscated during and after the inquisition process, which began in 1309 with Marguerite's arrest and ended with her death on June 1, 1310.[12] Thus, if Eckhart did have occasion to read her treatise during his last stay in Paris, the influence of *The Mirror of Simple Souls* would have extended over the greater part of Eckhart's preaching career in Germany.

Although Edmund Colledge has traced the themes of Meister Eckhart's sermon, the *Beati pauperes spiritu*, back to Marguerite, in the process he has disparaged her work and its influence on Eckhart.[13] In calling her the "high priestess of 'liberty of the spirit,'" and accusing her of being a "Valentinian Gnostic," Colledge displays the tendency of several modern interpreters to stand with her

---

[11] From the second inquisition process, we learn that Marguerite had actually given her book to another bishop, Bishop Jean de Château-Villain, the bishop of Châlons-sur-Marne, after its condemnation by Guy de Colmieu in 1306. See Verdeyen (78–80), who throws considerable doubt on this "obsequious" follower of the king's testimony.

[12] Herbert Grundmann, "Ketzerverhöre des Spätmittelalters als quellenkritisches Problem," *Deutsches Archiv für Erforschung des Mittelalters* 21 (1965): 519–75. He also tells of a note sent him by Josef Koch stating that he had "proof" of Marguerite's influence on Eckhart. Sadly, none of this "proof" survives (529).

[13] Edmund Colledge and J.C. Marler, "'Poverty of the Will': Ruusbroec, Eckhart and *The Mirror of Simple Souls*," in *Jan van Ruusbroec: The Sources, Content and Sequels of His Mysticism*, ed. Paul Mommaers and N. De Paepe (Leuven University Press, 1984), 14–47.

inquisitors in condemning Marguerite anew. In this paper, I will examine Marguerite's treatise, particularly its themes of knowing nothing, wanting nothing, and having no place for God, along with its larger ontological theme of *anéantissement*, the nothingness-in-God. I will then look at Eckhart's *abegescheidenheit* as a version of *anéantissement* which illustrates Caroline Walker Bynum's observation that in men's stories and symbols there are emphases on renunciations and reversals, while in women's there are gradual deepenings of ordinary experience.[14] Meister Eckhart, a highly original mind who yet reflects Marguerite's thought, has become, even with his differences, a mirror of the *Mirror*.

The mysticism of Marguerite's *Mirror* is actually both Dionysian and Beguine, and therefore both apophatic and cataphatic. The Beguine and Dionysian elements of Marguerite's mysticism occupy a peculiar dialectical space here. For at the heart of her apparently negative theology is the supreme value of Love as the affirmative revelation of the feminine divine. In Marguerite's Beguine *Minnemystik*, Love, as *Dame Amour*, replaces the Stoic-patristic Reason-Logos as the principle of the universe. The supremacy of Love in the treatise is its clearest mark of a Beguine spirituality,[15] following in the tradition of the love poetry of Hadewijch.[16] What remains in Marguerite of the early Beguine language of the Song of Song's mystical marriage and erotic union with Christ or visions of Christ's suffering humanity often mediated by the Eucharist is only the merest trace.[17] Marguerite is not primarily a visionary whose authority can derive from the authenticity of her visions as did Hildegard's.[18] Yet, in her adoption of *amour courtois* themes in the prologue to her treatise, Marguerite demonstrates the Beguine tendency to mingle secular and spiritual which is also found in Mechthild of Magdeburg.[19] Marguerite's borrowing from the genre of troubadour lyric and courtly love literature indicates that she

[14] See Caroline Walker Bynum, "Introduction: The Complexity of Symbols," in *Gender and Religion: On the Complexity of Symbols*, ed. Caroline Walker Bynum, Steven Harrell, and Paula Richman (Boston: Beacon Press, 1986), 13 and 277.

[15] Elizabeth Petroff describes early Beguine spirituality as employing the "language of the *Song of Songs* and of a certain kind of medieval love poetry, of *amour courtois* and *minnemystik*." *Medieval Women's Visionary Literature* (Oxford: Oxford Univ. Press, 1986), 174.

[16] See Paul Mommaers, "Preface," *Hadewijch: The Complete Works*, trans. and intro. Mother Columba Hart, O.S.B., Classics of Western Spirituality Series (New York: Paulist Press, 1980).

[17] See Caroline Walker Bynum, *Fragmentation and Redemption: Essays on Gender and the Human Body in Medieval Religion* (New York: Zone Books, 1992), 124.

[18] In one place she thanks God for visions of the Trinity as well as visions of "petites choses," but these visions are not the basis of her mystical treatise and theology. See Elizabeth Petroff, "Introduction," *Medieval Women's Visionary Literature*, 6, for the relation between visions and women's spiritual power.

[19] Petroff, 207.

wanted her book to reach a wide audience of both active and contemplative seekers and that, as a true Beguine, she wanted to move her treatise on mystical love of God out into the world.

But Marguerite's *Mirror* is equally and emphatically Dionysian in its insistence on the nothingness of God and of the soul brought to nothing in God. Marguerite's theology in its emphasis on "knowing nothing" as the way to the unknowable God may be considered a classic instance of the apophatic program of Dionysius. Yet, her mysticism might be said to assume the *cognitive* apophaticism of Dionysius and to concentrate more on a *conative* apophaticism aimed at "willing nothing." At the same time, it offers a critique of affective love-mysticism. Unlike the author of *The Cloud of Unknowing*, for example, she does not counsel love as final means of access to God. Although in describing the stages of ascent or really descent to God, the Beguine indulges in an erotic language of drowning in a sea of love, it is only in order to mark its inadequacy as an ultimate state. At the end, the terms allowing for a psychological *relation* to God have been burnt up, drowned, and annihilated precisely by this love that now becomes the Love of the only Lover left remaining— God. "All this, says Love, is like iron invested with fire which has lost its own semblance because the fire is stronger and thus transforms the iron into itself. So also this Soul is completely invested with this greater part, and nourished and transformed into this greater part, because of the love of this greater part, taking no account of the lesser" (*Mirouer*, 152; chap. 52).[20] Marguerite uses all the linguistic means at her disposal, particularly those of paradox and contradiction, to annihilate in language as in reality all understanding, will, love, and even the self itself. Her apophaticism can be seen as even more extreme than that of many Christian mystics in its ultimate rejection of a psychology of love and of the human person as the active, initiating lover.[21] In Marguerite's apophaticism, there may be a subtle critique of her Beguine legacy and a willingness to depart from the twelfth-century Bernardian union of love and will.[22]

Considerable tension therefore exists between the Beguine and Dionysian elements of Marguerite's mysticism. Marguerite may even have been alienated from her sister Beguines, as implied in a plaintive verse nearly ending the book:

---

[20] Translation of E. Babinsky, *The Mirror*, 130. I am grateful to Ellen Babinsky who made parts of her translation of the *Mirror* available to me while I was preparing this paper. Her translation will hereafter be cited in the text as Babinsky with the chapter and page number.

[21] See Bernard McGinn, "Love, Knowledge and *Unio mystica* in the Western Christian Tradition," in *Mystical Union and Monotheistic Faith: An Ecumenical Dialogue*, ed. Moshe Idel and Bernard McGinn (New York: Macmillan, 1989), 74.

[22] See McGinn, "Love, Knowledge, and *Unio Mystica*," 62–63.

Amis, que diront beguines,	O my Lover, what will Beguines say
et gens de religion,	and religious types,
Quant ilz orront l'excellence	When they hear the excellence
de vostre divine chançon?	of your divine song?
Beguines dient que je erre,	Beguines say I err,
prestres, clers, et prescheurs,	priests, clerics, and Preachers,
Augustins, et carmes,	Augustinians, Carmelites,
et les freres mineurs,	and the Friars Minor,
Pource que j'escri de l'estre	Because I wrote about the being
de l'affinee Amour.	of the one purified by Love.
Non fais sauve leur Raison,	I do not make Reason safe for them,
qui leur fait a moy ce dire.	who make them say this to me.[23]
(*Mirouer*, 344)	

But Marguerite's Dionysian apophaticism is also enriched by her Beguine spirituality. In her Dionysian-Beguine dialectic, Marguerite's pervasive concept of nothingness, *le nient*, is a metaphor of the primal maternal ground of being and seedbed of all possibilities. "And this Willing-Nothing sows the divine seed, which is taken from the heart of divine will. Such a seed can never fail, but so few folk are disposed to receive such a seed" (Babinsky, chap. 133, 216; *Mirouer*, 392). Here is an incipient and inchoate doctrine that resembles Eckhart's birth of the Son in the soul. Marguerite's work is a profound meditation on God as feminine *Amour* and feminine *Bonté* (Goodness) "which tends by the nature of love to give itself and to expand all its bounty" (*Mirouer*, 304; chap. 112), overflowing all boundaries. In Marguerite's dialectic, "God," the bountiful outpouring of a manifest Love, belongs to an unmanifest nothingness, which can be reached only by "knowing nothing," "willing nothing," and having no space for God.

Thus, arising out of a movement of semireligious women often considered an early feminist movement, and addressed to an exclusively female audience, Marguerite's mysticism was boldly gendered. The female gendering of all the major characters in her book with the exception of the courtly love figure, *Loingprès*, "FarNear," cannot be overlooked. *Dame Amour* is consistently addressed with the feminine pronoun and as *maitresse*, although the noun *amour* is masculine in French. The soul is described in female relational terms as "queen of the virtues, daughter of the Godhead, sister of Wisdom, and bride of Love" (*Mirouer*, 246; chap. 87). Marguerite affirms the scandal of particularity of the female gender as a viable political option for her sister Beguines, the "Great Church," and even for the

---

[23] This passage exists only in the Old French version; there is a lacuna in the Middle English at this point.

Deity. Paradoxically, in the exercise of this political option, by going through gender, one could finally be liberated from both externalized and internalized forms of oppression. Internally, the liberation from mental structures of domination took for Marguerite the radical form of annihilation. Externally, the notion of "gender," insofar as Marguerite entertained such a notion,[24] was not a matter of traits or of social roles, but of the prophetic possibility of dissent from and subversion of the predominant patriarchal order. In her feminine reordering of love over reason,[25] as well as the Great Church of God's true lovers over the Lesser Church, she subverted patriarchal structure and values. Gender was therefore for Marguerite a fulcrum for overturning ecclesiastical hierarchy both in its external form and its internal *raison d'être*. In this respect, Marguerite's was a Beguine program of what a recent critic has described as "fighting silently against the sclerosis of the hierarchical Church."[26] Although she never entirely collapsed the ontologized notion of hierarchy inherited from Dionysius, she did turn it on its head so that an upside-down hierarchy emerged in her new vision of church and society. By inverting prevailing patriarchal values, *The Mirror of Simple Souls* reflects a contemporary ecclesiastical world that was itself an inversion of women's experience and values.

Yet, at first glance, Marguerite's mystical theology does not resemble the sheer materiality and groundedness in female experiences of body of other women mystics such as Catherine of Siena or Angela of Foligno.[27] Marguerite's mysticism is not particularly affective, ecstatic, or visionary, and perhaps the real threat of her treatise was that it did not remain in the exclamatory, lyrical, emotional realm of language assigned to women, but passed over to an indicative, teaching, and literally "speculative" mysticism. Although her apophatic mysticism does not at first resemble the physicality of devotion to the humanity of Jesus or the eucharistic and ascetic piety of many women mystics, nonetheless her mystical theology is deeply gendered.

Although Marguerite's emphasis on physicality was much more subtle than that of contemporary women mystics such as Catherine of Siena, it was enough to

---

[24] The concept of sexual difference as a political option is discussed in Rosi Braidotti, "The Politics of Ontological Difference," and in Els Maeckelberghe, *Desperately Seeking Mary: A Feminist Appropriation of a Traditional Religious Symbol* (Netherlands: Pharos, 1992), 78–79.

[25] Love mysticism, Paul Mommaers asserts, "is a preeminently feminine phenomenon, and its essential hallmark, as shown by the term 'love' (*minne*), is that union with God is lived here on earth as a love relationship." "Preface," *Hadewijch: The Complete Works*, xiii.

[26] Odette Baumer-Despeigne, "Hadewijch of Antwerp and Hadewijch II: Mysticism of Being in the Thirteenth Century in Brabant," *Studia Mystica*, 14/4 (Winter 1991): 19.

[27] Caroline Walker Bynum, ". . . And Woman His Humanity": Female Imagery in the Religious Writing of the Later Middle Ages," in *Gender and Religion: on the Complexity of Symbols*, 259–60.

have caused her male inquisitors to read her as antinomian. Marguerite's body-soul integration unwittingly triggered a charge of antinomianism in a climate already primed for it. During the period immediately following the first burning of her book, Henry of Virneburg, Archbishop of Cologne, who later prosecuted Meister Eckhart, sent out a decree alleging that Beguines and Beghards of his diocese said that those moved by the Spirit were not under the law.[28] This challenge to traditional patriarchal categories whose ethic of renunciation derived from a dualism of physical and spiritual experience and resulted in hierarchies of the more "spiritual" over the bodily, was bound to be threatening to the established order. Marguerite's appropriation of "body" in a nature well ordered by transformation into Divine Love is a more subtle but consistent affirmation of body-soul integration. Marguerite's mysticism is gendered in its body-soul integration, its rejection of the pursuit of "virtue" over simplicity and nothingness, and its "theology" of a feminine Divine.[29]

Marguerite's entire treatise is in the form of a dialogue primarily between Love and the Soul, *Amour* and *Ame*.[30] The response to this Love is an increasing clarification and simplification, the soul's *anéantissement*, its annihilation. While the dialogue form functions to keep Love (God) and the soul separate, each maintaining her own standpoint, the subtext of the dialogue describes a oneness of being between Love and the Lover brought about by a transformation of the soul into Love.[31] The underlying logic of this transformation might be said to be that God *is* (and is becoming) "all in all." For Marguerite this logic is uncompromising in its power to encompass even that last vestige of "selfness," the will. What shows up in Marguerite's mirror is the utterly transparent, that is the no-thinged soul.

---

[28] Lerner, *The Heresy of the Free Spirit*, 66.

[29] For these reasons, I cannot subscribe to the "gender apophaticism" of Michael Sells (see Sells' essay in this volume). Despite the very real threat that the proclamation of difference entailed for her, with all characters in the treatise except "FarNear" gendered as female, I believe this difference mattered a great deal to Marguerite, and it was in part for that difference that she gave her life. To "unsay" gender to the point where it may unsay nature bespeaks a disregard for materiality and body that Marguerite did not share.

[30] In this it resembles another Beguine's, Mechthild of Magdeburg's, treatise, *The Flowing Light of the Godhead*, trans. Lucy Menzies; excerpted in Elizabeth Petroff, ed., *Medieval Women's Visionary Literature*. Yet, Mechthild clearly rejects the apophatic way advocated by Marguerite: "Thou must overcome . . . annihilation of self-will which drags so many souls back that they never come to real love" (Petroff, 218).

[31] Cf. Hadewijch's saying that "when the soul is brought to nought and with God's will wills all that he wills, and is engulfed in him, and is brought to nought—then he is exalted above the earth, and then he draws all things to him; and so the soul becomes with him all that he himself is." *Letter* 19, *Hadewijch: The Complete Works*, 90.

"The mirror returns its own image to the one who looks at herself there . . . the mirror evokes the knowledge of self, with the idea of a purification, of an assimilation to a perfect ideal."[32] As the mirror becomes empty, it more perfectly reflects the boundlessness of God's *Bonté*. The book itself is the mirror which reflects the soul reflecting the love of God. The mirror becomes therefore an image of wholeness and seamless simplicity rather than fragmentation and specialization, reflecting the mystic's experience of integration and transparency. The soul, the book, the love, the Lord, such are the many mirrors which become increasingly indistinguishable as their only "object," the soul, seems to disappear in its *anéantissement*.

The mirror, a medieval and modern image of women's vanity and narcissism, and of the superficial and false self, becomes transformed in this as in much mystical literature into a symbol of the honesty and depth of the true self before, in, and becoming God.[33] Even psychological interpretations of the mirror as an image associated with the alienations of self-consciousness, and the duality of subject and object, are overturned by its use here as a symbol of the oneness and freedom of the simple, "annihilated" soul. The transparency of this self prevents it from catching or putting out reflections, what some modern psychologists call "projections." The self alienated from itself, others, and from God, is replaced by its own absence. Absence then becomes presence. The mirror, an apparently apt symbol of woman's narcissism, in Marguerite's *Mirror* becomes emblematic of her willingness to lose herself in a most radical otherness.[34]

---

[32] Max Huot de Longchamp, "Introduction," *Marguerite Porete, Le Miroir des Ames simples et Anéanties* (Paris: Albin Michel, 1984), 16.

[33] Sr. Ritamary Bradley, in an article on the concept of mirror in the Middle Ages, (*Speculum* 29 [1954]: 100–119), discusses the mirror's "double function of showing the world what it is and what it should become" for the period from the fifth to the twelfth century. Jenifoy La Belle, *Herself Beheld: The Literature of the Looking Glass* (Ithaca, N.Y.: Cornell University Press, 1988), in surveying the literature of the nineteenth and twentieth centuries, states that "for women, mirroring is not a stage but a continual, ever shifting process of self-realization" (10).

[34] Modern French feminists have also taken up the image of the mirror: Julia Kristeva in *Tales of Love*, trans. Louis Roudiez, (New York: Columbia Univ. Press, 1987), and Luce Irigaray in *Speculum of the Other Woman*, trans. Gillian C. Gill (Ithaca, New York: Cornell, 1985). Irigaray's "La Mystérique," (191–202) a neologism which her translator says fuses "mysticism, hysteria, mystery, and the femaleness fundamental to the other three," offers an extremely close parallel to Marguerite's "specula-tions." Irigaray asks, "What if everything were already so intimately specularized that even in the depths of the abyss of the 'soul' a mirror awaited her reflection and her light. Thus I have become your image in this nothingness that I am, and you gaze upon mine in your absence of being. . . . When I look upon you in the secret of my 'soul,' I seek (again) the loss of specularization, and try to bring my 'nature' back to its mirroring wholeness" (197).

Marguerite's hermeneutic of restoration speaks of the true self, no longer the self-identity-as-same of an exclusive psychology and exclusive theology, but the self as fluid transparency, as burning glass.[35] In classical mythology, the symbol of the failure of mirroring and its hermeneutic of suspicion is the myth of the male figure Narcissus. On the other hand, the female figure *Prudentia* or *Sophia* in the medieval Alan of Lille's *Anticlaudianus*, holding a threefold effulgent mirror, "perceives how the composite is simple: the heavenly, mortal; the different, identical; the heavy, light; the moving stationary; the dark, bright . . . the eternal, temporal; the revolving, fixed."[36] Marguerite's specular experience is the paradoxical one of both-and, body-soul, self-other. Such paradoxes of self-as-other and self-in-other and body-as-soul underlie the dialectic of Marguerite's *Mirror*.

In the apophatic-cataphatic dialectic sustained by the dialogue, then, the soul's annihilation is paradoxically its liberation. "Thus, the Soul wills nothing, says Love, since she is free; for one is not free who wills something by the will within him, whatever he might will. For when one is a servant of oneself, one wills that God accomplish His will to one's own honor. . . . To such a one, says Love, God refuses His kingdom" (Babinsky, chap. 48, 126–27; *Mirouer*, 144). Only a most radical *nient-vouloir* releases one from servitude even to oneself. The soul becomes more and more free as it comes to know nothing and to will nothing, not even to will to do the will of God![37] It is as free of projections, the screen of objects thrown up by the mind's attempt to know something, as it is free of projects, the set of plans thrown out by the will's attempt to will something. In her more extreme formulations of this doctrine, Marguerite declares,[38] "how much better to will nothing in God, than to will the good for God," even to work miracles, to accept

---

[35] Irigaray remarks of the "embrace of fire that mingles one term into another,": "This is the place where 'she'—and in some cases he, if he follows 'her' lead—speaks about the dazzling glare which comes from the source of light that has been logically repressed, about 'subject' and 'Other' flowing out into an embrace of fire that mingles one term into another, about contempt for form as such, about mistrust for understanding as an obstacle along the path of jouissance and mistrust for the dry desolation of reason. Also about a 'burning glass.' This is the only place in the history of the West in which woman speaks and acts so publicly" (Ibid., 191).

[36] Quoted in Edward Peter Nolan, *Now Through a Glass Darkly: Specular Images of Being and Knowing from Virgil to Chaucer* (Ann Arbor, Mich., Univ. of Michigan Press, 1990), 290.

[37] "Se ceste Ame Adnientie veult la voulenté de Dieu—et qui plus la veult et plus la vouldroit vouloir—ce ne peut elle avoir par la petitesse de creature . . . comment peut l'Ame avoir vouloir, puisque Clere Congnoissance cognoist qu'il est ung estre entre les estres, le plus noble de tous les estres, lequel creature ne peut avoir, se elle ne l'a par nient vouloir?" *Mirouer*, chap. 12, 52.

[38] See also the modern French translation in *Marguerite Porete: Le Miroir des âmes simples et anéanties et qui seulement demeurent en vouloir et désir d'amour*, intro., trans., and notes Max Huot de Longchamp (113).

martyrdom daily, or be ravished into heaven and visions of the Trinity as was St. Paul (*Mirouer*, chap. 49, 148; Babinsky, 128).[39] Willing-Nothing, *le nient vouloir*, becomes in Marguerite almost a positive, transitive act whose ultimate effect is transformation into the nothingness of God.[40]

Without the knowing or the willing of an object-God, it is no longer possible to "have" God. "For all that this soul has of God in herself by gift of divine grace seems to her nothing from the standpoint of what she loves, which is *in* God. . . ." (*Mirouer*, chap. 13, 60). When it is no longer possible to "have" God by way of ownership, possession, or place, then one has entered into the deepest poverty of spirit, into *anéantissement*. The deeply experiential nothingness of Love does not cling to the names, modes, or attributes of a rational theology or the virtues, acts, or means of a moral theology.[41] One loses God and the way to God to be brought to nothing-in-God.

Annihilation, as willing nothing and knowing nothing, brings liberation to God as well as to the soul. One's bringing the will to nothing leaves God to become all in all, to be in fact truly God.

> He is, says this Soul, and nothing is lacking to Him. I am not, and so nothing is lacking to me. And so He has given me peace and I live only from Peace, which is born from His gifts in my soul without thought. I can do nothing if it is not given to me to do. He is my All and my Best Good. Annihilation by the unity of divine righteousness has such power (Babinsky, chap. 52, 130; *Mirouer*, 154).

Neither the gifts of God in this life nor the rewards or punishments in another can attract or intimidate the annihilated soul. To emphasize that all such intentionality must cease, Marguerite has Love proclaim, "Whoever would ask such free Souls, sure and peaceful, if they would want to be in Purgatory, they would say no; or if they would want to be certain of their salvation in this life, they would say no; or if they would want to be in paradise, they would say no. But then with what would they will it? They no longer possess any will, and if they would desire anything, they would separate themselves from Love." (Babinsky, chap. 9, 86–87; *Mirouer*, 32). Annihilation is necessary to expand the space where Love will be.

---

[39] Cf. also her statement that "This soul knows only one thing, which is to know that she knows nothing, and wills only one thing, which is that she wills nothing. And this nothing-knowing (*nient savoir*) and this nothing-willing (*nient vouloir*) give her everything." *Mirouer*, 130; chap. 42.

[40] Cf. Mechthild's affirming that one must love *das nicht*. See Frank Tobin, "Mechthild von Magdeburg and Meister Eckhart," 44–61.

[41] Both Marguerite and Eckhart are at one in a dismissal of the path of virtues.

In freeing the soul and God, Marguerite insists that the soul is no more dependent on fasting, prayer, Masses, and sermons. Not only do these methods of mediation enslave the soul, but they bind God to works and sacraments. Marguerite discloses her Beguine "worldliness" in saying, "It seems to beginners that certain people, who thus seek God in mountains and valleys hold that God must be subject to his sacraments and to his works. . . . But those have a good and profitable time who no longer seek God only in temples or monasteries but in all places, through being in union with the divine will" (*Mirouer*, chap. 69, 196).

Marguerite's most objectionable expression of the nonmediational and antinomian element of her work, cited by the continuator of the Nangis chronicle as part of the Inquisition's list of heretical statements, goes even further:

> [L]et us take one Soul for all, says Love, which Soul neither desires nor despises poverty nor tribulation, nor Mass nor sermon, nor fast nor prayers, and gives to Nature all that is necessary for it, without remorse of conscience; but such nature is so well ordained by transformation of unity of Love, to which the will of this Soul is conjoined, that nature asks nothing which is forbidden (*Mirouer*, chap. 9, 32).

Read in the context of her whole work, this statement, far from being antinomian, does, however, dismantle the hierarchy of soul and body so prevalent in the tradition of Christian Platonism. As elsewhere throughout her text, Marguerite is presupposing what mystics call "holy indifference" or an equanimity based on greater body-soul unity than her inquisitors could accept. In support of her ethic of integration and affirmation of nature, she has Divine Justice say, "We take the service of the four elements in all the ways that Nature has need of, without reproach of Reason; . . . and all such souls use all things made and created, of which Nature has need, in such peace of heart, just as they use the earth on which they walk" (*Mirouer*, 72; chap. 17).[42] Marguerite's ethic refuses to deny the place of materiality in the all-encompassing action of God's grace.

Marguerite's rejection of intermediaries extends even to the practice of the virtues, a subtlety that was unfortunately lost on her inquisitors. The first article condemned in the process against her and later by the Council of Vienne can be found in one of its explicit formulations in Chapter Twenty-one:

> It is true that this Soul has taken leave of the virtues, as to their exercise and as to the desire of what they demand, but the Virtues have not taken leave of her, for they are always with her, but in perfect obedience of her . . . this

---

[42] See also her statement that the Sun of Justice never healed the soul without the body (*Mirouer*, 220; chap. 78).

Soul has gained so much with the Virtues, that she is beyond the Virtues, for she has in her all that the Virtues know how to teach, and still more, without comparison. For this Soul has in her the mistress of the Virtues, that is called Divine Love, which has transformed her into Herself, and united with her, by which this Soul is no more in herself nor in the Virtues (*Mirouer*, 80–82).

As this passage indicates, the liberated soul is no longer in bondage to the individual virtues, no longer in willful pursuit of their achievement. No longer needing to turn to this or that partial goal, the liberated soul is in full possession of these more elementary practices of the spiritual life. The virtues are in her, and she has only taken leave of willing them. Marguerite's refined spirituality will not let the virtues become self-aggrandizing acquisitions contaminating the soul with self-will. She understands that whoever aims at this or that particular goal, no matter how virtuous, aims at something less than God. The virtues belong to a works theology superseded by her more complete transformation into Love. Marguerite's mirror refuses to reflect a specialized, fragmented self in pursuit of one or the other of the virtues (from *vir*, "man"), a literally masculine spirituality which she intuitively rejects.

However, Marguerite's kicking out the ladder of mediation actually comes near the end of a seven-stage process.[43] These seven stages are actually an elaboration of a broader three-stage movement from grace through spirit to the life of unity in God. From keeping the commandments to imitating Christ in the counsels of perfection, she accomplishes the works of goodness in the first three states, but she is so attached to doing these works that the will must then be put to death, martyred, pulverized, "to enlarge the place where love would want to be, and to encumber the self by several stages in order to unencumber the self to attain one's being" (Babinsky, chap. 118, 190). It is at this stage that the will must begin to be annihilated. The soul then passes into the embrace of union of the fourth state where she becomes "so dangerous, noble and delicious" that she mistakenly believes this to be the highest gift God can give.

In her pride over her abundance of love and in seeing herself as the mistress of resplendence, the soul is, however, greatly deceived. Love, says Marguerite, and here she means the affective, psychological movements of soul shared with courtly love,

---

[43] Marguerite actually makes two attempts to convey her doctrine of annihilation. The first is stageless and ateleological. One is not on a journey or climbing the steps of a ladder as in St. John Climacus' influential *Ladder of Perfection*, but only present before the mirror. Near the beginning of her treatise, she describes the soul in terms without projects or stages, "No one can find her; she is saved by faith alone; she is alone in love; she does nothing for God; she leaves nothing to God; she cannot be taught; she cannot be robbed; she cannot be given anything; she has no will" (*Mirouer*, chap. 29).

"has deceived many souls by the sweetness of the pleasure of her love" (ibid.). Just where one might expect a lingering in the delights of a *Brautmystik* or a Beguine *amour courtois*, Marguerite passes beyond this state, thereby offering a subtle critique of its *amor sensibilis*. Retrospectively reflecting on this state of psychological love, which she associates with the life of the spirit, she comments:

> But she thinks that she possesses this love toward God, by whom she is wounded; but, to be sure, it is herself whom she loves, without her knowing it and without her perceiving it. And there they are deceived who love through the tenderness which they have by affection, which does not allow them to arrive at understanding. And thus they remain as children in the works of children, so they remain as long as they have affection of the spirit (Babinsky, chap. 133, 216; *Mirouer*, 392).

However, in the fifth stage, the soul begins to move toward a more essential, ontological union; the dialectic here is between Being and Non-Being, God's Being and her not-being without God. Now, delivered from her own will, standing in the blinding light of Love, the soul in this state sees "what God is, that God IS." "The Soul considers that God is Who is, from whom all things are, and she is not if she is not of Him from whom all things are" (Babinsky, chap. 118, 191; *Mirouer*, 324). Her will to love is replaced by the will *given* her by the God who is Being and an overflowing Goodness, and her own resplendence disappears in the flood of Divine Light poured into the soul to move her will (ibid.). She stands abashed at the sight of God's infinite goodness giving free will even to her nothingness.

In contrast to the preceding state of violent love and the warfare of her will, her transformation into Love in this state is accompanied by peace. The "Spouse of her youth," the erotic relation of a less mature spirituality, has now become the One. The soul then finds herself in a profundity so great that there is no beginning or measure or end, but an abyss without foundation ("une abysme abysmee sans fons; la se trouve elle, sans trouver et sans fons" *Mirouer*, 326). "Now this Soul has fallen from love into nothingness, and without such nothingness she cannot be All. The fall is so deep, she is so rightly fallen, that the soul cannot lift herself from such an abyss" (Babinsky, chap. 118, 193; *Mirouer*, 328). Her fall is perfect, for it humbles the once *dangereuse* spirit blinded by feelings of love at the height of contemplation of the fourth state. In the sixth state the soul no longer sees herself or God, but rather God sees God in her so that she sees that none is but God. "But this Soul, thus pure and clarified, sees neither God nor herself, but God sees Himself of Himself in her, for her, without her. God shows to her that there is nothing except Him" (ibid.; *Mirouer*, 330). At this point the terms of the dialectic disappear into a nothingness that has become All, an all that has become Nothingness.[44] At this final earthly stage, even before the seventh state's heavenly beatitude, the soul, returned to her origins, "is in the stage of her prior being, and so has left three and has made of two One" (Babinsky, chap. 138, 219; *Mirouer*, 400).

Turning now to Meister Eckhart's celebrated *Predigt* 52, the *Beati pauperes spiritu*,[45] we encounter what could be seen as a summary of the apophatic themes of Marguerite's mysticism. In Eckhart's sermon, which Colledge speculates was written as a "gesture of defiance" after his Defense of 1327,[46] Eckhart describes a truly poor person as one who wants nothing, knows nothing, and has nothing. The person who wants nothing has no attachment to penances or other external exercises, a frequent theme throughout Eckhart's work as in Marguerite's. Furthermore, this person is so poor that he or she no longer wills to fulfill God's will (*ES*, 200). This person should even be as free of created will as when he was nothing ("dô er niht enwas," DW 2: 491).[47] For then this person had no "God," no other outside himself to want, to know, or to "have." One with God in this precreated preexistence, there is no need for God or for anything: "What I wanted I was, and what I was I wanted," says Eckhart.[48] He even prays to God to be free of "God," that is to be free of the created relationship to God. The parallels to Marguerite's work are here quite striking, for Marguerite had said, "for she is no one in this one and then she has no more to do for God than God has to do for her. For God is and she is not. . . . for she is without being, in that place where she was before she was" (*Mirouer*, 396; chap. 135).[49] In both Marguerite and Eckhart, the paradigmatic relation to God is

[44] See Romana Guarnieri, "Frères du libre esprit," in *Dictionnaire de spiritualité* V (1964): 1257–59.

[45] This sermon can be found in DW 2: 478–516 and is translated in *Meister Eckhart: The Essential Sermons, Commentaries, Treatises, and Defense*, trans. and intro. Edmund Colledge, O.S.A., and Bernard McGinn, Classics of Western Spirituality Series (New York: Paulist Press, 1981), 199–203. Cited hereafter as *ES*.

[46] Edmund Colledge, O.S.A., and J.C. Marler, "'Poverty of the Will': Ruusbroec, Eckhart and *The Mirror of Simple Souls*," in *Jan van Ruusbroec*, 14–47.

[47] In Eckhart's work "On Detachment," where he echoes the language of the *Beati pauperes*, he refers to a mysterious "teacher" who says: "The poor in spirit are those who have abandoned all things for God, just as they were his when we did not exist." (*ES*, 292–93). Since this "teacher" has never been identified, we can at least speculate on whether this could have been Marguerite.

[48] "Dô enwolte ich niht, noch enbegerte ich niht. . . daz ich wolte, daz was ich, und daz ich was, daz wolte ich," DW 2: 492.

[49] This passage exists only in Middle English translation as found in *Mirouer*, 396. We might compare to both Eckhart's and Marguerite's statements of this preexistent willessness, this from Augustine, "The will loses what the will acquires, for the soul already existed with power to will its conversion toward its Source, but before it existed it was not there to will to be a soul." *De Trinitate*, 8.3.5.

no relation but a return to the self-sufficient Source or ground of Being,[50] what Eckhart calls the Godhead and Marguerite calls Nothingness. Even to remain in the relation of love in Marguerite or of creature in Eckhart is to have a God and thus to negate God.[51]

Eckhart continues that the truly poor person knows nothing, not even that God lives in her. This introspective knowing of God within, expressed throughout the Fathers as the power of the image of God, allows for distinction, and Eckhart is after complete indistinction, even if it costs him "God"! In both Marguerite and Eckhart, only a dismantling of the dualistic structures of knowing and willing, structures which erect a narcissistic world of self-and God-projections, can give the uncompromising unity they seek. Yet, while Marguerite's tendency is to express the nonduality of the highest states in terms of selflessness or acosmism ("and what is, is God's self, . . . which shows that there is none other than God," *Mirouer*, 330), Eckhart's tendency is to express it in terms of an a-theistic self-avowal ("When I stood in my first cause, I then had no 'God,' and then I was my own cause," *ES*, 200).[52]

Having treated the poverty of willing nothing and knowing nothing, Eckhart goes on to give an even more "intimate" and radical degree of poverty. Reversing his previous position, he now says that a poor person should not have a place for God, but that God should be God's own place to work. Eckhart is aware that he is here transcending "grace and being and understanding and will and longing," all the structures in which God might occupy a space in the human, or the human have a place for God.[53] Before Eckhart, Marguerite had said, "There she no longer prays, any more than she did before she was ought . . . for this she has no place, nor does she take account of anything that may happen to her. She has no more bottom or floor than she has place, and if she has no place, then she has no love of herself" (*Mirouer*, 398; chap. 136).

From the state of total poverty Eckhart has been describing in *Predigt* 52, where a person is free of self-will and God's will, of God's works and of God's-self (*ES*, 203), there is now the breaking-through into the God beyond God. Here is the

---

[50] Colledge maintains that Eckhart is adopting the usual scholastic distinction between God in himself and God in creatures. He interprets Eckhart's "poverty" as "identified with the beatific self-sufficiency which only God, considered in himself, can give." "'Poverty of the Will,'" 17. Surprisingly, the absence of relation in Eckhart's *Gotheit* actually recalls the absence of real relation between Aquinas' God and the world.

[51] Technically, it is the negation of the *Deus pro nobis*, not of the *Deus in se*.

[52] I am tempted to make the observation that Marguerite's self-annihilation and Eckhart's God-annihilation at this point are gender-related.

[53] "Nû schînet disiu rede obe gnâde und obe wesene und obe verstantnisse und obe willen und ob aller begirde." DW 2: 501.

collapse of the God who can be grasped and snatched into time for use "before and after." In this *durchbrechen* to the Godhead, one reaches a place beyond the splintering multiplicity of events in time with their power to divide us from ourselves and from God. "For in this breaking-through," says Eckhart, "I receive that God and I are one" (*ES*, 203).[54] Without a God, without a self, one is back where one was before one existed, in eternal being.

Both Eckhart's breakthough and Marguerite's fall from love into nothingness are a drive beyond union, and beyond any semblance of duality in which one can have or even be related to a God who is essentially a projection of desire and will. Just there, all dualisms, of inner and outer, higher and lower, self and God, dissolve into that simple point of oneness where all is gathered into silent unity. Just there, even the name Godhead leaves too much trace in the desert, too much echo in the stillness. Just there, One is living without a why,[55] even the why of God.[56] Just there, one is released into a joy destined to ebullience.[57]

On the one hand, Marguerite's and Eckhart's paths into that breaking-through are amazingly similar. Eckhart's *abegescheidenheit* or detachment, like Marguerite's *anéantissement*, or annihilation, relentlessly purifies the soul of attachment to works, to the will of God, or to heavenly reward.[58] Yet, where Eckhart has an *abegescheidenheit* that is literally a cutting away, reflecting the tendency of men's symbols to involve renunciation and reversal, Marguerite has an *anéantissement*, a gradual "becoming what one is most deeply" that Bynum sees as characteristic of women's stories.[59] Marguerite's concept of the annihilated soul does not employ an ethic of renunciation of nature as found at times in men's spirituality, but an ethic of integration so total and seamless that the reflection of

---

[54] "Wan ich enpfâhe in disem durchbrechen, daz ich und got einz sîn," DW 2: 505.

[55] It should be noted that Marguerite has first used this phrase the *sans nul pourquoi*, in several places in her treatise.

[56] See Reiner Schürmann, who states "Before things come to appear, they are 'teeming' with a respiration without a why in the bosom of the Godhead." *Meister Eckhart: Mystic and Philosopher* (Bloomington: Indiana Univ. Press, 1978), 120.

[57] Cf. the *ebullitio* of Eckhart's Latin works.

[58] See the linkage that Schürmann makes between detachment and annihilation in Eckhart: *Mystic and Philosopher*, 167. He states, "No less than the concepts of being or detachment, the concept of nothingness can serve as a guiding thread for the exploration of the Eckhartian universe" (168).

[59] In addition to sources previously cited, see Caroline Walker Bynum, *Fragmentation and Redemption: Essays on Gender and the Human Body in Medieval Religion* (Berkeley: Univ. of Calif. Press, 1992). Bynum asks, "Is it not rather a reflection in image of the woman's own experience of the irrelevance of structure, of continuing to strive without resolution, of going beyond only by becoming what one is most deeply?" (49).

the integrated self disappears. In Marguerite the physicality of "nature" enfolded into the simplicity of a whole self is brought to nothing in God. While Marguerite's simple, annihilated soul mutes any opposition between nature and soul, Eckhart's soul "cuts away" and detaches from time, multiplicity, and images. Here are differences occasioned by different experiences and perspectives based on gender, but not "essential" because not ultimate. Ultimately, as both their mystical ways so eloquently attest, there is left in essence the Nothingness of God and the breakthrough of freedom from all perspectives. The hallmark of both their ways of radical negation is freedom, a freedom which their inquisitors saw as an antinomian "freedom from," but which was for both really a freedom for and liberation of God.[60]

The paths of detachment and annihilation therefore open onto an ethic of presence and of affirmation of God everywhere in the world. Marguerite's annihilated souls turn the world upside down, as they make up the "Great Church" of God's true lovers, whose task it is to teach and nurture the "Lesser Church," the Church of Reason (*Mirouer*, 132). For these souls of the Greater Church, "find God everywhere. . . . And because all things are consonant with God, these souls find God in all things" (*Mirouer*, 98; chap. 30). Grounded in unity with a God in whom there is no outside except self-will, they in one sense never "go out" (and Marguerite stresses this so much that she sounds quietistic). Though Eckhart holds the terms of the dialectic between God and the Godhead painfully apart, in the simultaneity of eternity they are ontologically present to each other. The Nothingness is therefore the ground out of which flows the life of the Trinity. In Eckhart's birth of the Son in the soul and in Marguerite's transformation of the soul into Love, one's breakthrough into the Godhead has made one fruitful with God. From annihilation and the fall into nothingness issues a way into the world that is free from preoccupation with the self's manipulations and ideologies.

In concluding, when we attempt to assess the extent of the influence of Marguerite on Eckhart, we come up against at least two equally astounding theories of transmission. It is just as astonishing that Eckhart read this condemned mystic's work and appropriated it, as it is to suppose that he did not actually read it but arrived at its message through the commonality of their mystical destinies. By whatever mode of communication, Eckhart could not help but recognize in Marguerite one who knew the *wüste Gotheit* as well as the birth of Love in the soul. Although we may never know just how profoundly Marguerite has influenced the Meister, we can at least put the question, "What is the source of Eckhart's *Predigt*

---

[60] As Eckhart so beautifully says, "Every attachment . . . deprives one of the freedom to wait upon God in the present . . . , free and renewed in every present moment" (*ES*, 178).

52?" We should certainly listen to Eckhart's own response to this question when he tells us it is "a truth beyond speculation that has come immediately from the heart of God" (*ES*, 203). It has indeed come from there, but by way of the radically annihilated mysticism of Marguerite Porete. For her own spiritual poverty was so great that it had to suffer conflagration in order to be reborn out of the heart of God into the soul of Meister Eckhart.

5

Suffering Transformed

Marguerite Porete, Meister Eckhart, and the Problem
of Women's Spirituality

Amy Hollywood

A certain narrative concerning late medieval piety is becoming increasingly familiar. It runs something like this. In the later Middle Ages, women are associated with the bodily aspect of human nature. Understood as intrinsic to human personhood, the body is subject to both sin and redemption. The association of women with bodiliness is therefore not only, or even primarily, a means by which women are denigrated and a debilitating hierarchy of male over female inscribed within the social order, but also the means by which women achieve sanctification. Insofar as women are associated with the body, they are able to align themselves with the humanity of Christ through which the redemption of human nature is affected. In this way, women's reputed ties to the body become the source of their salvation; the spirituality of late medieval women is bodily, both in its language and its practice.

Such a view, presented most notably in the work of Caroline Walker Bynum, offers an essential corrective to the false picture of medieval Christianity as unqualified in its denunciation of the body and of femaleness insofar as it is tied to bodily nature.[1]

---

[1] See Caroline Walker Bynum, *Holy Feast and Holy Fast: The Religious Significance of Food to Medieval Women* (Berkeley: University of California Press, 1987); and Caroline Walker Bynum, *Fragmentation and Redemption: Essays on Gender and the Human Body in Medieval Religion* (New York: Zone Books, 1991), especially chap. 6. The account is problematized, particularly with regard to Bynum's attempts to revaluate medieval women's somatic sanctity, but basically remains intact in much current work on medieval women's spirituality, particularly in the United States. See Karma Lochrie, *Margery Kempe and the Translations of the Flesh* (Philadelphia: University of Pennsylvania Press, 1991); Elizabeth Robertson, "The Corporeality of Female Sanctity in *The Life of Saint Margaret*," in *Images of Sainthood in Medieval Europe*, ed. Renate Blumenfeld-Kosinski and Timea Szell (Ithaca: Cornell University Press, 1991); Elizabeth Robertson, "Medieval Medical Views of Women and Female Spirituality in the *Ancrene Wisse* and Julian of Norwich's *Showings*," in *Feminist Approaches to the Body in Medieval Literature*, ed. Linda Lomperis and Sarah Stanbury (Philadelphia: University of Pennsylvania Press, 1993); Laurie A. Finke, *Feminist Theory, Women's Writing* (Ithaca: Cornell University Press, 1992), chap. 3; Danielle Régnier-Bohler, "Voix litteraires, voix mystique," in *Histoire des Femmes en Occident: Le Moyen Age*, ed. Christiane Kalpisch-Zubar (Paris: Plon, 1991); and Kathleen Biddick, "Genders, Bodies, Borders:

Yet the picture requires shading in order to capture the complexities of late medieval religiosity and of women's bodies and voices within it. Most importantly, attention must be paid to the currents and countercurrents through which "feminine spirituality" defines itself historically and has been defined by modern scholarship. This requires careful attention to particular texts and figures, firmly located within specific historical moments and locations.

In late thirteenth-century northern Europe clear differences can be discerned between male and male-defined understandings of women's religiosity and women's own texts. In fact the Beguine writers, and most clearly Marguerite Porete, directly protest the form of spirituality described and prescribed as feminine in the male-authored hagiographical traditions surrounding the thirteenth-century women's religious movement. The gender relations are complex, however, for one of Porete's closest followers in rejecting bodily and ecstatic forms of spirituality is the Dominican preacher and theologian, Meister Eckhart. Both Porete and Eckhart sought to subvert the association of women with the body, suffering, and Christ's suffering humanity through the transfigurative operations of apophasis. Whereas male hagiographers looked to the Beguinal religious and social movement and created individual religious heroes, women whose extraordinary bodies signaled their sanctity, Porete and Eckhart reject the pain intrinsic to this spirituality, arguing for a form of mystical consciousness in which the relation of the soul to the world is transformed.

In the following essay, Michael Sells delineates the apophasis of gender which occurs (although in different ways) in Porete and Eckhart as a central part of their rejection of culturally defined gender hierarchies. Here I will focus upon their desire to surpass visionary, imagistic, and ecstatic spiritualities, understood as defining women's religiosity and grounded, in complex ways, in human suffering. While the former can be seen in the use of gender imagery and in the gender dynamics of their thought, the latter becomes clear when attention is given to the place they accord to the ascetic, contemplative, and visionary lives. The rejection of these modes goes together with their subversions of gendered language and images.

In demonstrating the gendered role of suffering and its refusal in Porete and Eckhart, I hope also to suggest the historical limitations of this more broadly defined apophasis of gender and the different ways in which it was pursued and experienced by women and men.[2] For while the interplay of individualism and democratization

Technologies of the Visible," *Speculum* 68 (1993): 389–418. Bynum's work shares in a current intellectual reappraisal of asceticism. For a range of texts dealing with this issue, see the two issues of *Semeia* 57–58:1 and 2 (1992).

[2] For more on Porete and contemporary feminist debates around essentialism, see Amy Hollywood, "Anti-Essentialism in the Middle Ages: The Conjunction of Feminist and Medieval Studies," in *Breviloquium: Reinstating Medieval Studies*, ed. Catherine Conybeare and Bert Roest (forthcoming).

or, perhaps less anachronistically, of esoterism and equality in the texts of Porete and Eckhart is complex, Porete's execution and Eckhart's condemnation demonstrate their inability to provide an alternative legitimate space for women's speech within the late medieval world. The work of Porete and Eckhart, its fate, and that of women's spirituality within fourteenth-century northern Europe, then, suggest the limitations of individual transformation within a world still dominated by men. Those women who follow, as witnessed in the convent chronicles and mystical texts emanating from German Dominican convents linked to Eckhart and his circle, will return to the body, albeit bodies whose manipulation is the basis for group religiosity and communal women's voices.[3]

Caroline Walker Bynum succinctly summarizes the distinctions many scholars have made between male and female forms of religiosity in the later Middle Ages:

> Thus, as many recent scholars have argued, the spiritualities of male and female mystics were different, and this difference has something to do with the body. Women were more apt to somatize religious experience and to write in intense bodily metaphors; women mystics were more likely than men to receive graphically physical visions of God; both men and women were inclined to attribute to women and encourage in them intense bodily asceticisms and ecstacies. Moreover, the most bizarre forms of bodily occurences associated with women (e.g. stigmata, incorruptibility of the cadaver after death, mystical lactations and pregnancies, catatonic trances, ecstatic nosebleeds, miraculous inedia, eating and drinking pus, visions of bleeding hosts) either first appear in the twelfth and thirteenth centuries or increase significantly in frequency at that time. [4]

Bynum here distinguishes female from male spirituality in three ways: with regard to harsh asceticism, paramystical bodily phenomena, and bodily metaphors. Less clear from her text is that while the first two are central in the predominantly male-authored

---

[3] See, for example, Karl Schröder, ed., *Der Nonnen von Engelthal Büchlein von der Genaden Überlast* (Tübingen: Literarischer Verein in Stuttgart, 1871); Ferdinand Vetter, ed., *Das Leben der Schwestern zu Töss beschrieben von Elsbet Stagel* (Berlin: Weidmannische Buchhandlung, 1906); Jeanne Ancelet-Houstache, ed., "Les 'Vitae sororum' d'Unterlinden. Edition critique du Manuscrit 508 de la Bibliothèque de Colmar," *Archive d'histoire et littéraire du moyen âge* 5 (1930): 317–509. For further references and discussions of this extensive literature, see Otto Langer, "Zur dominikanische Frauenmystik im spätmittelalterlichen Deutschland," in *Frauenmystik im Mittelalter*, ed. Peter Dinzelbacher and Dieter Bauer (Ostfildern: Schwabenverlag, 1985), 70–104; Otto Langer, *Mystische Erfahrung und spirituelle Theologie. Zu Meister Eckharts Auseinandersetzung mit der Frauenfrömmigkeit seiner Zeit* (Munich: Artemis Verlag, 1987); and Peter Ochsenbein, "Leidensmystik im dominikanische Frauenklöstern des 14. Jahrhunderts am Beispiel der Elsbeth von Oye," in *Religiöse Frauenbewegung und mystische Frömmigkeit im Mittelalter* (Cologne and Vienna: Bohlau, 1988), 353–72.

[4] Bynum, *Fragmentation*, 194.

hagiographical traditions, only the third occurs in the female-authored mystical texts of the thirteenth century.

There is no doubt that thirteenth-century male hagiographers, particularly in northern Europe, view women's sanctity as peculiarly somatic, both with regard to their harsh ascetic practices and the bodily transfigurations ascetic and mystical practice bring about within and upon the saintly woman's body.[5] This is particularly the case for those women who spend all or part of their lives as semireligious. Accounts of ascetic practices, ranging from the moderate demands of the rule of Benedict to accounts of inedia, miraculously long periods of sleep deprivation, and bodily mutilation are found in the hagiographies of almost all of the early Beguines and Cistercian nuns.[6] Causal correlations between such practices and the transformation of the saint's body into a miraculous one are not always made explicit, yet the juxtaposition of these two elements throughout the hagiographical literature of the thirteenth century points to their intimate relation.[7]

---

[5] Among the Beguines or semireligious women of whom lives survive from the period are Marie of Oignies (d.1213), Odilia (d. 1220), Christina the Astonishing (d. 1234), Ivetta of Huy (d. 1228), Margaret of Ypres (d. 1237), and Douceline (d. 1274). Other women who had strong interactions with Beguines and spent some portion of their lives within Cistercian houses are Lutgard of Aywières (d. 1246), Julianna of Mont-Cornillon (d. 1257/58), Ida of Nivelles (d. 1231/32), Ida of Léau (d. ca. 1260), Ida of Louvain (d. ca. 1255), and Beatrice of Nazareth (d. 1268). Most of these lives are available in the Bollandists' *Acta Sanctorum* (abbreviated AASS), although more specific references for certain texts will be given below.

[6] The most "spectacular" examples are those of Marie of Oignies, who cut off a sizable portion of her own flesh, and Christina the Astonishing, who threw herself into ovens, icy rivers, boiling water, and turned herself on a wheel, among other things. Through all of this her body remained unharmed; for Christina, the actions provided the spectacle and her closed body the miracle. See Jacques of Vitry, *Vita Mariae Ogniacensis*, AASS 23: n. 22, 641–42 and n. 67, 654; and Thomas of Cantimpré, *Vita Christianae Mirabilis*, AASS 31: 637–60. Almost all of the vitae include some reference to bodily castigations, food, and sleep asceticism. For the inedia of many women saints from this and other periods, see Bynum, *Holy Feast*; and Rudolph Bell, *Holy Anorexia* (Chicago: University of Chicago Press, 1985).

[7] The sanctification of the flesh through asceticism can be seen in both the life of Marie of Oignies and the Supplement written by Thomas of Cantimpré, in which he reports that her body and relics brought about miracles. Thus a man was healed from illness by touching her hair and Jacques of Vitry traveled with a bodily relic of Marie, affording him protection from bodily harm. Similarly, the asceticism of Margaret of Ypres sanctified her tomb and all the things which had touched her body. A headband which her mother had buried, assuming it was rotten and infected from Margaret's final illness, was found by her confessor Siger uncorrupted. See *Vita Mariae Ogniacensis* n. 108, p. 665; Thomas of Cantimpré, *Vita Mariae Ogniacensis supplementum*, AASS 23: nn. 6–7, 20, 668–69, 674; and Thomas of Cantimpré, *Vita Margarete de Ypris*, ed. G. Meersseman, in "Les Frères Prêcheurs et le Mouvement Devot en Flandre au XIIIe siècle,"*Archivium Fratrum Praedicatorum* 17 (1947): chap. 53–54, pp. 128–29. For more on the cult of relics and its role in medieval society, see Patrick Geary, *Furta Sacra: Thefts of Relics in the Central Middle Ages* (Princeton: Princeton University Press, 1978).

Furthermore, in the hagiographies of women from this period, such ascetic and paramystical phenomena are associated with the life of contemplation and ecstatic prayer also described, although in slightly different language, by those women who produced mystical texts. As Bynum has cogently argued, the use of bodily language and metaphors by women, as evidenced in their mystical texts, makes comprehensible male hagiographers' transposition of internal experience onto women's bodies. What was important for the medieval writer and reader, according to Bynum, was the fact of suffering; where that suffering occurred was relatively insignificant. While I would agree with the interrelations between internal and external suffering, I think that the distinction *was* important in the medieval context and carried gender implications.[8] This can be demonstrated by reexamining briefly the gap between hagiographical and mystical modes of discourse elided in the above account.[9]

The slide from mystical to paramystical language becomes evident in texts such as the *Life* of Beatrice of Nazareth, which in translating her mystical treatise, "On the Seven Manners of Loving," into Latin externalizes what are described by Beatrice as internally apprehended experiences.[10] Whereas Beatrice uses bodily metaphors to evoke the strength and madness of love within her, her hagiographer stresses the externally perceptible nature of these events.

> *Treatise*: And at times the soul becomes so boundless and so overflowing in the soul, when it itself is so mightily and violently moved in the heart, that it seems to the soul that the heart is wounded again and again, and that these wounds increase every day in bitter pain and in fresh intensity. It seems to the soul that the veins are bursting, the blood spilling, the marrow withering, the bones softening, the heart burning, the throat parching, so that the body in its every part feels this inward heat, and this is the fever of love.[11]

---

[8] David Aers has recently reemphasized the importance of interiority in medieval spiritual traditions. See David Aers, "A Whisper in the Ear of Early Modernists: or, Reflections on Literary Critics Writing the 'History of the Subject,'" in *Culture and History 1350-1600: Essays on English Communities, Identities and Writing*, ed. David Aers (Detroit: Wayne State University Press, 1992), 177–202.

[9] Bynum, *Holy Feast*, 212.

[10] Although Ursula Peters has recently contested the claim that the fourth book of Beatrice's *Life* is a translation of the treatise, the similarities in order, structure, and images demand such a reading. See Ursula Peters, *Religiöse Erfahrung als literarisches Faktum: Zur Vorgeschichte und Genese frauenmystischer Texte des 13. und 14. Jahrhunderts* (Tübingen: Max Niemeyer, 1988), 32–33; and Amy Hollywood, *The Soul as Virgin Wife: Mechthild of Magdeburg, Marguerite Porete, and Meister Eckhart* (forthcoming), chap. 2.

[11] "Ondertusschen so wert minne so onghemate ende so ouerbrekende in der sielen also har seluen so starkeleke ende so verwoedelike [berurt] int herte, dat hare dunct, dat har herte menichfoudeleke wert seere gewont ende dat die wonden dagelix verueerschet werden ende

Beatrice uses visceral language to convey the immediacy and violence of the soul's passion and the way in which her desire blurs all distinctions between bodily and spiritual experience. Yet the phrase "it seems" and the reference to "inward heat" show that in thus disrupting boundaries Beatrice does not wish to (re)instate the body as the sole or prime arena of divine action.

Beatrice's hagiographer makes precisely this transposition from internal to external experience, and in ways that point to the importance of the distinction within his text.

> *Life*: Indeed her heart, deprived of strength by this invasion, often gave off a sound like that of a shattering vessel, while she both felt the same and heard it exteriorly. Also the blood diffused through her bodily members boiled over through her open veins. Her bones contracted and the marrow disappeared; the dryness of her chest produced hoarseness of throat. And to make a long story short, the very fervor of her holy longing and love blazed up as a fire in all her bodily members, making her perceptibly hot in a wondrous way.[12]

The hagiographer takes Beatrice's mystical experience of divine love and makes it visible upon her body; the "visionary" is made into a "vision" for the viewing pleasure of her contemporaries.[13] As such, the spectacle of her body becomes the legitimation of her sanctity and also the source of her salvific power for other bodies.

This dynamic is visible throughout thirteenth-century hagiographies of women, and of men whose sanctity was not guaranteed by their clerical roles and or political and ecclesiastical power.[14] The body marked by harsh asceticism and

verseert, in smerteliker weelicheiden ende in nuer iegenwordicheiden. Ende so dunct hare dat har adren ontpluken ende hare bloet verbrent ende hare ede gevuelen der hitten van binnen ende des orwoeds van minnen." L. Reypens and J. Van Mierlo, *Seven maniernen van minne* (Leuven: S. V. de Vlaamsche Boekenhalle, 1926), 19–20; and Beatrijs of Nazareth, "There are Seven Seven Manners of Loving," trans. Eric Colledge, in *Medieval Women's Visionary Literature*, ed. Elizabeth Alvida Petroff (Oxford: Oxford University Press, 1986), 203.

[12] "Siquidem ipsum cor, ad illius invasionem viribus destitutum, frequenter, ipsa sentiente simul et a foris audiente, quasi vas quod confringitur [sonitum] fractionis emisit; ipse quoque sanguis, per corporalia membra diffusus, apertis venis exiliens, ebulliut, ossibusque contractis ipsa quoque medulla disparuit, pectoris siccitas ipsius gutturis raucitatem induxit, et, ut paucis multa concludam, ipse fervor sancti desiderii et amoris omnia membra corporea, mirum in modum sensibiliter estuanti, incendio conflagravit." Roger de Ganck, trans. and annot., *The Life of Beatrice of Nazareth*, (Kalamazoo, Mich.: Cistercian Publications, 1991), 308–11.

[13] This formulation is similar to that of Elizabeth Castelli's, made with reference to the transpositions between Perpetua's autobiographical prison narrative and the account of her martyrdom in which it is embedded. See Elizabeth Castelli, "Mortifying the Body, Curing the Soul: Beyond Ascetic Dualisms in *The Life of Saint Syncletica*," *Differences* 4/2 (1992): 151.

[14] On reading hagiography as evidence, see Bynum, *Holy Feast*, 87–8; Michael Goodich, *Vita Perfecta: The Ideal of Sainthood in the Thirteenth Century* (Stuttgart: Anton Hiersemann, 1982),

paramystical phenomena increasingly becomes the visible sign by which sanctity can be demonstrated and read. The degree to which such legitimating strategies are internalized by late medieval women can be gauged both by the repetition of such tropes within female-authored hagiography and by their incorporation within female-authored mystical writings.[15] While the former occurs within the thirteenth century, the later move does not begin to surface until the fourteenth century when persecution of Beguines and other religious women was given new impetus by the decrees of the Council of Vienne.[16] Before this period, women's mystical treatises found their primary form of legitimation in the depiction of visionary experience and the erotic mystical language of the Song of Songs, both of which lend themselves to, yet without enacting, the movement towards externalization and somatization seen in the *Life* of Beatrice of Nazareth.

While her text shares an emphasis upon the language of love, Marguerite Porete rejects the forms of spirituality associated with women both in the hagiographical traditions and in certain aspects of the thirteenth-century female-authored mystical literature. As such, she completes a movement begun in the Beguine authors Hadewijch and Mechthild of Magdeburg and the Cistercian Beatrice, by which they

1–20; Siegfried Ringler, "Die Rezeption mittelalterlicher Frauenmystik als wissenschaftliches Problem, dargestellt am Werk der Christine Ebner," in *Frauenmystik im Mittelalter*, ed. Peter Dinzelbacher and Dieter R. Bauer (Ostfildern: Schwabenverlag, 1985), 178–200; Jane Tibbetts Schulenburg, "Saints Lives as a Source for the History of Women, 500–1000," in *Medieval Women and the Sources of Medieval History*, ed. Joel Rosenthal (Athens: University of Georgia Press, 1990), 285–320; and Hollywood, *Virgin Wife*, chap. 2. For the increasingly important role of asceticism in thirteenth-century definitions of sanctity, see André Vauchez, *La Sainteté en Occident aux derniers siècles du moyen âge d'après les procès de canonisation et les documents hagiographiques* (Paris: Ecole Française de Rome, 1981), 450–55; and Donald Weinstein and Rudolph Bell, *Saints and Society: The Two Worlds of Western Christendom, 1000-1700* (Chicago: University of Chicago Press, 1982), 123–37, 153–57, and 236–37.

[15] There are few hagiographies of women from this period known to have been authored by women. Book One of Gertrude of Helfta's *Herald* is remarkable for its lack of ascetic reference only within the context of male-authored lives, not other women's writings. The *Life of Douceline*, however, written by one of her fellow Beguines, gives some attention to her own ascetic life and tells an unpleasant story of her beating a seven-year-old girl bloody when she looks at a man working nearby. Finally, Marguerite of Oingt, who is clearly uncomfortable with any form of extreme asceticism, nevertheless recounts such practices in the opening of her *Life of Beatrice of Orniceaux*. See Gertrude of Helfta, *Getrude d'Helfta: Oeuvres spirituelles II: Le Heraut (Livres I et II)*, ed. Pierre Doyere (Paris: Editions du Cerf, 1968); J. H. Albanes, *La Vie de Douceline* (Marseilles: Camoin, 1927), 50–51; and Marguerite d'Oingt, *Les Oeuvres de Marguerite d'Oingt*, ed. Antonin Durraffour, Pierre Gardette, and Paulette Durdilly (Paris: Belles Lettres, 1965), 106–15.

[16] On the decrees against the Beguines and the association of the movement with the heresy of the Free Spirit at the Council of Vienne, see Robert Lerner, *The Heresy of the Free Spirit in the Later Middle Ages* (Berkeley: University of California Press, 1972), 78–84. Lerner goes on to discuss the subsequent harassment of Beguines.

attempt to resolve the anguished dialectic between God's presence and absence to the loving soul.[17] Grounded in an experiential interpretation of the Song of Songs,[18] this opposition together with its dialectical resolution is central to Porete's thought.

The texts of Hadewijch, Beatrice, and Mechthild delineate a two-fold response to the suffering engendered by God's absence. On the one hand, the soul is called upon to suffer with Christ in his humanity in order to be one with him in his divinity.[19] As Hadewijch and Mechthild make clear, and as Bynum has brilliantly captured in her work, the associations of women with the body, and by extension with the humanity of Christ, serve as the basis for this divinizing identification.[20] But, whereas the suffering of Christ was both internal and external, Hadewijch, Beatrice, and Mechthild stress the internal suffering of the soul forced to experience the exile and alienation of one who has tasted divinity and then been forsaken. Their refusal or bypassing of physical suffering is remarkable in the context of thirteenth-century hagiographical traditions in which externally marked bodies are a paramount sign of sanctity.[21]

The desire to spare the suffering body, furthermore, leads ineluctably to a desire to spare the suffering soul. This movement, central to the thought of Porete, can be clearly seen in that of Mechthild and Beatrice, both of whom use the image of the soul as God's "housewife" to convey their understanding of the well-ordered soul for whom divine presence and absence have become one.[22]

---

[17] See Hadewijch, *The Complete Works*, trans. Mother Columba Hart, Classics of Western Spirituality Series (New York: Paulist Press, 1980); Mechthild of Magdeburg, *Mechthild von Magdeburg 'Das fliessende Licht der Gottheit': Nach der Einsiedler Handschrift in kritischem Vergleich mit der gesamten Überlieferung* [*FL* hereafter] ed. Hans Neumann (Munich: Artemis Verlag, 1990); and Beatrice, *Seven manieren*.

[18] For the importance of the Song of Songs in medieval culture and mysticism, see Friedrich Öhly, *Hohelied-Studien: Grundzüge einer Geschichte der Hoheliedauslegung des Abendlandes bis um 1200* (Wiesbaden: Franz Steiner, 1958); E. Ann Matter, *"The Voice of My Beloved": The Song of Songs in Western Medieval Christianity* (Philadelphia: University of Pennsylvania Press, 1990); and Ann W. Astell, *The Song of Songs in the Middle Ages* (Ithaca: Cornell University Press, 1990).

[19] Hadewijch, *Complete Works*, Letter 6, p. 61.

[20] Bynum, *Holy Feast*, 261–69; and *Fragmentation*, chap. 5.

[21] As suggested above, the Beguines share silence with regard to physical asceticism with other women writers. Perhaps what is remarkable in their texts is the emphasis upon the suffering and anguish of the soul, together with the movement away from such suffering. This would fit with the suggestion, emanating from Bynum's work, that semireligious women laid more emphasis upon female debility and the need for suffering than did those who were cloistered. Beatrice is an obvious exception, although her proximity to the Beguines, both biographically and theologically, has been noted. See Caroline Walker Bynum, *Jesus as Mother: Studies in the Spirituality of the High Middle Ages* (Berkeley: University of California Press, 1982), chap. 5.

[22] See Beatrice, *Seven manieren*, 25; and Mechthild, *FL*, Bk. VII, chap. 3, p. 260.

Leading to the central role of the death and renunciation of the will in Porete and Eckhart, the soul as housewife has learned to forgo the ecstacies of the bridal chamber and as such has a renewed sense of the underlying presence of God in all reality. Like the Virgin Mary, Mechthild argues, these souls can speak to God even in his apparent absence, thereby overcoming the soul's ecstatic joy and her alienated suffering.[23]

The role in Marguerite's work of the dialectic between God's presence and absence, and the suffering this engenders, is made clear from the opening prologue, in which Love, one of the main interlocuters in the dialogue, gives an exemplum which describes the *Mirror*'s genesis and function. Based in part on the Old French romance, Alexander of Bernay's *Roman d'Alexandre*, the story tells of a young princess who fell in love with Alexander the Great after having heard stories of his great courtesy and nobility. This love, however, is the source of great pain, for the princess neither knows Alexander, nor, due to the great distance separating them, has she any access to him. As Love tells the soul, when the princess

> . . . saw that this faraway love, who was so close to her within herself, was so far outside, she thought that she would comfort her unhappiness by imagining some figure of her love, by whom she was often wounded in her heart. Therefore she had an image painted which represented the semblance of the king who she loved as closely as possible to the presentation of that which she loved and in the affection of love by which she was captured, and by means of this image, together with other practices, she dreamed of the king himself. [24]

By making an image of her beloved, the princess is able to overcome the pain of his absence, even if only partially.

In the same way the *Mirror of Simple Souls* is given by God to the soul so that she might experience the divine presence in and despite its absence. Greater and more distant by far than Alexander is to the princess, the soul stresses God's agency in the overcoming of this space:

> . . . but he was so far away from me and I from him, that I did not know how to comfort myself, and so that I might remember him, he gave me

---

[23] Mechthild, *FL*, Bk. V, chap. 23, pp. 180–81.

[24] "Et quant elle vit que ceste amour loingtaigne, qui luy estoit si prouchaine ou dedans d'elle, estoit si loing dehors, elle se pensa que elle conforteroit sa masaise par ymaginacion d'aucune figure de son amy dont elle estoit souvent au cueur navree. Adonc fist elle paindre ung ymage qui reprentoit la semblance du roy, qu'elle amoit, au plus pres qu'elle peut de la presentacion dont elle l'amoit et en l'affection de l'amour dont elle estoit sourprinse, et par le moyen de ceste ymage avec ses autres usages songa le roy mesmes." Marguerite Porete, *Mirouer*, chap. 1, p. 12.

this book which represents in some manner his love itself (or "the love itself of him").[25]

An early instance of the ambiguities of phrase which run throughout the book, the passage anchors the text within its divine source and simultaneously suggests the unity of the soul and of the divine in the experience of love. For while *l'amour de lui mesmes* can be taken to refer to the love which the divine king has for the soul, it can also be understood, in a manner more closely paralleling the Alexander story archetype, as a representation of the love the soul feels for her lover. Presaging the unity of the soul and the divine as and in Love, the passage points both to and beyond imagination as the means by which the dialectic between presence and absence, and hence between joy and suffering, is overcome.

The princess can mitigate her suffering through the use of imagination; the soul longing for her Divine Lover ultimately refuses the mediation of any images, even that found within the *Mirror of Simple Souls* itself. Only an empty and pure mirror can reflect the simplicity of the divine and of the soul, leading to the difficulties and ambiguities of the text itself. This refusal of images coincides with and is causally related to Porete's rejection of the ascetic and visionary piety found among and prescribed for her female contemporaries.[26] She refuses the path to the divine which lies through humanity, and demands instead the renunciation of all createdness in order to become divine herself.

In doing so, Porete recognizes the affront her thought poses to contemporaries, among them her fellow Beguines. In the opening rondeau of her work she names only "theologians and other clerics" as those who must put aside reason in order to understand her words, but in the canzone which comes near the close the soul includes "Beguines" among those who will say that she is in error. [27] Such women, like the clerics, theologians, and others who the soul imagines accusing her, live by the lights of reason and the will rather than those of love, accept the paths to sanctity prescribed for them by the church, and therefore are unable to comprehend the freedom of the annihilated soul.

The unencumbered and free soul, according to the *Mirror*, is without a will and any created nature, and as such is one with its precreated ground and with the divine.

[25] "Mais si loing estoit de moy et moy de luy, que je ne savoie prandre confort de moy mesmes, et pour moy souvenir de lui il me donna ce livre qui represente en aucun usages l'amour de lui mesmes." Ibid.

[26] I make this distinction throughout, in order to keep in the reader's mind the important differences between hagiographical and mystical texts described above.

[27] *Mirouer*, chap. 122, p. 344. For Porete's use of poetic forms, see Peter Dronke, *Women Writers of the Middle Ages: A Critical Study of Texts from Perpetua (d. 203) to Marguerite Porete (d. 1310)* (Cambridge: Cambridge University Press, 1984), 218.

To attain this state the soul must pass through those lower stages which include the ascetic, churchly, and contemplative practices advocated by the majority of thirteenth-century religious and semireligious. In her descriptions of these lower stages, we can see with great specificity how Marguerite rejects those forms of ecstatic mysticism particularly associated with women. She argues that the soul must go through seven stages, marked by three deaths; those of sin, nature, and the spirit. Subsequent to each death are two stages, the first roughly characterized by a certain complacency and the second by a sense of dissatisfaction which leads to the next death.[28]

After the initial death, the soul is given divine grace and becomes free of mortal sin. In this stage, she willingly follows the twofold commandment to love God and her neighbor. When this minimal Christian life seems inadequate, however, and the soul begins to follow the apostolic way of humility and poverty, she has entered the second stage precipitating her death to nature. After this death, the soul has an abundance of love and wishes to excel in good works. This leads, paradoxically, to her desire to give up all external works as inadequate to divine Love. The fourth stage, therefore, is the life of contemplation, full of asceticism, poverty, prayers, meditations, ecstasies, and martyrdoms.

> The fourth state occurs when the Soul is drawn up by the height of love into the delight of thought through meditation and relinquishes all labors of the outside and of obedience to another through the heights of contemplation. . . . So the Soul holds that there is no higher life than to have this over which she has lordship. For Love has so greatly satisfied her with delights that she does not believe that God has a greater gift to give to this Soul here below than such a love as Love has poured out within her through love.[29]

The soul is so inebriated and blinded by the touch of love that she falsely believes no higher fate is possible.

Porete clearly believes many of her contemporaries are stuck on this level. Such "lost souls" are incapable of attaining freedom because of their refusal to see that the life of asceticism, contemplation, and spiritual delight in which they are ensconced does not represent the soul's highest perfection.[30] Rather than taking the divine

---

[28] See Porete, *Mirouer*, chap. 118, pp. and chap. 60, pp. 172–76.

[29] "Le quart estat est que l'Ame est tiree par haultesse d'amour en delit de pensee par meditacion, et relenquie de tous labours de dehors et de obedience d'aultruy par haultesse de contemplacion. . . . Adonc tient l'Ame que il n'est point de plus haulte vie, que de ce avoir, dont elle a seigneurie; car Amour l'a de ses delices si grandement resasié, que elle ne croit point que Dieu ait plus grant don a donner a ame ycy bas, qu'est telle amour que Amour a par amour dedans elle espandue." *Mirouer,* chap. 118, p. 322.

[30] *Mirouer*, chap. 55, pp. 158–60.

absence as an intrinsic part of union with God, such souls attempt to bring back the experience of divine sweetness through suffering, asceticism, and internal works, or contemplation. These "merchants" believe that it is possible to barter with Love, and as such are unable to merit her courtesy.[31] This blindness marks the greatest danger and temptation to the soul who would be free.

Freedom is attained only through the death to the spirit, which requires the rejection of both internal and external works. The first step toward simplicity is to become "bewildered"; although still "servants"and "merchants" possessed of will and works, bewildered souls are no longer lost, for they recognize that there is a being better than theirs.[32] Their confusion leads them to follow the path of willing nothing, upon which the spirit dies and is liberated. Porete's terms here become ambiguous, for after this death it is not clear what remains of the soul other than this "name." Yet, as she argues, the annihilated soul does not even have a name.[33] The death of the spirit requires that both of Reason [34] and of the will, and therefore includes all the essential features of the soul herself. This annihilation occurs only towards the end of the text, furthermore, and necessitates closure; without Reason or will, there is no protoganist in and on whom dramatic debate can center. The soul herself is destroyed and/or made absolutely indistinguishable from the divine. Language is inadequate to the soul, therefore, just as it is to God; the terms themselves occur only to be negated.

For this reason, Love and the soul can only describe the fifth and sixth stages with a language continually and negatively marked by its propinquity to Reason. The soul is now utterly transparent to the divine, without essence, substance, and name other than that divine Love in which she finds her true being. Whereas the fifth stage is one of absolute peace and simplicity, the sixth is radiant. In it, the Trinity displays her (the Trinity's and the soul's) glory.[35] The masculine FarNear (*Loingprès*) becomes feminized in his union with the soul. While the soul and Love strain language in their attempts to show this radiance to Reason and their hearers, the real work of the

---

[31] See, for example, *Mirouer*, chap. 63, p. 184. Also important here is the advice given by the soul and Love against feeling anxiety over sinfulness. They argue that the simple soul need have no shame or anxiety, using scriptural figures as models. See *Mirouer*, chap. 41, pp. 128–30; and chap. 76, pp. 210–12.

[32] *Mirouer*, chap. 57, pp. 164–66.

[33] On the relation of soul and spirit, see *Mirouer*, chap. 72, pp. 200–202 ; and chap. 74, p. 206. For the soul's "namelessness," *Mirouer*, chap. 83, p. 236. Love tells Reason that such a soul is both "without herself" and "belongs to herself." She is not "in" anything, but that annihilation which is the work of the spark. The language points to Eckhart. *Mirouer*, chap. 59, pp. 170–72.

[34] Reason dies in *Mirouer*, chap. 87, pp. 246–48. Love speaks for Reason in the following chapter and she has returned by chap. 98.

[35] *Mirouer*, chap. 61, p. 178.

dialogue and of language itself within the text is to break the hold of Reason upon the soul through negation, paradox, and contradiction. Through such mystical apophasis, the soul will be annihilated and her divine simplicity and radiance uncovered.

The text of the *Mirror* circles around and continually alights upon this moment, in which Reason and the will are annihilated. The decisive event occurs, as I have said, towards the close of the text. Here Porete takes up the language of love and the dialectic of presence and absence so central to many thirteenth-century mystical and hagiographical texts. She demands that the soul become not merely a housewife with a steady will, but that she annihilate herself through the destruction of her will. Like Hadewijch and Mechthild, Porete both uses and deconstructs courtly traditions, in this case through her portrayal of a trial of love in which the soul is challenged by Love in ways which ultimately destroy her.

> Then in my meditation I considered how it would be if he might ask me how I would fare if I knew that he could be better pleased that I should love another better than him. At this my mind failed me, and I did not know how to answer, for what to will nor what to deny; but I answered that I would ponder it.
>
> And then he asked me how I would fare if it could be that he could love another better than me. And at this my mind failed me, and I knew not what to answer, or will or deny.
>
> Yet again, he asked me what I would do and how I would fare if it could be that he would will that another love me better than he. And in the same way, my mind failed, and I did not know what to answer, any more than before, but again I said that I would ponder it.[36]

Love demands that the soul annihilate love itself. All creatureliness, all that is the soul's own, must be destroyed in order to attain the pre-Adamic state of freedom to which Love calls her.[37]

---

[36] "Et aprés ce, regarday en pensant, comme se il me demendroit comment je me contendroie, se je savoie qu'il luy peust mieulx plaire que j'amasse aultruy mieulx que luy; et adonc me faillit le sens, et ne sceu que respondre, ne que voulloir, ne que escondire, mais je respondi que je m'en conseilleroie.

Et aprés, me demenda comment je me contendroie, se il povoit estre qu'il peust mieulx aultruy amer que moy. Et ycy me faillit le sens, et ne sceu que respondre, ne que vouloir, ne que escondire.

Oultre plus, me demenda que je feroie et comment je me contendroie, se il povoit estre qu'il peust vouloir que ung aultre que luy me amast mieulx que luy. Et pareillement me faillit le sens, et ne sceu que respondre, nientplus que devant, mais je dis tousjours que je m'en conseilleroie." *Mirouer*, chap. 131, p. 384.

[37] For Porete's Edenic longing, see *Mirouer*, chap. 29, pp. 96–98, chap. 94, p. 264; and Romana Guarnieri, "Frères du Libre Esprit," *Dictionnaire de spiritualité, ascétique et mystique, doctrine et histoire*, ed. M. Villon et al. (Paris: Beauchesne, 1932-), vol. 5, col. 1263.

This soul who "lives without a why" has been freed from love by Love.[38] As such, she rejects all works of love and of the spirit, attachment to which are marks of servitude and "villainy." Whereas those lost souls who are merchants, exchanging prayers, fasts, masses, and contemplative works for the onslaughts of divine Love, are servants to the virtues, the unencumbered soul has been freed from this prison. Here Porete's aim, to free souls from their suffering servitude to works, asceticism, and the cycle of ecstasy and alienation, is made clear.

> *Love*: When Love dwells in them, and the Virtues serve them without any contradiction and without the work of such souls [they are free]. Oh, without doubt, Reason, . . . such souls who have become free, have known for many days what Dominion usually does. And to the one who would ask them what was the greatest torment that any creature could suffer, they would say that it would be to dwell in Love and to be in obedience to the Virtues. For it is necessary to give to the Virtues all that they ask, whatever the cost to Nature. For it is thus that the Virtues demand honor and goods, heart and body and life. It is to be expected that such souls leave all things, and still the Virtues say to this soul who has given all to them, retaining nothing in order to comfort Nature, that the just one is saved by great pain. And thus this exhausted Soul who still serves the Virtues says that she would be assaulted by Fear, and torn in hell until the judgment day, and after that she would be saved.[39]

To save "heart and body and life" and free the soul from that "great pain" demanded by the Virtues, Love must free the soul from Love. In annihilating self-will, paradoxically, the soul is restored to her nature.

The clarity of Porete's demand that Nature be freed from its burden and that the suffering of the soul be allayed is obscured by her apparent elitism, esotericism, and perfectionism. In demanding that the soul give up all of her will, Porete's Love demands a seemingly impossible perfection from those souls who would claim true nobility. The free soul goes so far as to express surprise that salvation will be attained by the peasants

---

[38] *Mirouer*, chap. 122, p. 344.

[39] "*Amour*. Quant Amour demeure en elles, et que les Vertuz servent a elles sans nul contredit et sans travail de telles Ames. . . . Hee, sans faille, Raison, . . . telles Ames qui sont si franches devenues, ont sceu mainte journee ce que Danger seult faire; et qui leur demanderoit le plus grant tourment que creature puisse souffrir, elles diroient que ce seroit demouree en Amour et estree en l'obedience des Vertuz. Car il convient donner auz Vertuz tout ce qu'elles demandent, que qu'il couste a Nature. Or est it ainsi que les Vertuz demandent honneur et avoir, cueur et corps et vie; c'est a entendre que telles Ames laissent toutes chouses, et encoures dient les Vertuz a ceste Ame qui tout ce leur a donné ne n'a rien retenu pour conforter Nature, que *a grant paine est le just saulvé*. Et pource dit telle lasse Ame qui encores sent aux Vertuz, que elle vouldroit estre demenes par Crainte, et en enfer tourmentee jusques au jugement, et aprés qu'elle deust estre saulvée." *Mirouer*, chap. 8, pp. 28–30.

and merchants who have reached only the early stages of divine grace and union.[40] The text distinguishes between Holy Church the Great and Holy Church the Little, pointing to two distinct, and hierarchically graded, paths to salvation.[41] Furthermore, Love continually warns the soul against disseminating her secrets among those who are unworthy and still living according to Reason. The text itself, however, belies this injunction and the hierarchies upon which it is based, for in it Love attempts to explain herself to Reason, albeit only in order to facilitate the later's destruction.[42] This contradiction points, I think, to the ways in which Porete's text continually undercuts its own hierarchies, for it is insofar as the soul has become nothing that she is all, and insofar as she achieves freedom that she is perfect; in that moment what is most hidden and distant becomes most clear. By calling for perfection through the annihilation of the will, Porete attempts to free the will, together with the "heart and body and life" from the impossible to meet demands of the Virtues and of contemplative life.

Porete's text also offers a response to the charges of antinomianism made against her by contemporaries. Although the unencumbered soul can give to Nature what she will, such a soul is so fully united with the divine that she can never will anything contrary to what God wills. As such, the soul can give freely to Nature, which has overcome its fallenness. Like Mechthild and Beatrice, Porete implies that the soul's true nature lies in her precreated state within the divine.[43] The somewhat anachronistic charge of quietism is thereby also diverted, for insofar as the soul is one with the divine, she becomes the place in which God works in the world. The text is authored by Porete, the soul, and Love, in ways which become increasingly difficult to distinguish. The problem, of course, is that the text must speak to those "lost souls" still governed by Reason. In order to teach such souls of freedom, the text dramatically enacts the process by which the soul annihilates reason, will, and affection in order to achieve absolute freedom and simplicity.[44]

---

[40] *Mirouer*, chap. 63, p. 184. Here Porete is concerned with the peasants who are only, apparently, at the first and second levels. The merchants on the third and fourth levels are willing to imitate Christ in his poverty and torment; yet ultimately, this suffering itself must be superceded. Elsewhere, Love suggests that God will refuse his kingdom to those who seek to do his will, rather than renouncing their own wills entirely. See *Mirouer*, chap. 48, p. 144.

[41] *Mirouer*, chap. 19, pp. 74–76; and chap. 43, pp. 132–36.

[42] *Mirouer*, chap. 121, pp. 338–40.

[43] Both Mechthild and Beatrice use the images of the fish in the water and the bird in the air to describe the way in which the soul finds her true nature in the divine. See Beatrice, *Seven manieren*, 25–26; and Mechthild, *FL*, Bk. I, chap. 44, pp. 30–31.

[44] I explore the textual dynamics, which are much more complex and tension-laden than I have evoked here, in greater detail in Hollywood, *Soul as Virgin Wife*, chap. 4. I believe that the great anxiety and ambiguity of the *Mirror* is also tied to gender, pointing to the tensions created for a woman who wishes to reject her culture's definitions.

Eckhart's sermons most clearly echo Porete's text in his descriptions of the process of detachment, his valuation of the way of works and contemplation, and his understanding of the freedom of detached, virgin souls. Furthermore, Eckhart makes much more explicit and thematically central the fruitfulness of such souls. He demonstrates the ways in which "living without a why" is an ethical imperative, both in its liberatory potential and its ability to engender the just work. Porete, perhaps constrained by the ideals of piety held before her as a woman, places much more emphasis upon the first pole of the soul's liberating experience, allowing the work of the soul to be exemplified implicitly by her text.

As Edmund Colledge and J. C. Marler have shown, Eckhart's most daring language with regard to the union without distinction between the soul and the divine directly parallels statements made by Porete in the *Mirror*.[45] Her radical understanding of the Beguine ideal of poverty leads to the claim that the truly simple soul does not even will to will according to God's will, for even such a level of independent volition would serve to separate the soul and the divine.

> Thus the soul does not will nothing, says Love, unless she is free, for no one is free who wills anything by the will within him, whatever he might will. For then he is a servant to himself since he wills that God accomplish his will to his own honor. The one who wills this only wills that the will of God be accomplished in him and in another. For such a person, says Love, God refuses his kingdom.[46]

Those who will to do God's will, according to Love, are "merchants" who believe they can barter with God for his love, a commercial metaphor used also by Eckhart, who calls those who attempt to will the good in order to attain salvation "servelings and traders."[47]

Eckhart also takes up the theme of spiritual poverty and emphasizes the necessity of complete detachment from self-will in order to become truly poor. Like Porete, he distinguishes between those who understand such true poverty and the

---

[45] Edmund Colledge and J. C. Marler, "'Poverty of the Will': Ruusbroec, Eckhart and *The Mirror of Simple Souls*," in *Jan van Ruusbroec: The Sources, Content and Sequels of His Mysticism*, ed. P. Mommaers and N. de Paepe (Leuven: Leuven University Press, 1984), 14–57. They suggest that *Predigt* 52 may have been written as a homage to Porete after Eckhart's unsuccessful defense. For a fuller account of the textual parallels, see Michael Sells in this volume.

[46] "Adonques ne veult lame nient, dit Amour, puis quelle est franche, car cil nest mie franc qui veult aucune chose de la voulenté de son dedans, quelque chose quil vieulle. Car de tant est il serf a luy mesmes, et cil qui ce veult ne le veult sinon pour la voulenté de dieu acomplir tant seulement en luy et en aultruy. Pour telle gent, dit Amour, refusa dieu son royaulme." *Mirouer*, chap. 48, p. 144.

[47] Pr. 39: DW 2: 253.

"donkeys" who believe that poverty lies in the works of the active and contemplative lives, thereby attempting to will God's will.[48] Such a freedom from works is elsewhere described as a disencumbering, directly paralleling Porete's language:

> So long as a person has this as his will, that he wants to fulfill God's dearest will, he has not the poverty about which we want to talk. Such a person has a will with which he wants to fulfill God's will, and that is not true poverty. For if a person wants really to have poverty, he ought to be as free of his own created will as he was when he did not exist. For I tell you by the truth that is eternal, so long as you have a will to fulfill God's will, and a longing for God and for eternity, then you are not poor; for a poor person is one who has a will and a longing for nothing.[49]

Eckhart uses the same threefold description of poverty as wanting, knowing, and having nothing found throughout the *Mirror*, and similarly follows Porete's description of those things for which the naked soul has no need: "possessions or honor or ease or pleasure or profit or inwardness, holiness or reward or the kingdom of heaven."[50]

Colledge and Marler have also shown how ideas from the *Mirror* can help to explain Eckhart's statements about the poor soul being the place in which God works. Even more radically, the soul who embraces true poverty becomes so poor that she does not even provide a place in which God can work, but rather God works in himself. This parallels the claim that the soul has no will with which to will God's will. As such, the soul becomes the divine, and his working in the soul and in himself are one. The use of such spatial language to describe the union without distinction of the soul and the divine is found throughout the *Mirror* and is tied to Porete's use of courtly images and tropes. The soul who is completely unencumbered is without a proper place, and is taken to God's place far from her own being.[51] Porete thereby evokes the image of the soul transported to God's faraway court, in which she finds her proper place and true being in the divine.

---

[48] This bestial metaphor is also found in Porete. See *Mirouer*, chap. 68, p. 192.

[49] *Essential*, 200 (translation modified). "Als lange als der mensche das hât , daz daz sîn wille ist, daz er wil ervüllen den allerliebesten willen gotes, der mensche enhât niht armuot, von der wir sprechen wellen; wan dirre mensche hât einen willen, mit dem er genuoc wil sîn dem willen gotes, und daz enist niht rehtiu armuot. Wan, sol der mensche armuot haben gewaerlîche, sô sol er sînes geschaffenen willen alsô ledic stân, als er tete, dô er niht enwas. Wan ich sage iu bî der êwigen wârheit: als lange als ir willen hât, ze ervüllenne den willen gotes, und begerunge hât der êwicheit und gotes, als lange ensît ir niht arm; wan daz ist ein arm mensche, der niht enbegert." Pr. 52, DW 2: 491–92.

[50] *Essential*, 85. "noch guot noch êre noch gemach noch lust noch nuz noch innicheit noch heilicheit noch lôn noch himelrîche." See Pr. 6, DW 1: 100.

[51] See *Mirouer*, chap. 136–37, pp. 398–400.

Perhaps the most important parallel between Porete and Eckhart, however, first pointed out by Bernard McGinn, is that between the idea of the virtual existence of the soul alluded to in the passage from *Predigt* 52 cited above, and the suggestions of such a precreated being found throughout the *Mirror*.[52] Insofar as the will is annihilated and the soul lives without a why and without imagistic or other mediations between herself and God, both Porete and Eckhart suggest, she has attained her true nature in the divine. Thus in chapter 91 of the *Mirror*, Porete likens the state of the annihilated soul to that of the soul before her creation:

> Now he [God] possesses the will without a why in the same way that he possessed it before the soul was made a lady by it. There is nothing except him. No one loves except him, for nothing is except him, and thus he alone completely loves, and sees himself alone completely, and praises himself alone completely by his being itself.[53]

The annihilated soul returns to her precreated state. This claim carries with it the implication that the soul in some way preexists within the Godhead, a suggestion found in the writings of Mechthild of Magdeburg as well and one upon which the Beguines' shared desire to allay the suffering of body and soul rests. For insofar as through the regulation and/or annihilation of the will the soul is able to attain the innocence of her precreated being, all works, both of the active and contemplative lives, become unnecessary and the body and soul are freed.

In his Latin works, Eckhart provides a metaphysical context for this claim that the soul preexists in the Godhead. There Eckhart appropriates Neo-Platonic ontology in order to distinguish between the virtual existence of all things within the Godhead and their actual existence as created beings in the world. This sets the stage for his discussions within the *Predigten* of the precreated spark of the soul through which she attains both virginity and fruitfulness. What has not been adequately recognized by scholars is that this theological development, dependent as it is upon Eckhart's Neo-Platonic and scholastic sources, has its genesis in the union without distinction first suggested in the writings of Hadewijch, Mechthild, and

---

[52] Bernard McGinn, "Love, Knowledge and *Unio mystica* in the Western Christian Tradition," in *Mystical Union and Monotheistic Faith: An Ecumenical Dialogue*, ed. Moshe Idel and Bernard McGinn (New York: Macmillan, 1989), 73–78.

[53] "Or l'a maintenant, sans nul pourquoy, en tel point comme il l'avoit, ains que telle en fust dame. Ce n'est nul fors qu'il; nul n'ayme fors qu'il, car nul n'est fors que luy, et pource ayme tout seul et se voit tout seul, et loe tout seul de son etre mesmes." *Mirouer*, chap. 91, p. 258. For similar texts see chap. 11, pp. 46–48; chap. 27, p. 94; chap. 45, pp. 138–40; chap. 51, pp. 150–52; chap. 64, pp. 184–86; chap. 70, pp. 196–98; chap. 82, pp. 232–36; chap. 89, p. 252; chap. 104, p. 284; chap. 110, pp. 298–300; chap. 111, pp. 302–4; and chap. 133, pp. 390–94. Also see McGinn, "*Unio mystica*," 74.

Beatrice, and elaborated by Marguerite Porete.[54] Through attaining her precreated state, the soul lives together with/as the divine; and, of course, it is in living divinely, without a why, that this precreated state is regained. Eckhart, by adopting this language from Porete, demonstrates his knowledge of her work and their commonality of purpose.[55]

Eckhart, like Porete, calls upon his listeners to reject the path of works, both active and contemplative, and its mixture of alienation and ecstasy, in favor of the life of detachment; through detachment the divine is present in its absence or absolutely immanent in its very transcendence. Grounded, paradoxically, in the absolute unlikeness between creatures and the divine, Eckhart elaborates this dialectic in numerous places and using a variety of languages, most famously his discussion of the indistinct and the distinct in the *Commentary on Wisdom*. There the point is made that God is absolutely unlike creatures, who are by their nature limited and distinct. God is absolutely indistinct, and as such transcendent to all created things. Yet, Eckhart goes on to argue:

> Everything which is distinguished by indistinction is the more distinct the more indistinct it is, because it is distinguished by its own indistinction. Conversely, it is the more indistinct the more distinct it is, because it is distinguished by its own distinction from what is indistinct.[56]

As McGinn has shown, this begins to make sense when translated into the language of immanence and transcendence.[57] Everything which is distinguished by transcendence is more transcendent the more immanent it is, for it is made transcendent by its own immanence. God, as the *esse indistinctum* which underlies all beings, is totally immanent to all creatures, and as such is distinct and unlike them. Thus God's radical otherness is dialectically related to his radical immanence, in the same way that for Porete the nothingness of createdness is its grounding in the all.

---

[54] See *Mirouer*, chap. 35, pp. 114–16; chap. 87, pp. 246–48; and chap. 107, pp. 90–92. The idea of all things preexisting in the divine Idea or Logos is, of course, traditional and central for Augustine. Eckhart, however, develops this idea in new ways through his reappropriation of Neoplatonic thought, in that he pushes preexistence back further into the Godhead.

[55] See *Mirouer*, chap. 91, pp. 256–58; and Eckhart, Pr. 5b, DW 1: 83–96.

[56] *Teacher*, 169. "Omne quod indistinctione distinguitur, quanto est indistinctius, tanto est distinctius; distinguitur enim ipsa indistinctione. Et e converso, quanto distinctius, tanto indistinctius, quia distinctione sua distinguitur ab indistincto. Igitur quanto distinctius, tanto indistinctius; et quanto indistinctius, tanto distinctius, et prius." *Comm. Wis.*, n. 154, LW 2: 490.

[57] Bernard McGinn, "Meister Eckhart on God as Absolute Unity," in *Neoplatonism and Christian Thought*, ed. Dominic J. O'Meara (Norfolk, Va: International Society for Neo-Platonic Study, 1982), 132.

In language which strongly echoes that of the earlier Beguine, Mechthild of Magdeburg, and also points to Porete's dialectic of all and nothing, Eckhart describes the intimate interplay between the breakthrough into the divine ground where God's ground and the soul's are one and the birth of the Son in the soul.[58] As in Mechthild's and Marguerite's work, the "lowness" and humility of the detached soul compels (*twingen*) God to share his gifts, for that which is on high must flow out to that which is below. This is made clear in a sermon devoted to Luke 1:28, "Hail, full of grace," in which Eckhart describes the Incarnation as God's making himself like humanity in order that humanity might be like him. The Incarnation occurs not only, and perhaps not even primarily, historically in the person of Jesus Christ, but also in the soul of each believer who humbles him or herself and achieves true detachment.

> If I were up here, and I said to someone, "Come up here," that would be difficult. But if I were to say, "Sit down there," that would be easy. God acts like that. If a person humbles himself, God cannot withhold his own goodness but must come down and flow into the humble person, and to him who is least of all he gives himself the most of all, and he gives himself to him completely. What God gives is his being, and his being is his goodness, and his goodness is his love.[59]

The soul free of all images and all creatureliness compels God's presence, reenacting the birth of the Son to the Virgin in the birth of the Son in the soul.

In calling upon his listeners to become detached so that they might enter into the "chamber" where God exists in his ground, Eckhart makes one of his few allusions to the Song of Songs tradition and the soul as the bride of the Son. The link with themes central to thirteenth-century women's texts—bridal imagery, the love song tradition, sinking humility, and the compulsion of the divine—is further underlined by a rare reference to physical suffering. Once again, the way in which the reference works in Eckhart is instructive, and points to the relationship of his aims to those of Porete. In discussing the good of the Incarnation, Eckhart tells a story of a rich husband and his wife. When the wife lost an eye in an accident, she

---

[58] See, for example Mechthild, *FL*, Bk. IV, chap. 19, pp. 135–36; Bk. V, chap. 4, pp. 156–58; Bk. V, chap. 12, p. 166, and Eckhart, Va, DW 5: 402–4 (*Essential*, 286).

[59] *Essential*, 194 (translation modified). "Waere ich hie oben und spraeche ich: ze einem: 'Kum her ûf!' daz waere swaerer. Mêr: spraeche ich: 'sitz hie nider!' daz waere lîht. Alsô tuot got. Swenne sich der mensche dêmüetiget, sô enmac sich got niht enthalten von sîner eigenen güete, er enmüeze sich senken und giezen in den dêmüetigen menschen, und dem allerminsten dem gibet er sich in dem allermeisten und gibet sich im alzemâle. Daz got gibet, daz ist sîn wesen, und sîn wesen daz ist sîn güete, und sîn güete saz ist sîn minne." Pr. 22, DW 1: 385.

grieved that she would no longer be worthy of her husband's love. To prove the
constancy of this love, the husband gouged out his own eye, thereby becoming like
his wife. So Christ, in becoming flesh, metaphorically gouges out his eye so that he
might become like us. Eckhart characteristically focuses not on the suffering taken
on by Christ, but rather on his act as one in which he transforms himself into the
likeness of humanity so that humans might be like the divine. Human suffering is
not demanded in order to perfect that likeness; rather, suffering is misfortune, one
which is made good and overcome through Christ's taking on flesh both historically and in the birth of the Son in the soul.[60] Christ's action transforms
suffering into union rather than demanding it. If God is the soul's suffering, as
Eckhart puts it in his treatise on divine consolation, then suffering itself is
transformed into God.[61]

Eckhart calls upon his hearers, then, to recognize that when the soul becomes
free of images and returns to her uncreated ground in the divine, she compels God,
making him present to her despite apparent absence. One should not fear God, but
rather love him, and in that love the soul renounces even her own love, thereby
becoming the ground out of which divine love acts. Such a soul is free of all created
things and even of God himself; in this freedom suffering and the demand for
suffering are superceded.

> The just person seeks nothing in his works, for those who seek something
> in their works are servelings and traders, or those who work something for
> a wherefore. Therefore, if you will be in or transfigured into justice, then
> intend nothing in your works and in-figure no wherefore in yourself,
> neither in time nor in eternity, neither reward nor blessedness, neither this
> nor that; for these works are all truly dead. Yes, and if you image God in
> yourself, whatever works you perform therefore, these works are dead, and

[60] Pr. 22, DW 1: 375–89. Some attention should be given as well to possible changes in
Eckhart's thought, particularly given the probable time of his introduction to Porete's work.
Eckhart's implicit reference to the fall as an accident or misfortune is echoed later by Julian of
Norwich. Although she sees suffering as a means of adding to and furthering the salvation
brought through Christ, this stance is in tension with her message of comfort, grounded in the
idea of a precreated being which never assents to sin. The gender implications of this tension
are worthy of further exploration. See Julian of Norwich, *Showings*, trans. Edmund Colledge
and James Walsh, Classics of Western Spirituality Series (New York: Paulist Press, 1978).

[61] See *Essential*, 234–35. Eckhart's discussions of suffering frequently turn upon the
identification of the divine and the soul in such experiences, thereby stressing the ways in which
God takes on human pain. This allows both consolation to those who *are* suffering, as well as
undercutting religious demands that one *imitate* the suffering of Jesus Christ. See Donald
Duclow, "'My Suffering is God': Meister Eckhart's *Book of Divine Consolation*," *Theological
Studies* 44 (1983): 570–86; and Jean-François Malherbe, "*Souffrir Dieu*"; *La prédiction de
Maître Eckhart* (Paris: Cerf, 1992), 35–42.

you will spoil good works; and not only will you spoil good works, but more; you will also sin.[62]

Just as Porete contrasts the princess's act of imagination as a means of overcoming the distance between herself and her beloved with the power of divine Love to transform the soul into herself through the dramatic dialogue of the *Mirror*, so Eckhart calls upon his listeners to go beyond images for the divine, to work without mediation and without a why, so that the imagination and its wounds might be displaced. For while imagination can partially bridge the suffering gap between the lover and her beloved, the distance is never fully overcome; distance remains and suffering is compounded insofar as the desire for his presence marks the body of the lover, either through ascetic practices, illness, or paramystical phenomena designed to demonstrate the divine presence.

Throughout these mystical movements, the role of the body, so central in thirteenth-century depictions of female sanctity, is consistently downplayed. Yet, as we saw above, Porete and Eckhart are radically incarnational in that the divine works in and through the soul who has become detached. Such souls embody Christ insofar as annihilation and the birth of the Son occur within them. This language is, of course, problematized by both Porete and Eckhart, for the detachment of such souls is so great that they have no "place" within which God works, but rather the divine works in himself. Properly understood, however, these claims underline the radically incarnational tendencies of their thought, for it is insofar as God or the Trinity works in his/her own ground that divine action is manifested upon earth.

Yet despite this, Porete and Eckhart both ignore, de-emphasize, and even vilify the role of the body and bodily practices in the movement of annihilation and detachment. This is a direct response to the forms of sanctity prescribed for women among their contemporaries and is an attempt to counter a situation of anxiety, struggle, moral rigorism, and bodily suffering. Porete and Eckhart, in rejecting the paths of suffering in body and soul, downplay the role of the body in the religious life, demanding the renunciation of all creatureliness, including and most importantly, that of the will and intellect. By establishing the moral neutrality of corporeality, they attempt to save it from suffering. They go further, moreover, and

---

[62] "Der gerehte ensuochet niht in sînen werken; wan die iht suochent in irn werken, die sint knehte und mietlinge, oder die umbe einic warumbe würkent. Dar umbe, wilt dû în- und übergebildet werden in die gerehticheit, sô enmeine niht in dînen werken und enbilde kein warumbe in dich, noch in zît noch in êwicheit, noch lôn noch saelicheit, noch diz not daz; wan disiu werk sind alliu waerlîche tôt. Jâ ich spriche: und bildestù got in dich, swaz dû werke dar umbe würkest, diu sint alliu tôt und dû verderbest guotiu werk; und niht aleine verderbest dû guotiu werk, mêr; dû tuost och sünde." Pr. 39: DW 2: 253–54.

argue that the suffering engendered by God's apparent absence to the soul can be overcome through the annihilation of the soul through which his abiding presence is made apparent. By recognizing that in which all things are equal, their uncreated ground in the divine, suffering, estrangement, and alienation are superceded and the soul is transfigured into love. Without such a move, furthermore, the body would continue to suffer, for it is the most obvious and visible site of difference from and hence absence from the divine.

Elaine Scarry argues that empathy is a function of the imagination, for it is through the work of the imagination that the suffering of physical bodies is displaced and the limitations of those bodies expanded. Whereas in portions of the Hebrew Bible, according to Scarry, the disembodied God marks his presence through the physical suffering of human flesh, the imaginative production of texts and artifacts displaces this physical suffering and thereby allays it. Imagination is therefore both grounded in human suffering and in attempts to overcome that suffering, understood and experienced as a central characteristic of embodiment.[63] Yet the work of the imagination is never done, for the immaterial divine, even after the Incarnation, continually eludes believers. The demands for harsh asceticism, bodily mutilation, and physical miracles during the later Middle Ages can be understood, at least in part, as the attempt by medieval men and women to make their God present in the world.

Porete and Eckhart, therefore, are dramatically aware of the limitations of the body and of the imagination, which continually haunt embodied experience thereby engendering further suffering. Insofar as one recognizes the equality of all things, an equality grounded in the absolute immanence of the divine which is the source of its transcendence, imagination becomes transfiguration and the limitations of embodied being are overcome. The created world, for Eckhart, is sanctified in the very process of detachment. Rather than depending upon the suffering of women, marked by visible wounds and dismemberment of their living and dead bodies, to embody the divine and ward off death, Porete and Eckhart seek to relieve the suffering and anxiety of their contemporaries by calling them, both women and men, to a new relation with God. The divine, immanent in its very transcendence, is made present to embodied natures not through wounds but through equality, justice, and the birth of the Son in the soul which engenders and is engendered by them.

---

[63] Elaine Scarry, *The Body In Pain: The Making and Unmaking of the World* (Oxford: Oxford University Press, 1985), 161–80 and chap. 4, 181–243. For a phenomenological reading of embodiment, which suggests why suffering is seen as one of its central characteristics, see Drew Leder, *The Absent Body* (Chicago: University of Chicago Press, 1990). I explore these issues further in Hollywood, *The Soul as Virgin Wife*, chap. 1.

If medieval people's great love of the body and understanding of embodiment as constitutive of human personhood lie behind their ascetic practices, clearly the burden of such ascetic sanctification did not fall equally upon all.[64] Rather, hagiographical traditions portray women as disproportionally responsible for such suffering, the bodily sanctification it enabled being shared by the men around them.[65] Similarly, the writings of women in northern Europe during the thirteenth century demonstrate that their experiences of divine sweetness, their love and enjoyment of such experiences, necessitate and justify the suffering brought about when these fleeting moments pass. Furthermore, the suffering of the exiled and alienated soul is understood as salvific, not only of the soul herself, but also of spiritual children on earth and in purgatory.[66] In their rejection of bodily asceticism, paramystical phenomena, and, most importantly, special visionary and unitive experiences, Porete and Eckhart are attempting to allay women's pain.

Yet the attempt is problematic for both Porete and Eckhart in ways further shaped by the gender hierarchies and assumptions of the culture in which they lived. Called a "pseudo-woman" by the chronicler who records her trial and condemnation, Porete's refusal of the forms of religiosity and sanctity ascribed to women within the thirteenth century led to her death.[67] Eckhart, in preaching to women and lay people of both sexes, drew the suspicion of his ecclesiastical superiors, leading eventually to the condemnation of portions of his work.[68] While their relationships to authority differed greatly according to gendered lines and the effacement of Porete and her work was more complete, both Porete and Eckhart were ultimately unable to provide means of legitimation and religious sanctification for women which bypassed the role of the suffering body. The suffering

---

[64] Philippe Ariès, *Western Attitudes toward Death from the Middle Ages to the Present*, trans. Patricia M. Ranum (Baltimore: Johns Hopkins University Press, 1974), 27–52.

[65] See the examples cited above in n. 7, although there are very many others.

[66] See, for example, Mechthild, *FL*, Bk. V, chap. 8, pp. 161–62.

[67] See Paul Verdeyen, "Le Procès d'Inquisition contre Marguerite Porete et Guiard de Cressonssart (1309–10)," *Revue d'Histoire Ecclésiastique* 81 (1986): 47–94.

[68] See M.-H. Laurent, "Autour du procès de Maitre Eckhart. Les documents des Archives Vaticanes," *Divus Thomas* (Piacenza), Ser. III 13 (1936): 331–38, 430–47; Franz Pelster, "Ein Gutachten aus dem Eckehart-Prozess in Avignon," *Aus der Geisteswelt des Mittelalters. Festgabe Martin Grabmann* (Beiträge Supplement III) (Münster, 1935),1099–1124; Gabriel Thery, "Édition critique des pièces relatives au procès d'Eckhart contenues dans le manuscrit 33b de la Bibliothèque de Soest," *Archives d'histoire littéraire et doctrinal du moyen âge* 1 (1926): 129-268; and Bernard McGinn, " Eckhart's Condemnation Reconsidered," *The Thomist* 44 (1980): 390–414.

of the female body becomes more necessary as a mark of suffering humanity, and hence of sanctity, in the fourteenth century.[69]

Eckhart, as a male member of an established teaching order and representative of the Church, was invested with the authority to expound Scripture, teach, and preach. He was, moreover, free to subvert that authority as a demonstration of the ethics of detachment. Evidence suggests that his teachings and his language would not have been considered dangerous if he had kept them within the schools, and hence among men. For medieval women, authority and legitimation were much more difficult to attain, for they were barred from the new schools, the interpretation of Scripture, and public preaching.[70] Almost every medieval women who wrote primarily on religious themes did so on the basis of some extraordinary form of religious experience, whether visionary, unitive, or both. This fact has too often been seen as telling us something about the nature of women, rather than about the nature of the power structures in which they found themselves, and in which they attempted to speak.[71] The visionary mode, including a divine command to write and some sign of ecclesiastical approbation of this injunction, can be found in almost all women's religious texts from the Medieval Period.[72] Porete, who eschews such explicitly visionary references, opting for an allegorical drama in which

[69] The fourteenth century sees the emergence of what can best be called autohagiographies, in which mystical and hagiographical discourses blend. This can be seen in the convent chronicles and other literature emanating from German Dominican convents and in the slightly earlier *Book* of Angela of Foligno. Angela's lay status and the fact that her text was written through a male intermediary both may help explain the use of this form in her text. As a lay woman, she was in need of greater legitimation. On the other hand, the references to bodily suffering and divine marks may have been added by the scribe, in much the same way that Beatrice's hagiographer (mis)-interprets her mystical text. See Angela of Foligno, *Il libro della Beata Angela da Foligno (Edizione critica)*, ed. Ludger Thier and Abele Calufetti (Grottaferrata: Collegii S. Bonaventurae, 1985); and for a much later although similarly positioned text, Margery Kempe, *The Book of Margery Kempe*, ed. Sanford B. Beech and Hope Emily Allen (London: Early English Text Society, 1940).

[70] See Petroff, "Introduction," in *Medieval Women's Visionary Literature*; and David Herlihy, *Opera Muliebria: Women and Work in Medieval Europe* (New York: McGraw Hill, 1990), 117–231.

[71] See, for example, Petroff, "Introduction"; and Emilie Zum Brunn and Georgette Epinay-Burgard's introduction to their collection, *Women Mystics in Medieval Europe*, trans. Sheila Hughes (New York: Paragon House, 1989).

[72] The literature is full of such accounts. For examples, see Hildegard of Bingen, *Scivias* in *Corpus Christianorum: Continuatio Medievalis*, vols. 43–43a, ed. Adelgundis Führkotter (Turnhout: Brepols, 1978), "Protestificatio," 3–6; Mechthild of Hackeborn, *Revelationes Gertrudianae ac Mechtildianae 2: Sancta Mechthildis virginis ordinis sancti Benedicti Liber specialis gratiae*, ed. monks of Solesmes (Paris: Oudin, 1877), Bk. 1, Prologue, pp. 5–7; Gertrude of Helfta, *Oeuvres spirituelles*, vol. 3: Héraut III, Prologue and chap. 1, pp. 12–16; and Mechthild, *FL*, Bk. IV, chap. 2, p. 113.

the fate of the soul can be enacted, is, together with Beatrice of Nazareth and Clare of Assisi, one of the rare exceptions. Beatrice's texts do not appear to have been circulated much in her lifetime, many of them apparently having been destroyed.[73] Clare's writings also are sparse and of a private and pedagogic nature.[74] In both cases, hagiographers immediately after their death provided an ascetic and visionary setting for the life and teachings, pointing to the importance of such features to the larger culture's understanding of female sanctity.[75] Porete, in actively arguing against such modes, was seen as intolerable and without legitimating authority, despite the claims that the text was written by Love herself.

By undercutting the place of asceticism, paramystical phenomena, and visionary experience in the religious life, Porete and Eckhart effectively undermine the main avenues of religious authority and expression open to women in their culture. While in a world governed according to apophatic principles such legitimation would be unnecessary, late medieval ecclesiastical culture demanded it. The ambivalence created by this situation is clearly reflected in the traditions influenced by Eckhart, and indirectly, Porete, in the years following their condemnations and deaths. Some texts demonstrate the liberating appeal of their teaching for women and its power to subvert traditional authoritative structures. In the work known as "Schwester Katrei," for example, the title character is depicted as attaining a state of perfect detachment in which she has authority over the master, Eckhart himself.[76]

Yet the convent chronicles of the fourteenth century, produced when many Beguines had chosen or been forced to accept the Dominican rule, are full of accounts of ascetic, visionary, and ecstatic experiences.[77] There is a movement back to and in continuity with earlier thirteenth-century traditions, as well as the explicit mingling of mystical and hagiographical elements. Heinrich Suso, a male follower of Eckhart, followed suit: the account of his life, written in part by Elsbet Stagel, includes grueling ascetic accounts. At the same time Suso urges women followers to

---

[73] On Beatrice's life and texts, see Simone Roisin, *L'hagiographie cistercienne*, 61–65; and Roger de Ganck, *Beatrice of Nazareth in Her Contexts*, 2 vols. (Kalamazoo, Mich.: Cistercian Publications, 1991).

[74] See Francis and Clare, *The Complete Works*, trans. Regis J. Armstrong and Ignatius C. Brady, Classics of Western Spirituality Series (New York: Paulist Press, 1982), 169–234.

[75] Beatrice's hagiography is discussed above. For Clare, see Ignatius Brady, *The Legend and Writings of Saint Clare of Assisi* (St. Bonaventure, N.Y.: The Franciscan Institute, 1953).

[76] "Schwester Katrei," in *Der Freiheitsbegriff der deutschen Mystik*, ed. Franz-Josef Schweitzer (Frankfort am Main: Peter Lang, 1981), 322–70; and discussion and translation by Elvira Borgstadt in *Teacher*, 10–14, 349–87.

[77] See the texts cited in n. 3.

mitigate their own suffering.[78] In a fascinating reversal of thirteenth-century norms, Suso replaces his suffering body with the female bodies of the early Beguines. Yet in attempting to lessen women's suffering, he seems to claim he makes a better model for Christ and his humanity, therefore usurping a central salvific role open to women. Whereas the convent chronicles offer communal accounts of female sanctity, which bring together Eckhart's "mysticism of everyday life" with the bodily demands of female spiritual authorization, Suso claims his own singularity as a new replacement for suffering female flesh. The choice seems to lie between women's active suffering or their silence.

Finally, without changes to the dominant social structures of late medieval Europe and the ecclesiastical structures of Christianity, the way of annihilation, detachment, and apophasis were inadequate to women's needs, although the continued attraction of forms of religiosity which saved the suffering "heart and body and life" can be seen in much of the subsequent mystical tradition. Porete and Eckhart desired to free their hearers by re(e)valuating the world and escaping its constraints. We might well ask whether such constraints can ever be overcome; clearly in the face of hierarchical power structures, individual projects of detachment reach an impasse. Porete's silence throughout her imprisonment and trial speaks powerfully her belief in such a path, despite an uncomprehending and intransigent male ecclesiastical world. Eckhart, at his defense, exhibits much more surprise at the cultural refusal of his teaching. In the face of this refusal, many women sought access to the divine and to authority by inscribing their bodies and souls with suffering, with wounds marking the presence of God and the limits of the imagination.

---

[78] See Heinrich Suso, "Life of the the Servant," in *Heinrich Seuse: Deutsche Schriften im Auftrag der Wurttembergischen Kommission für Landesgeschichte*, ed. Karl Bihlmeyer (Stuttgart: Kohlhammer, 1907) and *The Exemplum and Two Sermons*, trans. Frank Tobin, Classics of Western Spirituality Series (New York: Paulist Press, 1989). For his arguments against female asceticism, and his usurping of female roles, see Bynum, *Holy Feast*, 102–5.

6

The Pseudo-Woman
and the Meister

"Unsaying" and Essentialism

Michael Sells

S ince the startling discovery of a French manuscript of Marguerite Porete's mystical text, *The Mirror of Simple Souls*, the relationship between Porete's writings and those of Meister Eckhart has opened up central questions concerning Eckhart and women's spirituality in the Middle Ages.

Here I will focus upon one aspect of that conversation between Porete and Eckhart's mystical writings: the effort to keep both the deity and the human from falling into categories of being, substance, and entification. This effort is tied into the language of *apophasis*, a term I translate as "unsaying." Eckhart and Porete's mystical language of unsaying entails an effort to overcome three forms of essentialism: (1) it unsays the "being," "substance," or "essence," of transcendent reality not only by asserting that such transcendent reality is "beyond-being" or is "nothing," but by actively turning back upon the spatial, temporal, and causal reifications contained even in such assertions; (2) it unsays the monotonic, male, "He-God," and opens up the deity to a powerful and open-ended gender dynamic; (3) it unsays implicit gender essentialism within the roles of "male writers" and "female writers" prescribed and enforced by inquisitional authority in the Middle Ages, and reinforced, at least implicitly, in the language of some contemporary historians.[1] With Porete and Eckhart, each of these three "unsayings" entails the other two.

---

[1] Amy Hollywood has suggested that a conversation between Medieval Studies and Women's Studies offers a particularly intriguing possibility: "In discussing the points of intersection between Women's Studies and Medieval Studies, we are first confronted with the ambiguities inherent in both of these fields, ambiguities which must be explored without being destroyed. Both terms designate endeavors which cut across the academic disciplines as they have traditionally been defined in order to delineate new fields of research and sets of questions." See "Anti-essentialism in the Middle Ages: the Conjunction of Feminist and Medieval Studies," revised version of a paper presented at the May, 1991, International Congress of Medieval

Mystical language of unsaying, from a variety of traditions, shares some key characteristics.[2] It begins with the dilemma of ineffability. If we say that the ineffable is "beyond names," we are caught in an *aporia*, an unresolvable dilemma. Insofar as it is beyond names, then it is beyond the name "the ineffable" that was used to assert its being beyond names. Indeed, we cannot assert ineffability without using some name. The assertion of ineffability turns back upon itself. Rather than turning to silence, or positing a way of speaking about the "effable" aspect of the ineffable, the language of unsaying is in fact a continual movement within the *aporia* of ineffability. No single statement can stand on its own as a meaningful proposition, since any single proposition (x is beyond words, x is beyond the world) must use a name ("x"). *Apophasis* yields then to a language of double propositions, each correcting the previous proposition, and meaning is found only in the fleeting tension between the two propositions. Because the language-conditioned mind tends to reify the last proposition as a self-standing utterance, *apophasis* can never achieve closure. There must always be another, new statement.

Within this *apophatic* language, particularly as it appeared in medieval Christian thought, the metaphor of "emanation" becomes central and the paradox of emanation (that the procession *is* the return) is used in a radical way to destabilize the temporal, causal, and spatial structures of language. In doing so, the apophatic writer attempts to keep the transcendent from being reified and entified, from being limited within the sphere of substance or being. It is through the continual effort to undue the essentialisms inherent in the use of language that the writings of Porete and Eckhart arrive at their extraordinary reconfiguration of gender relations within the divine, within the human, and between the divine and human.

Porete's Work of Love

In 1946 the Italian scholar Romana Guarnieri discovered that the treatise known as the *Mirror of Simple Souls*, which had circulated for centuries in anonymous

Studies, Kalamazoo, Michigan, 1. Here I begin by focusing upon the medieval critique of theological "essentialism," then move to the transformation of a monotonic "He-God" into a vision of dynamic gender relations within deity, within the human, and between deity and human, and finally move on to the issue of gender essentialism. The effort is not to collapse the three issues into a sameness, but precisely to explore the ambiguities in terms like "essentialism" and to better understand the relationship between differing modes of essentialism.

[2] For a sustained argument concerned the nature and function of apophatic language, see M. Sells, *Mystical Languages of Unsaying* (Chicago: University of Chicago Press, 1994). The present essay contains some material from chapters five and seven of *Mystical Languages*, but is focused much more specifically upon the *conversatio* between the work of Eckhart and Porete, and their theology of "work."

versions in Latin, Italian, and English, was nothing other than the work of the famous heretic Marguerite Porete, who was burned at the stake at Place de la Grève in Paris on June 1, 1310. Guarnieri's discovery of an antique French manuscript, and even older Latin manuscripts, and her publication of them in cooperation with Paul Verdeyen, has stirred new interest in what is certainly one of the more remarkable works of medieval mystical literature. It has also raised intriguing questions concerning the relationship between the *Mirror* and the writings of the Dominican scholar, preacher, and administrator, Meister Eckhart, who was himself condemned some eighteen years after Marguerite's death. While Eckhart resided in Paris in 1311, only a year after Porete's execution, he stayed at the same Dominican house as William Humbert, Porete's inquisitor, where he may have had access to a copy of the *Mirror*.[3] We may never know whether Eckhart and Porete knew of one another's works firsthand. It has been established, however, that the writings of the two mystics share complex, detailed, and powerful affinities. Elsewhere, I have examined these affinities from a more general perspective, and I have suggested that they cluster around the complete abandonment of the will (willing nothing) and the radical apophatic dialectic to which it leads. The abandonment of will entails several interconnected themes: (1) the reversion to the state of precreation; (2) living "without a why"; (3) the relinquishment of all medium or mediation; (4) the nakedness of the soul that has given up all will and reason; and (5) the giving up of all works.[4] In this essay, I will focus on the concept of the "work" of the divine, first in Porete, then in Eckhart. I will examine how in each author the conception of the divine work is central to the destabilizing of essentialist notions of deity, of humanity, and of gender (in both the divine and the human realms). I will suggest

---

[3] See Kurt Ruh, "Meister Eckhart und die Spiritualität der Beginen," in *Kleine Schriften* (Berlin: Walter de Gruyter, 1984) II: 327–36; Alois Haas, "Meister Eckhart im Spiegel der marxistischen Ideologie," in *Sermo mysticus: Studien zu Theologie und Sprache der deutschen Mystik* (Freiburg, Switzerland: Universitätsverlag, 1979), 246–49; Edmund Colledge, O.S.A., and J. C. Marler, "'Poverty of the Will': Ruusbroec, Eckhart and The Mirror of the Simple Souls," in *Jan Van Ruusbroec: The Sources, Content, and Sequels of his Mysticism*, ed. P. Mommaers and N. de Paepe (Leuven, Belgium: Leuven University Press, 1984), 15. Cf. Herbert Grundmann, "Ketzerverhöre des Spätmittelalters als quellenkritisches Problem," *Deutsches Archiv für Erforschung des Mittelalters*, 21 (1965): 519–75. Particularly strong thematic parallels have been drawn between Porete's *Mirror* and Eckhart's *Predigt* 52, entitled *Beati pauperes spiritu* (Blessed are the poor in spirit). Colledge and Marler, "'*Poverty of the Will*.'" A short but particularly contextualized discussion of the parallels between Porete and Eckhart can be found in Bernard McGinn, "Love, Knowledge, and *Unio Mystica* in the Western Christian Tradition," in *Mystical Union and Monotheistic Faith: An Ecumenical Dialogue*, edited by Moshe Idel and Bernard McGinn (New York: Macmillan, 1989), especially pp. 73–79. It was the McGinn discussion that first introduced this author to Porete's masterwork, *The Mirror of Simple Souls*.

[4] For a detailed discussion of the far wider range of affinities between the works of Eckhart and those of Porete, see *Mystical Languages of Unsaying*, 180–205.

that it is within the theme of the divine work in the world that the conversation between Eckhart and Porete's mystical languages is at its deepest. The essay will close with some questions concerning the relationship of the standard categories of male writer and female writer to two major writers (and schools) that differ so radically from such categories.

The Mirror of Simple Souls takes the form of a dramatic allegory in which characters such as *Dame Amour* (Lady Love), *L'Ame Anneantie* (the Annihilated Soul), *Raison* (Reason), *Loingprès* (FarNear), and *Pure Courtoisie* (High Courtesy), engage in extended conversations on love and theology. The turning point in the drama occurs when Reason (clearly identified with the syllogistic reasoning of the schools and theologians) is so perplexed by the paradoxes of *Dame Amour* that it expires. This drama occurs within a seven-tiered cosmos of mystical stations, the fifth and sixth of which are the center of interest. (The seventh station is beyond all words and is associated by *Dame Amour* with the afterlife.)

Dame Amour's paradoxes begin when she radicalizes the notion that the soul must disencumber herself of her will, work, means, usage, and virtues; it is only when the soul has disencumbered itself to the point of self-annihilation that it can move beyond the stage of will and works (the fourth station) to the station of nothingness (the fifth station) and clarification (the sixth station).

The demand that the soul disencumber herself of works, virtues, will, and reason, is not a negation of action or reason, but a revisioning of them. At this point, the issue becomes not whether work is done, but who is the agent of the work. *Dame Amour* names several agents. At times it is God (*dieu, deus*): "And that is a work for God, for *God works in me*. I owe him no work as he himself works in me and if I did something, it would be undoing his work [emphasis added]."[5] At times it is FarNear: "This FarNear is the Trinity itself. The Trinity *works in this soul* showing her his/her glory. Of this no one can speak, except the deity itself [emphasis added]."[6] At times it is the Trinity by

---

[5] Marguerite Porete, *Mirouer* 84: 44–47, pp. 240–41: "A Dieu en est de ceste oeuvre, qui fait en moy ses oeuvres. Je ne luy doy point de oeuvre, puisque luy mesmes oeuvre en moy; et se je y mectoye le mien, je defferoye son oeuvre." See also *Mirouer* 41: 11–16, pp. 128–29: "This soul, says Love, is not with herself, and she is therefore excused by everyone. And he in whom she is, performs his work through her, for which she is well acquitted, with the witness of God himself, says Love, who is the worker of this work on behalf of this soul, a soul who has no work whatsoever within her." ("Ceste Ame, dit Amour, n'est mie avec elle, par quoi elle doit estre de tous excusee; et celluy en qui elle est fait son oeuvre par elle, pour laquelle chose elle en est bien acquictee, a tesmoing de Dieu mesmes, dit Amour, qui est ouvrier de ceste oeuvre ou prouffit de ceste Ame, laquelle n'a en elle point de oeuvre.")

[6] *Mirouer* 61: 27–31, pp. 178–79: "Le Loingprés est la Trinité mesmes, et luy monstre sa demonstrance, que nous nommons 'mouvement,' non mye pource que l'ame se meuve ne la Trinité, mais la Trinité oeuvre a ceste Ame la monstre de sa gloire. De ce ne scet nul parler, sinon la Deité mesmes."

name: "This soul has given all through the freedom of the *work of the Trinity* [emphasis added]."[7] Love also plays this key role. Reason asks how it can be true, as *Dame Amour* claims, that the annihilated soul has no concern for honor or dishonor, poverty or riches, comfort or discomfort, love or hate, hell or heaven. *Dame Amour* responds that an understanding of the annihilated soul cannot be found in scripture, that human sense (*sensus*) cannot apprehend it, nor human work merit it. It is a gift, one described as:

> Given by the Most High, in whom this creature is ravished [*ravie, perdita*] by the fullness [*planté*] of understanding, and becomes nothing in her understanding. And such a soul, who has become nothing, has everything, wills nothing and wills everything, knows nothing and knows everything.
>
> And how can that be, *Dame Amour*, says Reason, that this soul can will what this book says, which has already said earlier that she has no will.
>
> Reason, says Love, it is not her will that wills it, but the will of God, who wills it in her. For this soul does not remain within love which makes her will it by some desire. Love remains in her who has taken her will, and thus *love does her will with her, and love works in her without her* [emphasis added].[8]

This work within the annihilated soul is a nexus for various threads of Porete's thought and it is the point of transformation of her apophatic discourse. It is also the point of union for her various divine personae: Love, the Trinity, FarNear. Though Love is female and FarNear is male, though Love speaks and FarNear holds his peace, in the work within the annihilated soul they are one. And in this one work, the annihilated soul becomes one with them: "Love dwells in her and transforms her into herself so that this soul herself is Love, and Love has no discretion. In all things one should have discretion, except in love."[9] This

---

[7] *Mirouer* 89: 3–4, pp. 252–53: "Cest Ame a tout donné par franchise de noblesse de l'ouevre de la Trinité."

[8] *Mirouer* 7:11–25, pp. 26–27: "Ainsoys est ce don donné du Treshault, en qui ceste creature est ravie par planté de congnoissance, et demeure rien en son entendement. Et telle ame, qui est devenue rien, a adonc tout et si n'a nyent, elle vieult tout et ne vieult nient, elle sçait tout et ne sçait nient.

"Et que peut ce estre, dame Amour, dit Raison, que ceste Ame peut vouloir ce que ce livre dit, que desja a dit devant qu'elle n'a point de voulenté?

"Raison, dit Amour, ce n'est mie voulenté qui le vieult, mais ainçoys est la voulenté de Dieu, qui le vieult en elle; car ceste Ame ne demoure mie en Amour qui ce luy face vouloir par nul desirer. Ainçoys demoure Amour en elle, qui a prinse sa voulenté, et pource fait Amour sa voulenté d'elle, et adonc oeuvre Amour en elle sans elle."

[9] *Mirouer* 39: 26–29, pp. 124–25: "Car Amour demoure en elle, qui l'muee en luy. Si que ceste Ame mesme est Amour, et Amour n'a en luy poit de discrecion; mais en toutes choses convient avoir discrecion, excepté en amour." The Latin text reads: "Quia amor in ea manet qui eam in se mutavit. Ita quod talis anima adnichilata est amor, et amor not habet in se aliquam discretionem, licet in omnibus sit necessaria discretio praeterquam in amore."

transformation of the soul into love and the peace of love, "in which the soul lives and endures and is and was and will be without being [*en laquelle elle vit, et dure, et est, et fut, et sera sans estre*]" is compared to the transformation of molten iron into fire by the action of fire,[10] and—more radically—to a transformation into fire so complete that the fire burns without any matter.[11]

The union between annihilated soul and the deity is a union-in-act, the act being love's work within the soul. In the union the soul receives gifts from its divine lover as great as the giver. In one passage, the plural "gifts" suddenly changes, ungrammatically, to the singular. The divine gifts (*dons*) are as great "As he himself who has given it [*cecy*], which gift transforms her into him. This is Love and Love can do what she wills. Fear, discretion and Reason can say nothing against Love."[12]

Although this change from the plural (gifts) to the singular (it, this) could be explained as a scribal error, something more serious may be involved. The gifts are identical to the giver. The divine gift of itself to the soul will become a central theme with Eckhart as well.[13] Porete cites in evidence of the greatness of this gift John 14:12: "Whoever believed in me he will do the works I do and even greater."[14] This union is also spoken of as a union of form; in another passage with a precise analogue in Eckhart, the annihilated soul is imprinted (*emprainte, impressa*) upon the form of the divine, obtaining this impression from the union of love. The soul obtains the form of its exemplar as wax takes the form of the seal.[15]

The soul's abandonment of discretion reflects a paradox found within courtly love. The rules of courtly love or "courtesy" (*cortezia*) demand discretion, conforming to the conventions and norms of society, and *mezura*, avoiding of excesses of feeling and behavior. Yet the courtly lover (*fin aman*) continually violated these standards of *cortezia* and *mezura* and acted in a solitary, excessive manner.[16]

---

[10] *Mirouer* 52: 6–21, pp. 152–55.

[11] *Mirouer* 25: 10–19, pp. 90–93.

[12] *Mirouer* 95: 14–18, pp. 266–67: "Ses dons son aussi grans, comme est luy mesme qui a donné cecy, lequel don le meut de luy en luy mesmes. C'est mesmes Amour, et Amour peut quanqu'elle veult; a pource ne peut Crainte, ne Discrecion, ne Raison contre Amour rien dire."

[13] See below, p. 139.

[14] *Mirouer* 94: 13–15, p. 262.

[15] *Mirouer* 50: 2–6, pp. 148–49: "Ceste Ame est emprainte en Dieu, et a sa vraye emprainture detenue par l'union d'amour; et a la maniere que la cire prent la forme du seel, en telle maniere a ceste Ame prinse l'emprainte de cest vray exemplaire."

[16] See D. R. Sutherland, "The Love Meditation in Courtly Literature," in *Studies in Medieval French Presented to Alfred Ewert* (Oxford: Clarendon Press, 1961), 165–93, especially 165. In one category, however, *The Mirror* seems to differ from courtly love, and that is the emphasis on *melancholia*.

Porete has combined this language of cortezia with an apophatic language of mystical union. The union-with-and-in-love is *rapture*. Rapture is the act and work of love. The language of rapture includes a complex of interdependent terms and figures of speech (disrobing, nakedness, loss of discretion, loss of shame, abandon) that reinforce the basic sexual metaphor. As *Dame Amour* says, there is no "discretion" in love. The soul gives up her honor, her shame. She disrobes herself of will.[17] Her union with the Divine Lover occurs in nakedness. She gives herself over to abandon. She "falls" (in an expression that will have many levels of meaning) into love.[18]

The erotic tension is primarily temporal and is located between the fifth and sixth station. From the fifth station of annihilation the soul is rapt (*ravie, rapta*) into a sixth station of union with the divine lover, FarNear (*Loingprès*). However, "she cannot stay there long. It is an opening like a flash, quickly closing. There she is free and noble and disencumbered of all things. No one who has a mother can speak of this."[19] The instantaneous nature of rapture is evoked again in a passage of great lyrical beauty:

> The ravishing opening and expansion of this opening makes the soul, after its closing, of the peace of its work so free and so noble and so disencumbered of all things, as long as the peace which is given in the opening lasts, that she freely remains after this opening in the fifth station, without falling into the fourth, for in the fourth there is will while in the sixth there is no will. Thus in the fifth station of which this book speaks there is no will—there the soul remains after the work of ravishing FarNear which we call a flash because of the suddenness of its opening and loosening. No one can believe, says Love, the peace on peace of peace that this soul receives, unless he be she.[20]

Porete will occasionally evoke a spatial tension as well: "The exalting ravisher who takes me and unites me with the middle of the marrow of divine love in which

---

[17] *Mirouer* 88: 53–58, pp. 250–53.

[18] For similar themes in other Beguine mystics of the thirteenth century, see Sells, *Mystical Languages of Unsaying*, 125–26.

[19] *Mirouer* 58: 8–11, pp. 168–69: "Mais pou ce luy dure. Ca c'est une ouverture a maniere de esclar et de hastive closure, ou l'en ne peut longuement demourer, ne elle n'eust oncques mere, que de ce sceust parler."

[20] *Mirouer* 58: 12–23, pp. 168–69: "L'ouverture ravissable de l'espandement de celle ouverture fait l'Ame, après sa closure, de la paix de son oeuvre si franche et si noble et si descombree de toutes choses (tant comme la paix dure, que est donne en ceste ouverture), que qui se garderoit aprés telle avanture franchement, ou cinquiesme estat, san cheoir ou quart, se trouveroit, car ou quart a voulonté et ou cinquiesme n'en a point. Et pource que ou cinquiesme estat, dont ce livre parle, n'a point de voulenté—ou l'Ame demoure après l'oeuvre de Loingprés Ravissable que nous appellons eslar a maniere de ouverture et de hastive closure,—nul ne pouroit croire, dit Amout, la paix sur paix de paix que telle Ame reçoit, se n'estoit il mesmes."

I am melted."[21] Yet more often, it is the temporal paradigm that prevails. The sixth station is the intersection between time and eternity. From the temporal perspective, which is all that can be evoked (the eternal perspective of the seventh station being passed over in silence), eternity is perceived as a flash, both timeless and in time, both permanent and evanescent.

The Fall of Love

In regard to the fifth and sixth station, *Dame Amour* had said that once the soul has been rapt into the sixth station (of clarification and rapture), it stays in the fifth station (of annihilation) without "falling" into the fourth. Those in the fourth station cannot have peace unless they act against their own will and pleasure. "Such people do the opposite of the sensual, otherwise they fall back into the perdition of this life if they do not live contrary to their pleasure."[22] Up until this point, the spatial metaphor of mystical ascent is consistent. Those in the fifth station are rapt into the sixth. They return to the fifth without danger of "falling" into the fourth. Those in the fourth must continually fight their own will, sensuality, and pleasure lest they "fall back" into the earlier stages. Then in a sudden inversion, the ascent is figured as a fall. In contrast to those in the fourth station, the life of the spirit, who must fight their own will:

> Those who are free [*frans*] do the opposite. For, just as it is proper in the life of the spirit to do the opposite of the will, if one does not wish to lose peace, so—in contrast—the free souls do whatever pleases them, if they do not wish to lose peace, because they have come to the state of freedom [*franchise*], that is, they who have fallen back [*soient cheuz*] from the virtues into love and from love into nothing.[23]

This fall back from the virtues into love and from love into annihilation and freedom is related to *Dame Amour*'s statement that freed souls give to nature

[21] *Mirouer* 80:35–37, pp. 228–29: "Le sourhaulcement ravissable qui me sourprent et joinct au millieu de la mouelle de Divine Amour en quoy je suis fondue, dit ceste Ame." The Soul answers Reason's question as to who is her closest neighbor. She goes on to say that one should remain silent about this being, since it is impossible to say anything of it.

[22] *Mirouer* 90: 28–30, pp. 256–57: "Telles gens font le contraire de la sensualiuté, ou aultrement ilz rencherroiennt en perdicion de telle vie, se ilz ne vivoient au contraire de leur plaisance."

[23] Mirouer 90: 31–37, pp. 257–57: "Et ceulx qui sont frans, font tout le contraire. Car, tout ainsi comme il leur convient faire en vie d'esperit tout le contraire de leur voulenté, se ilz ne veulent perdre paix, ainsi, par le contraire, font les frans tout ce qu'il leur plaist, se ilz ne veulent perdre paix, puisque ilz sont venuz en l'estat de franchise, c'est a dire, qu'ilz soient cheuz des Vertuz en Amour, et d'Amour en nient."

whatever it demands. The *Mirror* assures us that the freed soul, though it can do what it wishes, will never wish anything contrary to the laws of the Church (though some of these assurances are later interpolations).[24] Even if these explicit disclaimers are not interpolations, however, by themselves they cannot resolve the issue. In order to evaluate *Dame Amour*'s claim that the soul is "excused" from everything, it is necessary to examine the view of agency upon which it is based. Those who act contrary to their own will and pleasure act through a kind of counter-will that is just as much tied to human will and works as the natural will. Such action is only another form of enslavement to will. As will be shown below, at the point of mystical union, the soul is free precisely insofar as it is not the soul who is acting. The divine (FarNear, *Amour*, or the Trinity) is acting in and through her.[25]

The sudden inversion of the metaphor of mystical ascent into one of descent is not unknown in medieval mystical texts.[26] Porete's reversal is distinct in the particular theological and cultural implications of sudden change in paradigm from ascent to descent. She associates the "fear of love" with the fear of nature. In this inversion of the Christian language of the fall, Porete brings together and affirms woman, love, the fall, and nature, four elements whose combination received a negative light in medieval Christianity.[27]

---

[24] See Edmund Colledge and Romana Guarnieri, "The Glosses by M. N. and Richard Methley to *The Mirror of Simple Souls*," *Archivio italiano per la storia della pietà* 5 (1968): 357–81.

[25] This argument entails an intricate set of apophatic transformations difficult to explain during an inquisitorial process bent on judging articles as single propositions taken out of context. Cf. chap. 6 in *Mystical Languages of Unsaying*.

[26] It occurs in the Jewish Hekhalot literature, where the ascent to the Merkevah or divine chariot can be replaced by a language of descent, as in *The Greater Hekhalot*, on which see G. Scholem, *Major Trends in Jewish Mysticism* (New York: Schocken, 1941), 46–47. In Eriugena, redemption was seen as a reversal of the fall in a way that inverted the temporal metaphor. There could be no fall until the redemption, because had humankind actually occupied paradise they could not have fallen from it. There is no paradise from which to fall until they return to it. See Sells, *Mystical Languages of Unsaying*, chap. 2.

[27] See M. Ruether, "Mysognynism and Virginal Feminism in the Fathers of the Church," in *idem*, ed., *Religion and Sexism: Images of Woman in the Jewish and Christian Traditions* (New York: Simon and Schuster, 1974), 150–83. The following passages cited by Ruether are particulary germane to Porete's view of nature, love, and the "fall of love": the first, on 161, from Jerome to the virgin Demetrias, Ep., 130.10: "You must act against nature or rather above nature if you are to forswear your natural functions, to cut off your own root, to cull no fruit but that of virginity, to abjure the marriage bed, to shun intercourse with men and, while in the body, to live as though out of it"; and the second, on 176, from Augustine's, *De Sermone Dom. in Monte*, 41: "A good Christian is found in one and the same woman to love the creature of God whom he desires to be transformed and renewed, but to hate in her the corruptible and mortal conjugal connection, sexual intercourse and all that pertains to her as a wife." For such views as they were reflected in twelfth-century Christianity, see Marie-Thérèse d'Alverny, "Comment les Théologiens et les Philosophes voient la femme," *Cahiers de*

The soul who ascends through the first five states undergoes a series of deaths and rebirths that end in a folding back into itself of the telescope of hierarchical articulations. Porete speaks of the death of sin and the life of grace, the death of nature and the life of the spirit, and finally of the death of the spirit and the "death of the life of works" as leading to the most genuine form of life.[28] The apophasis of desire includes the admonition to give to nature all that it desires, but that admonition applies to the annihilated soul in which nature and will and spirit have died. After the death of the will, the soul no longer needs to work contrary to her will and pleasure. As *Dame Amour* will suggest, the soul no longer is the worker; the deity works in her.

This self-abandon results in a dialectic of nothing and everything. The soul shrinks to a smallness where she can no longer find herself. She has "fallen" into the certainty of knowing nothing and willing nothing:

> Now this soul has rights [*droit*] to nothing in which she stays. And because she is nothing, she has no care of anything, not of herself nor of her neighbors nor of God himself. For she is so small that she cannot find herself. Everything created is far from her, so far that she cannot feel it. God is so great that she cannot comprehend. And through such nothing, she is fallen into certainty of knowing nothing and into the certainty of willing nothing. And this nothing, of which we speak, says Love, gives her all.[29]

---

civilisations médiévale 20 (1977): 105–26. Cf. Augustine, *Opus/Imperfectum Contra Julianum* 6, 25: "Nature, which the first human being harmed, is miserable . . . What passed to women was not the burden of Eve's fertility, but of her transgression. Now fertility operates under this burden, having fallen away from God's blessing," as translated by Elaine Pagels in *Adam, Eve, and the Serpent* (New York: Random House, 1988), 133. For a comparison of Porete and Eckhart on the issue of fertility, see below, 142–44.

[28] Edmund Colledge has suggested that Marguerite was confused in the way the stages were presented and that the seven stage schema contradicts another schema in the *Mirror*: that of the three deaths. Hollywood shows, however, that the three deaths and seven stages fit together well. The first two stages correspond to the life of grace born of the death of sin. The second two stages correspond to the life of the spirit born of the death of nature. The final stages correspond to the death of the spirit and the death of the life of works. Stages one and three are stages of contentment with one's position. Stages two and four are stages of struggle to move beyond it. A. Hollywood, *The Soul as Virgin Wife*, chap. 2.

[29] *Mirouer* 81: 3–11, pp. 230–31: "Or a ceste Ame, dit Amour, son droit non du nient en quoy elle demoure. Et puisque elle est nient, il ne luy chault de nient, ne d'elle ne de se proesmes ne de Dieu mesmes. Car elle est si petite, que elle ne se peut trouver; et toute chose creee luy est si loing, qu'elle ne le peut sentire; et Dieu est si grant, que elle n'en peut rien comprendre; et pour tel nient est elle cheue en certaineté de nient savoir et en certaineté de nient vouloir. Et ce nient, dont nous parlons, dit Amour, luy donne le tout."

The freed soul is disencumbered of all things and has no care for anything, self, neighbors, or *Dieu mesme*. The soul is liberated (*enfranchie, libera*) in complete abandonment of all will and all its "usages." Love tells her that she is "passed away in love and remains dead" (*estes vous pasmee et more demouree; in nihilo syncopyzastis et mortua remansistis*), [30] and thus is able to live truly.

In addition to will, reason also dies. The death of reason had been intimated earlier when the annihilated soul was said to be: "Dead to all the feelings of within and without, insofar as such a soul engages no further in works, neither for God nor for herself, and has lost her senses [*sens, sensus,* wits] in the usage, that she knows not how to seek God nor find him nor guide herself."[31]

In this stage discursive reason passes away. In the *Mirror*, the death of Reason is acted out theatrically. Love states that this soul is "lady of Virtues, daughter of Deity, sister of Wisdom, and spouse of Love" (*dame des Vertuz, fille de Deité, soeur de Sapience, et espouse d'Amour*).[32] Soul predicts that Reason will not be able to bear the paradoxes of these marvels (*merveilles*), even as she declares herself "nothing but love." Reason then cries: "O God! how can anyone say such things? I do not dare to hear them. I fail, Lady Soul, in hearing you. My heart has failed. I live no more."[33] Lady Soul laments at the death of Reason, but her lament carries a ruthless twist; her lament is that Reason had not died long before.[34]

---

[30] *Mirouer* 59:28 (Latin, l. 24). The full passage, 59:17–30, pp. 150–53, reads: "This is the end of my work, says this soul, to will nothing always. For just as I will nothing, says this soul, I am alone in him without myself, and completely freed, and when I will anything, she says, I am with myself and I lose my freedom. But when I wish nothing and have lost everything out of my will, then I lack nothing. Free being maintains me. I will nothing in anything.

"O very precious Hester, says Love, who has lost all your usages, and through this loss have the usage of doing nothing, you are truly precious. For in truth this usage and this loss is made in the nothingness of your love, and in this nothingness, says Love, you are passed out and remain dead. But you live, beloved, says Love, in his will in all. That is his chamber and it pleases him for you to stay there."

[31] *Mirouer* 41: 7–10, pp. 128–29.

[32] *Mirouer* 87: 3–4, pp. 246–47.

[33] *Mirouer* 87: 11–13, pp. 246–47: "Hay, Dieux, dit Raison, comment ose l'en ce dire? Je ne l'ose escouter. Je deffaulx vrayement, dame Ame, en vous oïr: le cueur m'est failly. Je n'ay point de vie."

[34] *Mirouer* 87: 14–25: pp. 248–49. Reason has been subsumed into that higher knowledge called *entendement d'amour* in the *Mirror*. For one of several references, see 9:29–39, pp. 34–45, where Dame Amour places this entendment beyond the reach of *maistres de sens de nature, maistres d'escripture, and ceulx qui demourent en amour de l'obedience des vertuz.* In the prelude, even the Beguines are included in the list (122: 96–101, p. 344):

> Beguines dient que je err,
>   prestres, clers, et prescheurs,
> Augustin, et carmes,
>   et les freres mineurs

Apophatic mysticism entails a moment of letting go of distinctions. With Porete's apophasis of desire, figured in terms of rapture, there is a similar moment of risk. Rapture entails complete abandon, abandon of will, of works, of reason, of self-vulnerability.[35] It can occur only in a context of absolute trust. At the moment of abandon, the soul gives up all defenses, control, security. The soul annihilated in love of the divine no longer exists in the formal sense as a subject that wills and acts—the only will and act are the will and act of the deity.

The mystical union occurs at the moment that will is abandoned, but that abandonment of will (the theological implications of which will be examined below) does not entail a lack of consent. In the past two decades, the more sinister aspects of the courtly love tradition have been explored, particularly the way rape has been both exploited and disguised with the romance.[36] In appropriating the language of courtly love, Porete was not merely borrowing conventions and tropes, but in many cases was inverting them. A language of "rapture," and "ravishment" which in the courtly tradition could become a code for the enactment of rape and for the disenfranchisement of the woman is transformed in the *Mirror*. For a closer look at the inversions and transformations within Porete's apophasis of desire, we turn to *Dame Amour*'s distinctive understanding of the soul's reversion to what she was "as she was before she was."

As She Was Before She Was

The annihilation of the soul (with its reason, will, and works) entails a reversion to a precreative state of being, to what the soul was "when she was not." The reversion is evoked through puns made upon the word *pourquoy* (for what, i.e., why) and related terms such as *de quoy* (of what, concerning what). The annihilated soul has no "why," and acts "without a why,"[37] without a "what."

Dame Amour states that one who truly believes "is said to live and to be" what he believes. "He has no more to do with himself or with another or with God

See also chap. 12 of the Mirror where the important concept of the "understanding of love" is figured as a character in the court of love, as *La Haultesse d'Entendement d'Amour*, 49–52.

[35] In Plotinus and Eriugena, abandon and absolute trust are figured primarily as ontological, the giving up of being. As was shown above, at the point of mystical union, this nothingness or beyond-beingness cannot be distinguished discursively from mere nothingness.

[36] The literature in this area is large. For one study, see Kathryn Gravdal, *Ravishing Maidens: Writing Rape in Medieval French Literature and Law* (Philadelphia: University of Pennsylvania Press, 1991). Of particular interest (1–12) is Gravdal's excursus on the semantic field and legal definitions of raptus.

[37] This expression occurs earlier in Beatrice of Nazareth where love for deity is spoken of as "without a why," *sonder enich waeromme: Seven manieren*, II, p. 7, ll. 4–6. See Zum Brunn and Epiney-Burgard, *Women Mystics*, 81, and 198, n. 24.

himself, not more *than if he were not*, though he is [emphasis added]."[38] In another passage, the paradigm shifts from the conditional (than if he were not) to the temporal (when she was not). Out of its overflowing good (*bonté*) the deity gave free will to the soul. But this freedom is only realized when the soul gives up her will and gives back her free will to the divine. There, where she was before she was, the soul has no "of what" (*de quoy*) for the deity to reprehend. She participates with the deity in many works, but always flows back into the deity where "I was created of him without me." There the deity and the soul carry out works together as long as the soul continues to reflow (*refluss*) back into the divine. The deity's act of giving "without a why" (*sans nul pourquoy*) echoes the soul's acting without a why.[39] Just as through its *bonté* the deity gave the soul her free will freely, without a why, and just as the freed soul acts without a why, so the deity takes back the free will from the soul without a why.[40]

Porete combines here the Neo-Platonic emanation paradox of procession and return, her own inversion of the language of the fall, and a distinctive notion of "exchange of wills."[41] The exchange of wills occurs after the soul has fallen from the virtues into love, from love into nothingness, and from nothingness into divine clarification. At the moment of divine clarification, as the soul returns to its precreated state, the deity dissolves into its three actions of self-seeing, self-loving, and self-knowing. The soul no longers sees, loves, or knows the divine: the actions

---

[38] *Mirouer* 100: 22–25, pp. 276–77: "Il n'a nient plus a faire de luy ne d'aultruy ne de Dieu mesmes, nient plus que se il ne fust mie; si que il est."

[39] *Mirouer* 111: 10–21, pp. 302–3: "Love: But he who has peace, stays willing nothing there where he was before he had a will. The divine *bonté* has nothing 'for which' it might reprehend him.

"O God, how well said! says the freed soul. But it is appropriate for him to do this without me, just as he created me without me of his divine *bonté*. Now I am, says this soul, a soul created of him without me, to work between him and me many works of virtue, him for me and me for him, as long as I flow back into him. I cannot be in him until he places me with him without me, just as he placed me without me of himself. It is the uncreated *bonté* that loves the *bonté* which it has created. Now the uncreated *bonté* has its own free will. It gives us our own free will of its *bonté*, outside of its power, without a why, except for ourselves and the very being of *bonté*.

"Mais celluy a paix, qui demoure en nient vouloir la ou il estoit, ains qu'il eust vouloir. La divine bonté n'a de quoy reprendre. Hee, Dieux, comme c'est bien dit! Dit l'Ame Enfranchie; mais il convient qu'il face ce sans moy, ainsi comme il me crea sans moy de sa bonté divine. Or suis je, dit ceste Ame, ame cree de luy sans moy, pour ouvreer entre luy et moy fortes oeuvres de vertuz, luy pour moy et moy pour luy, tant que je reffusse en luy; et si ne puis estre en luy, se il ne my' mect sans moy de luy, ainsi comme il me fist sans moy de lui mesme. C'est la Bonté increee qui ayme la bonté qu'elle a creee. Or a Bonté, de son propre, frache voulenté; que nous donne de sa bonté aussi franche voulenté, hors de sa puissance, sans nul pourquoy, sinon que pour nous mesmes, et pour estre de sa bonté."

[40] *Mirouer* 89:1–11, pp. 252–53.

[41] See chap. 7 of *Mystical Language of Unsaying* for details of this theme.

are now reflexive. At this point the deity, which had given over its freedom to the soul in making her "lady," receives back its freedom as the soul abandons her own will. In this courtly exchange, the divine "cannot take this free will back from himself without the pleasure of the soul." Marguerite continues:

> She has fallen from grace into the perfection of the work of the virtues, and from the virtues into love, and from love into nothingness, and from nothingness into the clarification of God who sees himself with the eyes of his majesty, who at this point has clarified her through himself. She is so returned into him that she sees neither herself nor him. He sees himself alone from his divine *bonté*; he is of himself in such *bonté* that he knew of himself when she was not, before he entrusted his *bonté* to her and made her lady of it. This was free will, which he cannot take back by himself without the pleasure of the soul. Now he has it, without a why, at that point that he had it before she was lady. There is no one else. No one else loves but he, for no one is outside of him and he alone loves and sees and praises from his own being.[42]

This freedom is ecstatic; the soul lives and is without itself, outside itself, or beyond itself. The ecstatic freedom occurs simultaneously with two events: (1) a highly erotic version of the mystical union of the lover and beloved (in which the two parties are now only one party), and (2) the courtly exchange whereby the deity entrusts the soul with its goodness and the soul hands back her will to the deity. *Dame Amour* dramatizes this radical freedom through complex puns on the word *pour quoy* (why, for what). To the implicit question, "why [*pour quoy*] should the soul live or act," *Dame Amour* states that the soul has no what (*quoy*) for (*pour*) which or on account of which it might act. *Dame Amour*'s colloquial language of living "without a why" contains within it the notion that the annihilated soul lives

---

[42] *Mirouer* 91: 10–23, pp. 256–59: "Sa voulenté est nostre, car elle est cheue de grace en parfection de l'oeuvre des Vertuz, et des Vertuz en Amour, de d'Amour en Nient, et de Nient en Clarifiement de Dieu, qui se voit des yeulx de sa majesté, que en ce point l'a de luy clarifiee. Et si est si remise en luy, que elle ne voit ne elle ne luy; et pource il se voit sout seul, de sa bonté divine. Il sera de luy en telle bonté ce qu'il savoit de luy ans que elle ne fust mie, quant il luy donna sa bonté, dont il la fist dame. Ce fut Franche Voulenté, qu'il ne peut de luy ravoir sans le plaisir de l'ame. Or l'a maintenant, sans nul pourquoy, en tel point comme it l'avoit, ains que telle en fust dame. Ce n'est fors qu'il; nul n'ayme fors qu'il, car nul n'est fors que luy, et pource ayme tout seul, et se voit tout seul, et loe tout seul de son estre mesmes."

The Latin offers an interesting and clearer alternative to the difficult passage (ll. 14–18) beginning with *Et si est si remise* ("And she is so returned"): "Et est ita in ipsum resoluta quod videt nec se nec ipsum. Et ideo ipse deus videt se solum sua divina bonitate. Ipse ita se rehabet de ipsa in tali bonitate, sicut se habebat de se, antequam esset, quando dedit ei suam bonitatem de qua fecit eam dominam."

without means (*moyens*, or in the Latin, *intermedium*). The term *moyens* can be read two ways: as a living without means or usages, a living without will, in other words, without a why; and as a lack of a medium between the divine and human, a complete immediacy of contact. Ultimately the two meanings are fused in Porete's thought. One aspect of this "why" consists of the rewards of heaven and the punishments of hell, neither of which, *Dame Amour* insists, are of any concern whatsoever to the freed soul. Similarly, the Virgin Mary lives without her will. She lives the life of the Trinity without any *entredeux* or "go between."[43]

In the annihilation and the clarification that take place in the fifth and sixth stations respectively, the referential distinction between reflexive and nonreflexive, self and other, human and divine, begins to break down. Although referring to an absolute unity, only the gender distinction between the annihilated soul (feminine) and the Divine Lover (masculine) keeps Porete's language from a complete fusion of pronominal antecedents. At times, however, we can see signs of stress in this distinction.[44] Thus, the Latin text, which for the most part echoes faithfully the French, diverges from it in the depiction of the "clear" life. One particularly difficult problem here is that the French text is late (fifteenth century) and probably does not reflect the pronouns that Porete may have used in her thirteenth-century dialect. In earlier French, the gender distinction within the dative pronouns was fragile and

---

[43] The Latin gives *intermedium* for *entredeux*. The French *entredeux* provides a more personal play—"go-between" or "interloper"—upon the giving up of all medium (*moyens, intermedium*). *Mirouer* 93: 23–24, pp. 262–63: "Et pource eut elle, sans nul entredeux en l'ame d'elle, en ung corps mortel de la Trinité glorieuse vie."

The stage of "clarification" of the soul in Porete can be viewed along two vectors of comparison. One vector reaches toward the strikingly similar conception in the Sufism of the twelfth through fourteenth centuries, while the second moves through the courtly and theological context of thirteenth-century Europe, and particularly the Beguine tradition. The reversion to the precreative state in which one "was before one was" has a close analogue within the classical Sufi exposition of mystical union. For Junayd (d. 911), the goal of the mystic is to reach that state where he is "as he was when he was before he was." *An yakūn, kamā kāna idh kāna qabla an yakūna*. See Abdel Kader, *The Life, Personality and Writings of Al-Junayd* (London: Luzac, 1962), Arabic text, 56–57.

Behind Junayd's formula was the theory of the early Sufi, Sahl al-Tustari, in which this precreative state is identified with a Qur'anic passage in which the preexistent souls of humankind pledge their allegiance to their lord. Sahl ibn ʿAbdallah at-Tustarī, Tafsīr al-Qur'ān al-ʿAzīm (Cairo: Dār al-Kutub al-Gharbiyya al-Kubrā, 1329/1911), 40–41. For a translation of the relevant passages and a discussion of this important theory in Tustari, see Gerhard Böwering, *The Mystical Vision of Existence in Classical Islam: The Qur'a-nic Hermeneutics of the Sufi Sahl at-Tustarī, d. 283/89* (Berlin: Walter de Gruyter, 1980), 153–57.

[44] For an example of the kind of complete reference fusion that can occur in a text without such gender distinction, see Sells, *Mystical Languages of Unsaying*, 70–77.

could be ambiguous.[45] The composers of the later French text and the Latin may have been trying to interpret an older French in which the gender distinctions, already fragile, are breaking down at the point of mystical union. One example of this frequent breakdown can be found in the following passage. I have marked the discrepancies between the Latin and French versions with a slash:

> I call [this life] clear [clere] because she has surmounted the blindness of the life of annihilation. . . . She does not know who she is, God or humankind. For she is not, but God knows of himself in him/her for her of her/himself. Such a Lady does not seek God. She has no "of what" [de quoy] with which to do that. She need not do that. For what [pour quoy, why] would she seek then? [46]

Daughter of Deity

The distinctiveness of Porete's language is found not only in the subtle way in which she configures the various themes just discussed, particularly her version of the

[45] See M. K. Pope, *From Latin to Modern French with Especial Consideration of Anglo-Norman* (New York: Barnes and Noble, 1934, 1961), 322–24, especially on the confusion of *lui* with *li* (#840:1), 324. I wish to thank Professor Penny Armstrong of Bryn Mawr College for her help on issues concerning the evolution of the French language.

[46] *Mirouer* 100: 27–32, pp. 276–77: "Pource l'appelle je clere, que elle surmont l'aveugle vie adnientie; l'aveugle soustient a ceste cy ses piez; la clere est la plus noble et la plus gentile. Elle ne scet que soit, ne Dieu ne homme; car elle n'est mie; mais Dieu le scet de luy, en luy, pour elle, d'elle mesmes [Latin: Sed Deus scit hoc de se in ipsa, pro seipsa de seipso]. Telle dame ne quiert mais Dieu; elle n'a de quoy, elle n'a de luy que faire. Il ne lui fault mie; pourquoy le querroit elle donc?"

See *Mirouer* 81: 21–22, pp. 230–31. "If God works his work in her, it is of him in her without her for him/her" ("Se Dieu fait son oeuvre en elle, c'est de luy en elle, sans elle, pour elle. // Si Deus facit in ea opus suum, hoc est de se in ipsa propter se sine ipsa").

The ambiguity recurs in verses 24–27 of the same passage. A similar ambiguity occurs in *Mirouer* 95: 13–16: (translated and discussed above, p. 119): "Ses dons son aussi grans comme est luy mesmes qui a donné cecy, lequel don le meut de luy en luy mesmes // Ista enim dona sunt ita magna, sicut est ipsemet, cuius sunt quae donat isti animae. Quae etiam dona mutant eam in illummet propter ipsam."

In this context, the term "annihilated soul," its combination with the reversion to the precreative state, and the reference fusions that take place at the point of mystical union show a multifold affinity to Sufi thought that can hardly be dismissed as pure coincidence. The issue is not whether the Beguine "borrowed" the concept from Sufi-influenced writings or developed it out of the courtly love tradition on her own—for the courtly love tradition is itself implicated with Arabic and Islamic culture. No claim is made here of any particular textual influence; these ideas must have been circulating freely—probably more through oral traditions and "fall," but also in her reinterpretation of biblical and theological themes from the perspective of *Dame Amour*'s court. The moment of annihilation in love of the divine is represented not only by the Virgin Mary, but also by Mary Magdalene in the desert. When she began seeking God, Mary Magdalene lost God because the "of which" (her will, her work) interposed itself.[47] *Dame Amour* says of Magdalene that she "did not know when she sought him that God was everywhere and that she had, without any intermediary, the divine work within herself." The text continues:

> But when she was in the desert, love took her and annihilated her and thus love works in her through her without her. She lived, then, the divine life which gave her the life of glory. Thus she found God in her, without seeking him, and also she did not have any "of which" since Love had taken it. [48]

In another pun, *Dame Amour* contrasts the sorrowful or "marred" soul (*marrie*) with Marie (the Virgin Mary, but perhaps with allusions to Mary Magdalene and to Martha's sister, who also represent the life of the soul annihilated in love). The Latin term for *marrie* is *maesta*. Those in the fourth stage live the sorrowful life, the life appropriate for a fallen nature and a fallen world. A further aspect of the pun may be the association of this sorrowful life with the married life, but loss of the original French text and the fluidity of accents makes this supposition difficult to demonstrate.[49]

Porete's distinction between the sorrowful life of works and the life of the three Marys can be seen as conventional. She takes up the very popular contrast between

conversations than the translations of particular texts. On the one hand, Porete's understanding of mystical union is remarkably close to the formulations of her Sufi contemporaries. On the other hand, it is grounded within the European milieux, particularly within the Beguine appropriation (going back at least to Mechthild of Magdeburg) of courtly love, with the themes of the nakedness of the soul, the union of the lover with the divine beloved. Her writing is situated at the intersection of the Beguine and the Sufi traditions. Her originality and genius are one major testimony to the simultaneous culmination of apophatic traditions in Judaism, Christianity, and Islam. They also suggest that at this particular moment in the history of Western mysticism, Sufism, and European Christian mysticism were part of a larger multireligious cultural entity.

[47] *Mirouer* 93: 13–20, pp. 262–63: especially 16–17: "Elle ne savoit mie, quant elle le queroit, que Dieu fust partout."

[48] *Mirouer* 93: 8–13, pp. 260–61: "Mais quant elle fut ou desert, Amour l'emprint, qui l'adnientit, et pource oeuvra adonc Amour en elle pour elle sans elle, et vesquit adonc de divine vie, qui luy fist avoir glorieuse vie. Adonc trouva elle Dieu en elle, sans le querir, et aussi elle n'ot de quoy, puisque Amour l'ot emprinse."

[49] See Ioan Culianu's discussion of the medieval understanding of life as *maesta* in *Eros and Magic in the Renaissance*, trans. M. Cook (Chicago: University of Chicago Press, 1987), 46–52

Martha, busy about many things and thus representative of the active life, and Mary, who represents the contemplative life. Yet she uses this contrast as she uses the themes of courtly love, with a sudden reversal, in this case a reversal of the contemplative piety that saw itself as embodying the life of Mary, the life of contemplation. For *Dame Amour*, what others might call a life of contemplation is only a different form of enslavement to will and works. Such a life is caught up in the pleasure of its own mortification of the body and the pleasure of its own existence contrary to its pleasure. A similar critique is to be found in the writings of Porete's Beguine contemporaries and Meister Eckhart.

An unconventional twist lies beneath Porete's conventional use of the Martha and Mary figures. Similarly, beneath what appears to be a conventional understanding of the Christian Trinity is a truly radical implication. In several places within the *Mirror* she takes up the issue of the Trinity more explicitly and seems to be taking pains to show that her trinitarian position is traditional.[50] These passages on the Trinity from a Beguine with no formal theological training, sensitive as they are, were unlikely to have impressed her inquisitors. The bull *Cum quibusdam mulieribus* shows particular contempt for Beguines who would presume to engage in discussions of the Trinity.

It is in the relationship of the Trinity to the personae of *Dame Amour's* court of love that Porete achieves one of her most far-reaching theological breakthroughs. Porete identifies FarNear with the Trinity both implicitly (when she uses the Trinity and FarNear interchangeably as the agent that works in the freed soul) and explicitly. Her use of triadic formulations for the divine work in the soul (self-seeing, self-knowing, self-loving) could also be interpreted in trinitarian terms. Despite Porete's care to repeat the traditional credal formulations of Trinity, another Trinity appears within the *Mirror*, though it is never named as such, that of *Dame Amour*, FarNear, and the Freed Soul, the three prime actors in the court of love. *Dame Amour* and FarNear are by nature divine and, as mentioned above, are identified with one another. The Freed Soul that is born of the death of the spirit is divine within them, or within their work within her. Heralding the death of Reason, Lady Love announces that the Freed Soul is nothing less than the "daughter of divinity" (*fille de deité*). It is through these three persons (who are yet one) that Porete's reconception of deity within Christianity unfolds, a deity who is gendered male and female and who speaks through the female voice. This voice speaks on the margins

---

[50] See chap. 15 of the *Mirror*, for example, where memory, understanding, and love in the annihilated soul are associated with the Father, the Son, and the Spirit. De Longchamp sees in this trilogy the reflection of Augustinian trinitarian anthropology. Cf. De Longchamp, *Le Miroir*, 242, n. to 9.1. De Longchamp points to chaps. 9, 10, 57, 80, 92, 95 in particular as reflecting the "Augustinian climate" that permeates the *Mirror*.

of institutional theology and its categories of reason, which Dame Amour refers to as "Holy Church the little."

The triad of *Dame Amour*, FarNear, and Freed Soul is not a Trinity in the formal sense; the soul is not divine by nature. As Love declares: "I am God, for love is God and God is love, and this soul is God by condition of Love; I am God by divine nature and this soul is so by right of love, so that this precious friend of mine is taught and led by me without herself for she is transformed into me."[51] Even so, the three persons are placed in a suggestively analogous position to the Trinity of the church fathers. They each have a particular personality and yet are identical with one another as the agent of divine movement and work. The result is a daring vision of a gender balance in the deity.

Mary, Martha, and Mary

In turning to Eckhart, I will approach the issue of divine work in Eckhart by contrasting his notion of the divine work as the "birth of the Son in the soul" as it appears in his discussion of the Martha and Mary story and in his remarkable transformation of the Virgin Birth motif.[52]

Four areas of contemporary feminist thought will help bring into higher relief the gender dynamic within and between Porete and Eckhart's interpretation of Martha, Mary, and the Virgin Birth: (1) the critique of trinitarian theology as a theological archetype for an all male society of "processions";[53] (2) the critique of

---

[51] *Mirouer* 21:44–47, pp. 82–83: "Je suis Dieu, dit Amour, car Amour est Dieu, et Dieu est amour, et ceste Ame est Dieu par condicion d'amour, et je suis Dieu par nature divine, et ceste Ame l'est par droicture d'amour. Si que ceste precieuse amye de moy est aprinse et menee de moy sans elle, car elle est muee en moy."

[52] Elsewhere, I take a deliberately minimalist approach to using uppercase in connection with terms like "Son," "Father," "Daughter" when used in connection with the deity. For the sake of the stylistic coherence of this volume, I have used the more traditional uppercase. For a discussion of the hermeneutical issues and dilemmas entailed by this uppercase convention when dealing with classical texts which lacked an uppercase/lowercase distinction, see M. Sells, "Remarks," in *Mystical Union and Monotheistic Faith*, 163–73, and *Mystical Languages of Unsaying*, "Introduction."

[53] Mary Daly, *Gyn/Ecology: The Metaethics of Radical Feminism* (Boston: Beacon Press, 1978) 37–38. This naming of "the three Divine Persons" is the paradigmatic model for the pseudogeneric term"person," excluding all female mythic presence and denying female reality in the cosmos. For Daly, these male processions are an active principle for patriarchal "possessing" of women, and the alleged "feminity" of the Holy Spirit is not authentic. The theological is reflected in the social. As a prologue to her discussion of trinitarian processions, Daly cites the following passage from Virginia Woolf's *Three Guineas*: "There it is, then, before our eyes, the procession of the sons of educated men, ascending those pulpits, mounting those steps, passing in and out of those doors, preaching, teaching, administering justice, practicing

conventional Christian symbolism of the Virgin Mary as a religious paradigm for the passive, subservient female;[54] (3) the recent critical attention given to the association in many medieval Christian writings, of woman, nature, fall, and sexuality; and most importantly (4) the critique of the Martha and Mary story in the *Gospel of Luke* and its use within Christianity as a paradigm for spiritual choices. According to Luke 10:38–42:

> Now as they went on their way, he entered a village and a woman named Martha received him into her house. She had a sister called Mary who sat at the Lord's feet and listened to his teaching [*ton logon autou*]. But Martha was distracted with much serving [*diakoinian*]; and she went to him and said: "Lord, do you not care that my sister has left me to serve alone. Tell her to help me." But the Lord answered her: "Martha, Martha, you are anxious and troubled about many things; one thing is needful. Mary has chosen the good portion, which shall not be taken away from her" [Luke 10:38–42].

Elizabeth Schüssler-Fiorenza has interpreted the Lucan Martha-Mary account as a later reaction (by the author of Luke) against the active role of women in the primitive church. For Fiorenza, the story puts woman against woman in competition for the approval of a male authority, and places women within roles easily controlled and defined by the male authority. A history of interpretation finds the story engendering four hierarchical polarities: abstractionist (Martha and Mary as abstract principles—works versus faith; Judaism versus Christianity; worldly

---

medicine, making money." As with apophasis, Daly's language is as notable for how it works as it is for what it says, and this paraphrase cannot possibly do justice to the manner in which Daly turns words against the embedded mythopoetic meanings she considers to be controlled by patriarchal myth makers and myth stealers. Daly relates processional theology to what she sees as the central episode in the feminist account of Christianity: the witch burnings that took place from the mid-fifteenth century until the seventeenth. These burnings are viewed as a foundational event for modern language, institutions, and cultures, a hidden atrocity still silencing women through its inscription within the fabric of culture, and through its covering over of its own traces. The covering over of the intensity, extent, and true horror of the witch burnings is one more aspect of the witch burnings themselves.

[54] Daly, *Gyn/Ecology*, 82, gives a compelling analysis of this subject. She begins by stating that "It should not be imagined that Mary had any real role in this conception and birth." Daly then goes on to discuss the critiques of Helen Diner and Anne Dellenbaugh which focus on the the Virgin Mary's passivity. For Diner, the virgin birth is opposite of parthenogenesis, because "Mary does nothing, whereas in parthenogensis the female accomplishes everything herself." Dellenbaugh discusses the myth as stripping women of their integrity, portraying the female as a mere "hollow eggshell." For Daly, the Virgin Mary is a symbol of the tamed goddess whose creativity and power have been appropriated and taken over by the patriarchal domination of Christian myth.

versus spiritual; this world versus the world to come; active versus contemplative); nonabstractionist (good woman versus bad woman, woman serving God versus woman serving man; nun versus housewife); apologetic feminist (Jesus' supposed acceptance of a contemplative and scholarly role for women as opposed to the alleged rabbinic rejection of the same); and psychological (sibling rivalry and sexual rivalry, in which women are defined by the relation to men). In each of the four, hierarchical structures predominate. Mary, who sat and listened in apparent silence, is praised. The outspoken Martha is put in her place.[55]

Eckhart's unsaying of the monotonically male "He-God" begins, as is often the case with apophatic discourse, at the semantic microlevel; in this case with the preposition "in" of "in the soul." A theology in which a series of processions descend from the divine source to fill the emptied, passive soul (figured as feminine), would be yet another example of androcentric discourse—with its movement of male processions into a passive receptacle figured as feminine. Yet the receptacle paradigm is undone with the transformation of "in the soul."[56] The "in" also refers to the principle that what proceeds, insofar as it remains "in" its principle, is equal to and identical to that principle. At the moment of mystical union, the "in" refers not to the descent of a procession into a lower vessel, but rather to the higher reality of something "in" its principle. A look at the transformations of the spatial senses of "in" within the metaphor of emanation and return will demonstrate one precise and creative moment of conversation between the vernacular theology exemplified by Porete and Eckhart's *Predigten*, and the Latin theology of Eckhart's *Commentary on John*.

In the *Commentary on John*, the notion of "in its principle" is explicated in connection with the opening of John: "In the beginning/principle (*in principio*) was

---

[55] Elizabeth Schüssler-Fiorenza, "A Feminist Critical Interpretation for Liberation: Martha and Mary: Luke 10: 38–42," *Religion and Intellectual Life* 3 (1986): 21–35. Fiorenza's constructive hermeneutics reads Luke's story as a reaction against the role of women's service (*diakoinia*) within pre-Lukan "housechurches"—a role that combined service and proclamation within the eucharistic setting.

[56] Eckhart's trinitarian, processional theology could be viewed as a reaction against the rich gender dynamic among *Dame Amour*, FarNear, and the annihilated soul. Eckhart was capable of statements that reflected the very associations inverted by Porete in her "fall of love." At the end of Pr. 20b, Eckhart compares the soul to a man when it is gazing upward toward the deity, and to a woman when it turns down to the world. This statement contrasts of course with the equality between male and female asserted by Eckhart in Pr. 6 as well as in Pr. 27. By placing the "work" of the divine within the language of trinitarian processions rather than that of Lady Love and FarNear, Eckhart may be thought to risk losing that dynamic. Eckhart's language at times seems to dwell obsessively on the "fatherly heart." A central danger in Eckhart's birth imagery would be that it represents yet another appropriation by the male power (in this case the deity) of female power and creativity. However, the movement toward the domination of the male gender in the deity occurs (almost as a reflex) in contexts where, on the mythic and theological level, the univocal maleness of the deity is most radically undone.

the Word." In his Latin works, Eckhart uses the emanation metaphor with two distinctive images of his own. In *bullitio* (boiling over), what proceeds remains within its principle. This paradoxical emanation (flowing out) which yet remains within is the world of trinitarian relations. In *ebullitio* (boiling over or out) what proceeds is outside (*extrinsecus*) its principle. The "within" and "without" emanation language is then directly tied to semantics. That which remains in its principle is in univocal relations with it, equal to it, and—in Eckhart's radical reading of the unity of nature in trinitarian theology—identical with it. What flows out of its principle is in equivocal or analogical relations with its principle. If the principle is life, being, and justice, it cannot be described as having life, being, or justice. If it is described as life, then its principle must be beyond life.

The principle of trinitarian relations is given a double paradigm by Eckhart. On the one hand it is the Father as the source of the Son. But, given the fact that the Son is identical to the Father (that they are the same thing, *unum*, although not the same person, *unus*), then the Father begets himself in begetting his Son. Also, in correlative terms, there cannot be a father without a son. Thus, the principle is the Godhead or ground of deity beyond all trinitarian relations.

Eckhart radicalizes trinitarian language by reading back the difference in persons through the identity in nature. He also integrates the male metaphor of "begetting" into the metaphor of birth, viewing trinitarian, univocal relationships as a self-birth (*parturitio sui*). The introduction of the female metaphor of birth into the Trinity will be the foundation upon which Eckhart's language will unsay the essentialized and gender-monotonic "He-God."

This notion of "in" as the basis for the reversions of the various hierarchical strata backs up into a point of absolute equality. The concept of "inness" is the principle whereby the existence of something "in its principle," leads to its existence in the transcendent beyond-essence. At the moment of the birth of the Son in the soul, however, the "in" of "in the soul" is revealed to be the same as the "in" of "in the principle." The procession (emanation of the Son into the soul) is the return. For the deity, as Eckhart states strongly, does not give birth to itself in the soul as a place, or locus, or receptacle: it becomes the place of its own self-birth, its own "work."[57] In other words, the self-birth takes place really within the ground of the soul which is identical to the ground of the deity, that primal source of reality, naked-being, nothingness. When the soul becomes "equal to nothing" then the

---

[57] See the detailed discussion of Eckhart's "reading" back of difference of persons into union of nature, his transformation of the meaning of "in," and the apophatic significance of that transformation in chap. 6 of *Mystical Languages of Unsaying*, and in Michael Sells, "Emanation and Mysticism in the Writings of Meister Eckhart," *Listening: Journal of Religion and Culture (Eckhart Issue)* (1994), ed. Michael Demkovic, O.P..

divine gives itself to it; but by becoming "equal to nothing" the soul has reverted to
the nothingness of the ground of reality. This is the paradox of *bullitio*, the bubbling
out of, in and into itself into which the virgin soul is taken up (*assumptam*). This
"assumption" then is not the "assumption" of a passive Mary, nor is it the
"assumption" of human nature by a salvificatory male, but rather a theological
inversion in which the virgin soul becomes the ground and source of the one real
work that always has occurred and always is occurring. At this point, the virgin soul,
the Virgin Mary, has a real role in the birth of the deity. She is revealed to be the
mother of God in a literal sense, rather than the "catatonic" virgin[58] whose
motherhood of God is so often treated as a kind of purely formal honor.

The unsaying of the gender monotony of deity is grounded in the metaphor
of birth and self-birth that is implicated in turn in the transformation of the
meaning of "in-ness." By translating the language of procession into a paradigm of
self-birth, Eckhart displaces the male autogenesis that can be read in other examples
of processional and generational theology. The deity is both a self-birth and a self-
genesis. Birthing becomes the central event in divine and cosmic history. When the
Son is born in the soul, and the soul is taken up through that birth into equal
relations, or to use the alternate paradigm, when the soul becomes "equal to
nothing" and the Son is thereby born "in" the nothingness that is the ground of
reality—at that moment the gender components of deity become fluid. The soul is
the mother of deity and gives birth to it, but is also equal to (and identical to) the
Son and therefore the Father in the process. Eckhart does not stress the feminine
components of the Trinity here in explicit terms; he remains faithful to traditional
language in his formulations. But his paradigm of self-birth transforms the
traditional gender paradigms from within.

The gender implications of Eckhart's apophatic writings can be found most
clearly in his *Predigt* 2, which begins, fittingly, with the Martha and Mary story:
"Jesus entered into a certain little town and a certain woman, Martha by name, took
him up into her home." (*Intravit Jesus in quoddam castellum et mulier quaedam,
Martha nomine, excepit illum in domum suam.*) Eckhart rephrases this citation in
German as: "Our master Jesus Christ went up into a little castle and was received by
a *virgin who was a wife* [emphasis added]."[59] Through this verbal and translation
play, Martha becomes the symbol for the virgin wife and for the mystical
reconception of the virgin birth. The reconception is signaled by two expressions in
the German rewording of the Latin text on Martha and Mary. The first expression

[58] "Catatonic" is Mary Daly's term from *Gyn/Ecology*.

[59] Pr. 2, DW 1: 24: "Unser herre Jêsus Kristus der gienc ûf in ein bürgelîn und wart enpfangen
von einer juncvrouwen, diu ein wîp was."

is "up in" (*ûf in*) which alludes to transformation of "inness" and the paradox that the procession is the return, discussed above as central to Eckhart's apophasis of gender. The second expression is the term (*enfangen*) which Eckhart used to translate the Latin *excepit*, a term that can mean both receive and conceive, and paves the way for Eckhart's discussion of the wife who gives birth.[60]

The explication of the virgin who was a wife begins with the figuring of virgin as lacking all images. There is a further wordplay; the term for free, *ledic*, also means unattached in the sense of unmarried: "Now then, pay close attention to this word: it was necessarily by a virgin that Jesus was received/conceived. 'Virgin' designates a person who is free of all foreign images, as free as he was when he was not yet."[61] Switching to the first person, the voice in the sermon speaks of being as free of images "as I was when I was not"—the familiar theme of reversion to the precreated state.[62] Eckhart is combining both intellect and will in his notion of foreign images. By refusing all foreign images and all attachment to images, the soul is free and virginal. At this point the soul is ready to receive the impression, which in this sermon is compared to the fruit which the soul bears. The analogy of "bearing" evokes the birth-of-the-Son-in-the-soul. The sermon then moves on into the birth-of-the-Son-in-the-soul passage, a passage in which the birth takes place in an eternal moment that must be reenacted in each new moment in time. The passage is constructed around an opposition between "spouses" who give birth only every year and a "wife" who is perpetually giving birth each new moment. "Spouses" are defined as those who carry out their own work with *eigenschaft*. I have translated *eigenschaft* as "attachment," but it also connotes "possessiveness" and "self [*eigen*] regard." In more abstract philosophical terms, *eigenschaft* denotes a quality or property of a thing, and Eckhart is playing upon that sense as well. Later in the same sermon, he will speak of the spark of the soul. The deity, in order to see the spark, must give up his *eigenschaft*, its attachment to and its quality of persons.[63] Those who are attached are those who still have their own qualities; they have not yet become nothing. Such attachment takes a period of time before it can bear fruit,

---

[60] The play on *enpfangen* was noted in Colledge and McGinn, *Meister Eckhart*, 335, nn. 2, 3, and 4.

[61] Pr. 2, DW 1: 24–25: "Eyâ, nû merket mit vlîze diz wort: ez muoz von nôt sîn, daz si ein juncvrouwe was, der mensche, von der Jêsus wart enpfangen. Juncvrouwe ist alsô vil gesprochen als ein mensche, der von allen vremden bilden ledic ist, alsô ledic, als er was, dô er niht enwas."

[62] Pr. 2, DW 1: 26.

[63] Pr. 2, DW 1: 43: "Got selber luoget dâ niemer în einen ougenblik und geluogete noch nie dar în, als verre als er sich habende ist nâch wîse und ûf eigenschaft sîner persônen."

a period Eckhart calls "a year." By contrast, those who are free are said to be—in a
phrase that recalls the "willing nothing, having nothing, knowing nothing" of
Eckhart's sermon on the poor in spirit (Pr. 52)—those who have, will, and can (do)
nothing other than what the divine wills for them in each new moment.

> Any attachment to any work that takes from you the freedom to wait upon
> God in this present now [*disem gegenwertigen nû*] and to follow him alone
> in the light in which he informs you what to do and what to let be, in each
> now free and new [*in einem ieglîchen nû vrî und niuwe*], as if you possessed,
> desired, and were capable of nothing else. Such an attachment and every
> premeditated work [*vürgesetzet werk*] which takes from you this freedom
> that is new in each moment [*alle zît niuwe*], I now call a year.[64]

The sermon then turns in apostrophe to the reader (or hearer) in order to
delineate the consequences of such attachment. To live in long periods (with
attachment to a particular work or image) is contrasted with the giving up of works
and images in a kind of perpetual birth and rebirth in every moment.

> Your soul brings forth no fruit until it has accomplished the work to which
> you were attached. You trust neither God nor yourself, until you have
> carried out the work that you have seized upon with attachment; otherwise
> you have no peace. So you bear no fruit unless you complete your work. I
> consider this a "year" and even then the fruit is small, for it comes from
> attachment to the work and not from freedom. I call such people spouses
> [*êlîche liute*] because they are bound to attachment.[65]

The text goes on to discuss the *wip* that gives birth in each moment. The term *wip*
(wife, woman) was often used disparagingly, and by choosing it, Eckhart is
validating both the role of giving birth (disparaged by a certain trend in virginal
Christian piety) and the social role of the woman likely to be called a *wip*. This

---

[64] Pr. 2, DW 1: 28–29: "Ein ieglîchiu eigenschaft eines ieglîchen werkes, daz die vrîheit
benimet, in disem gegenwertigen nû gote ze wartenne und dem aleine ze volgenne in dem
liehte, mit dem er dich anwîsende waere ze tuonne und ze lâzenne in einem ieglîchen nû vrî
und niuwe, als ob dû anders niht enhabest noch enwellest noch enkünnest, ein ieglîchiu
eigenschaft oder vürgesetzet werk, daz dir dise vrîheit benimet alle zît niuwe, daz heize ich nû
ein jâr."

[65] Pr. 2, DW 1: 29: "Wan dîn sêle bringet dekeine vruht, se enhabe daz werke getân, daz dû
mit eigenschaft besezzen hâst, noch dû engetriuwest gote noch dir selber, dû enhabest dîn werk
volbrâht, daz dû mit eigenschaft begriffen hâst; anders sô enhâst dû dekeinen vride. Dar umbe
sô enbringest dû ouch dekeine vruht, dû enhabest dîn werk getân. Daz setze ich vür ein jâr,
und diu vruht ist nochdenne kleine, wan si ûz eigenschaft gegangen ist nâch dem werke und
niht von vrîheit. Dise heize ich êlîche liute, wan sie an eigenschaft gebunden stânt. Dise
bringent lützel vrüte, und diu selbe ist nochdenne kleine, als ich gesprochen hân."

short passage applies all the major elements of Eckhartian apophasis to the gender dynamic. The virgin who is a wife is "equally close" (*glîche nâhe*) to God and herself, and the dialectic of equality, distinction, and indistinction (those who are equal to nothing, are equal to all) is evoked. This virgin who is a wife is bearing forth fruit in each moment, neither more nor less than God, and the notion of eternity as the birth that always has occurred and always is occurring is evoked. In its specific language, in which the virgin who is a wife bears "a hundred or thousand times a day" the sermon gives a direct response to tradition, extending from Jerome to Augustine to Aquinas, that places the virgin over, against, and above the wife. Aquinas, in his affirmation of the superiority of virginity to other forms of chastity, had offered a succinct summary of that tradition:

> Jerome attributes a hundredfold fruit to virginity, on account of its superiority to [the chastity] of widowhood, to which he attributes sixty-fold; and to that of matrimony, to which he attributes thirty-fold. However according to Augustine, a hundred-fold fruit is for martyrs, sixty-fold for virgins, and thirty-fold for spouses.[66]

For Eckhart, the virgin who is a wife bears a hundred or thousand times daily and bears forth the only begotten Son from the noblest ground of all (*ûz dem aller edelsten grund*). Here the dialectic of nobility and equality, the noble and the common, is evoked.

> A virgin who is a wife is free and unbound with attachment is at all times equally close to God and herself. She bears much fruit, which is great, neither more nor less than Godself. This virgin who is a wife brings about this fruit and this birth, and brings forth fruit, a hundred or a thousand times a day, countless fruit, giving birth and by becoming fruitful from the most noble ground of all. To say it even better: from the same ground from which the Father is bearing his Eternal Word, she is fruitfully bearing with him.[67]

The virgin who gives birth to the Son of God is clearly to be identified with the Virgin Mary—what other virgin birth of the Son of God occurs in Christian

---

[66] Aquinas, *Summa Theologiae*, 2a2ae. 152, 5 (Blackfriars edition), 186, translation mine.

[67] Pr. 2, DW 1: 30–31: "Ein juncvrouwe, diu ein wîp ist, diu ist vrî und ungebunden âne eigenschaft, diu ist gote und ir selber alle zît glîch nâhe. Diu bringet vil vrüte und die sint grôz, minner noch mêr dan got selber ist. Dise vruht und dise geburt machet disiu juncvrouwe, diu ein wîp ist, geborn und bringet alle tage hundert mâl oder tûsent mâl vruht joch âne zal gebernde und vruhtbaere werdende ûz dem aller edelsten grunde; noch baz gesprochen: jâ ûz dem selben grunde, dâ der vater ûz gebernde ist sîn êwic wort, dar ûz wirt si vruhtbaere mitgebernde." Immediately after this extraordinary passage the sermon, almost as a reflex, turns to a continual repetition of the words "father" and "fatherly heart."

tradition? However, any soul, of male or female, that is empty of attachment to its own images and desires is the virgin that gives birth to the Son.

Eckhart does not evoke the name of the Virgin Mary at this point. Instead, his reinterpretation of the Virgin Mary as the actual source or ground of the deity—in most radical, literal sense—is superimposed here upon his inversion of the standard interpretation of the Martha and Mary story. That reinterpretation was effected through the subtle play upon the translation of the sermon's introductory quote from the Martha and Mary account in which "going up to a little town" was rephrased as being "received by a virgin who was a wife." Contemplation, as figured by the empty, silent, virgin soul, is no longer placed above activity (as figured by the wife who gives birth). The silent Mary is no longer put above the silenced Martha. Martha is now the prototype of the virgin who is a wife, the *wip*, who represents the fullest life (for male or female), or life itself, as birth (and self-birth) in every moment. Contemplation and proclamation are part of the same moment, as dialectically linked as are letting go and giving birth. The just act is the birth of the Son in the soul, the only just act that ever has occurred and ever is occurring. The contemplative and the active are fused into the one eternal work and birth that always has occurred and always is occurring. Mystical union is not an experience of the extraordinary, it is a new vision of the ordinary—the most humble act of justice, insofar as it is just, is nothing other than the birth of the "only begotten" Son of God. It is not a one-time experience, but a work that must be realized anew in each moment.

At the end of *Intravit Jesus*, the virgin soul and virgin wife are identified once again with the virgin/wife who received/conceived (*enfangen*) Jesus into her little town (*bürgelîn*). In that little castle, God is "blooming and growing as he is in himself." He is bringing to birth his only begotten Son as truly as in himself. In that little town, "God is gleaming and shining with all his richness."[68] The "in" is transformed from an indication of containment to an indication of the existence of something in its principle. Again we see the androcentric grammar and vocabulary (where God gives birth to Himself) is countered by the gender dynamic operative on this mythic level where the little town and the virgin who is a wife are revealed as the (groundless) ground of reality and the Mother of Deity.

The "Pseudo-Woman" and the Meister

From what we know, Porete had no formal training in theology and was considered unqualified to engage in theological discussion, while Meister Eckhart was placed in the prototypical position of patriarchal authority as spiritual and intellectual

[68] See Pr. 2, DW 1: 42.

guardian of women. He was an intellectual champion of the Dominicans, sent by them to Paris to do battle with the Franciscan Gonsalvo. His honorific, "Meister," became so attached to him that we do not even know for certain what his given Christian name was. He was placed in a position of authority over nuns and other women; yet both the nature of his sermons and the history of their transmission suggest that rather than controlling the powerful currents of women's spirituality, he was part of them. After his death, many of his sermons were passed on in an oral tradition by nuns and Beguines. Eckhart was a preacher and many in his audience would have been nuns or Beguines. Yet instead of telling them "how" they should live, his sermons subverted the question of "how to live" by turning to a discourse of living "without a how" or "without a why," without a *dar umbe*. When his sermons reach the point of "without a why" they collapse the hierarchical structure from which the preacher gains his teaching authority. When Eckhart uses the expression "a master says," this collapse of hierarchy into radical equality is signalled by the transfiguration of the monolithic voice of the "Meister" into a continual conversation in which each statement of a Meister is subject to an apophatic turn by the statement of another meister: "Now we say." At other key points, the voice of the preacher is transformed into the voice of the just person insofar as he or she is just. This transformation echoes and validates key themes (nakedness of the soul, abandonment of words and will, the word of the deity in the soul, the dialectic of nothingness and everything, the reversion or precreation, living without a why) of the great women mystics (Mechthild, Hadewijch, Beatrice, Hadewijch II, Porete) even as it links them, in often revolutionary ways, to the classical traditions of Neo-Platonic mysticism and Christian trinitarian theology.[69]

When viewed from the perspective of the four feminist critiques listed above, the achievement of Porete and Eckhart's apophatic discourse becomes clearer. Porete's court of love, while offering homage to the traditional Trinity, in effect displaces it with a new divine triad (*Dame Amour*, FarNear, the Annihilated Soul) whose interactions form the central cosmic, religious, and literary dynamic of the *Mirror*. The gender dynamic in the *Mirror* is distinctive in several areas. The deity is given a thoroughly interactive gender configuration in terms of *Dame Amour*, FarNear, and the Annihilated Soul. The divine speaker, *Dame Amour*, is feminine. The tradition of courtly love is reconfigured. Common medieval notions of the fall, woman, nature and sexuality are inverted in the figuring of the last stages of mystical ascent as a "fall of love."

---

[69] Eckhart's use of "a master says . . . but now I say" in reference to his own previous pronouncements in order to destabilize his position as authoritative master, and his turning the sermon into an ironic counter-sermon are discussed in detail in chap. 6 of *Mystical Languages of Unsaying*.

By placing virginity above the married, Mary above Martha, Porete had adopted the standard hierarchical paradigm of medieval piety that is the object of feminist critique. Yet by incorporating this paradigm into the mythos of courtly love, she also subverts that paradigm. While Mary is praised by Luke's Jesus for sitting at his feet and listening—in contrast to the outspoken Martha—in the court of *Dame Amour* it is for the most part females who speak. FarNear, the only major male character in the drama, is silent. The tension between the ideal of the silent Mary and the court of outspoken women is reflected in Porete's ambivalence about her own status as author. She refers to her act of writing the *Mirror* as the "work" of a poor begging creature and as an "encumbrance." Yet she also suggests that the work may be nothing other than the reflection of the annihilated soul, in which case it would be the work of the divine within the annihilated soul. However we interpret the *Mirror*'s complex portrayal of Porete as author, within her life her position is clear. It was her unbreakable resolve to continue writing and circulating her book that led to her execution at the stake.

From the perspective of this conversation between Porete and Eckhart, it would seem futile to try to rank them. Porete's apophasis of desire and the mysticism of love finds a perfect complement in Eckhart's mysticism of birth. In appropriating, combining, and inverting the mythos of courtly love and the paradigms of Martha, Mary, and the Virgin Mary, Porete may have also run up against the limitations within traditional understandings of those paradigms. Yet she succeeded in creating a court of love with an exceptionally rich gender dynamic within the divine, within the human, and between the divine and human. She figured the deity in terms of both male and female, and she figured the voice of the deity as feminine. In her passages on the "fall of love" she enacted an inversion of the themes (interlinked in medieval Christianity) of fall, femininity, nature, and desire. And by making the Divine Lover dependent upon the annihilated soul (he cannot have back what he has given except at her pleasure), she achieves a sense of mutual interdependence that transcends the original metaphor associating the naked soul with pure receptivity.[70] Eckhart's gender dynamic is less explicit. Yet in its revolutionary

---

[70] Margaret Miles has said the following about the "naked soul" metaphor: "Similarly, in the fourteenth-century mystical tradition founded by Meister Eckhart and carried to Martin Luther by Tauler and Suso, nudity received the less literal interpretation of the soul's divestment of cares, attachments, and ideas in order to expose the 'core of the soul' where God is to be found. Ironically, the soul, departing from the body at death, was painted as a tiny, colorless naked body, carried to heaven in a napkin by angels. " See M. Miles, *Carnal Knowing: Female Nakedness and Religious Meaning in the Christian West* (Boston: Beacon Press, 1989), xiii–xiv. This statement attributes to Eckhart the metaphor of the naked soul, without ever even mentioning the Beguine tradition (from Mechthild to Hadewijch, Hadewijch II, and Porete) in which that metaphor was developed. Eckhart uses the metaphor, but his notion of mystical

reinterpretation of the Virgin Birth (as occurring in the ground of any soul—male or female—which is the ground of God), inversion of the Martha and Mary paradigm, and refiguring of trinitarian processions in terms of birth and self-birth, Eckhart's apophatic discourse stands beside that of Porete as a radical reconception of gender in divine and human realms. His validation of birth and his emphasis upon the fruitful *wip* (wife) breaks with a tradition of associating birth with the fall and sin of Eve. It also collapses the hierarchy that places contemplation in opposition to, and over works; contemplation and works are united in the one genuine work, the birth of the Son.

Porete's writings and her life as a Beguine (neither clergy nor lay, neither married nor in a convent) threatened established social, intellectual, and theological boundaries and acquired for her the inquisitorial epithet of "pseudo-woman." Eckhart , as a Dominican "Meister," was placed in a position of administrative and theological control over nuns and other women, but rather than controlling the powerful currents of late thirteenth-century women's spirituality, he joined them.

But the gender roles that Porete and Eckhart challenged were not only the gender roles as defined at their own time. Contemporary historians have also attempted to define gender roles for medieval authors: how medieval "women" and "men" wrote. Caroline Walker Bynum argues, for example, against the view that medieval women either interiorized misogynistic categories and formed themselves upon them, or attempted an inversion of such categories. Yet, alongside her call to pay attention to the complexity of gender in medieval life, she has felt comfortable in establishing clear-cut categories for male and female writers. Only a few key categories can be cited here. Male writers view the issue of motherhood in terms of authority and as a counterbalance to the severity of fatherly judgment. They value the mind over the body. Female writers are less inclined to put motherhood in opposition to the authority and judgment of fatherhood. And of course, the imagery of female writers is dominated by images of corporality, sensuality,

---

union is based more on the notion of virginity and virgin birth than upon the erotic and sexual imagery in which the "nakedness of the soul" metaphor was used by the Beguines. In the Beguine writings, the nakedness of the soul is at the center of a wide range of related motifs: self-abandon, loss of discretion, ravishment. The statement that the soul was painted "as a tiny, colorless naked body, carried to heaven on a napkin"—without any specification of those who painted the soul in that way—is hardly a fair representation of this central theme from Beguine literature. The image in Porete and Eckhart has little to do with being carried to heaven on a napkin. With both writers, the naked soul image entails an abandonment of attaining heaven and avoiding hell as a religious goal. With Porete, the image entails a reappropriation and valorization of what had been negatively associated with women, the fall, nature, and sexuality. With Eckhart, it is partially subservient to his reinterpretation of virginity and virgin birth and his placement of the birth metaphor within the Trinity.

nurturing, and food, with the Eucharist as the prime symbol of mystical union.[71] There is historical fact behind these generalizations. Yet they exclude writers such as Porete and Eckhart and the large movement they represented.

Bynum gives the following explanations for her selection of "male writers" and "female writers": "With the predictable and fascinating exception of the 'heretic' Marguerite Porete, all thirteenth-century women who wrote at length on spiritual matters emphasize the Eucharist."[72] Later in the same work, she says:

> To demonstrate the difference in male and female perspectives, I shall explore a variety of female images in late medieval spiritual writing, taking care to locate the particular images in the clusters of other images among which they appear. So as not to prejudice my conclusions by my initial choice of texts, I shall compare those male and female writers who are, on the surface, most similar. After all, to compare the university-trained Thomas Aquinas or Meister Eckhart with a virtually illiterate Italian nun or tertiary would reveal differences in educational background and philosophical sources so vast that differences owning to gender or social experience could never be determined. Not only do I limit myself to comparable genres by male and female authors (vision collections, saints' lives and devotional texts); I also limit myself to those male writers whose spirituality is most "affective"—that is, to those male writers who, in style of religious life and style of devotion, came closes to the piety of twelfth, thirteenth, and fouteenth-century women. I concentrate here therefore on men such as Bernard of Clairvaux, Francis of Assisi, Richard Rolle, and Henry Suso, whose spirituality has been called "emotional," "lyrical" and "nuptial," and on men such as Thomas of Cantimpré, James of Vitry and John Tauler, who cultivated and were influenced by female followers.[73]

These criteria for selection raise several questions. While Eckhart was "university trained" (thus in the excluded category), he is perhaps the prime medieval example of a male mystic who cultivated and was influenced by female followers (and thus should be in the included category). Indeed, not only did

---

[71] See Caroline Walker Bynum, ". . . And Woman His Humanity: Female Imagery in the Religious Writing of the Later Middle Ages," in Bynum, S. Harrel, and P. Richman, eds., *Religion: On the Complexity of Symbols* (Boston: Beacon Press, 1986), 257–88. Cf. Bynum, *Holy Feast and Holy Fast* (University of California Press, 1986); and *Jesus as Mother: Studies in the Spirituality of the High Middle Ages* (1982).

[72] See Bynum, *Fragmentation and Redemption: Essays on Gender and the Human Body in Medieval Religion* (New York: Zone Books, 1992), 24.

[73] Bynum, *Fragmentation*, 157.

Eckhart spend much of his career speaking with women and in positions explicitly dealing with women, many of his sermons were memorized by women followers and passed on through a largely female oral tradition. The sermons themselves are highly colloquial—indeed in his vernacular sermons Eckhart communicated more directly to the "virtually illiterate" nun or tertiary than did Bernard of Clairvaux in his Latin writings. And although Porete, in Bynum's terms, may have been a "heretic," she had a large following not only in her own time, but down through the centuries, as her work was translated in various languages and circulated in medieval Christian life. Porete and Eckhart represented and culminated major movements of thought and writing, and in women's spirituality (much of Eckhart's audience consisted of women, and women were central in carrying on the Eckhartian tradition after his confirmation). These movements were contained (though never extinguished) only with the sustained and massive apparatus of inquisitorial repression. By excluding them, on the grounds that they were "heretics" or on the mistaken assumption that Porete was a totally isolated figure without followers and Eckhart a university trained scholastic writing for the intelligentsia or elite, we risk ratifying the roles of male and female writer that were prescribed by the inquisition.

From the apophatic perspective, authorial protestations that the named God is not bound in space and time are impotent in the face of the power of language and the implicit temporal, spatial, and substantialist categories created within it. Similarly, from the apophatic perspective on gender, protestations that expressions such as "male writers" and "female writers" are not meant to essentialize gender difference are ineffective against the power of the language used. Porete and Eckhart's breaking out of gender roles—as radical a break as is likely to be found in western Christianity—took place within an apophatic discourse that can never rest secure. Just as the nonsubstantialist and unnamed is continually reified and deified into the distinction between God and "God," so gender constructions are continually being essentialized. Similarly, our recognition of historical and social gender boundaries and simultaneous effort to transcend those boundaries—to prevent ourselves from living out monotonic essentialist categories as "male writers" and "female writers"— requires a continual movement of unsaying.[74]

[74] Tobin, in *Meister Eckhart*, 195, n. 33, criticizes the use of the term "feminist" in connection with Eckhart and points out Matthew Fox did not provide an argument to demonstrate his claim that Eckhart was influenced by the Beguines. Cf. Matthew Fox: *Breakthrough: Meister Eckhart's Creation Spirituality in New Translation* (New York: Image Books, 1980), 35–40. While it may be anachronistic to project back a term like "feminist" upon medieval writers, the apophatic gender dynamic outlined above suggests that it is equally dangerous to view the medieval period as a monolithic whole, to underestimate the power and the rigor of its dissenters, and the manner in which they may have addressed concerns that are still very much with us today.

Marguerite Porete was referred to as a "pseudo-woman" (*pseudomulier*) in the inquisition documents. She clearly did not fit the inquisitorially validated categories of "female writer." Meister Eckhart was referred to in the inquisitorial documents as "a certain Eckhart" (*quisdam Echardus*), in a literary disinvestiture of his status as a master. Among the charges brought against Eckhart was his defense of Beguine women mystics and the influence they had upon his thought. After Eckhart's condemnation, many of his vernacular sermons were passed on orally, by women.

We may never know whether Porete and Eckhart ever met one another, conversed in person, or read firsthand one another's works. In many ways, it really does not matter. For it is clear that what occurs between the works of Eckhart and those of Porete is a sustained and intricate *conversatio* between the Beguine tradition of vernacular theology that in some ways culminated with Porete and the formal traditions (Neo-Platonism, scholasticism) that reached another sort of culmination with Eckhart. Neither the vernacular with Porete nor the formal with Eckhart are pure; each is already imbued with the other form. At this delicate moment of intersection between the vernacular and the formal, Porete and Eckhart achieved then a three-fold unsaying of essentialism (perhaps as far-reaching as any in the history of western thought): the unsaying of the essentialist God, the unsaying of the monogendered deity and the monotonic gender relation between deity and human, and an unsaying of proscribed roles, always in danger of being essentialized, for "male writers" and "female writers."[75]

This essay, building upon the previous comparisons, has emphasized the depth and range of affinity between between Beguine writings, especially the *Mirror* and Eckhart's work. This affinity is not dependent upon any direct textual influence or upon any personal relationship between the two writers. The resonances between the two sets of writings would be just as profound in the unlikely event that Eckhart had never read or heard any of Porete's ideas. Eckhart and Porete were each taking part in a cultural revival in which "influence" could move by more subtle and supple channels than direct textual transmission or personal acquaintance.

[75] Recent writers have commented—some more sympathetically than others—on Bynum's ease with a gender "essentialism" which would tie the biological sex of the author to a particular mode of writing. See Elizabeth Robertson, "Medieval Medical Views of Women and Female Spirituality in the *Ancrene Wisse* and Julian of Norwich's *Showings*," in Linda Lomperis and Sarah Stanbury, eds., *Feminist Approaches to the Body in Medieval Literature* (Philadelphia: University of Pennsylvania Press, 1993), 163, n. 1: "I shall only say here that Bynum and I differ in general in that she seems to wish to soften the misogyny that informs medieval female mystical experience whereas I wish to explore it, and that Bynum seems more comfortable with essentialist views of women than am I."

Conclusion

Women and Men in the Development of Late Medieval Mysticism

Richard Woods, O.P.

E ach of the preceding essays illuminates one or more of the variegated dimensions of shifting paradigms of gender-relationships in the Middle Ages and, by implication, today. For the deeper psychological and spiritual issues underlying current conflicts between the sexes, at least in the Northern Hemisphere, are largely medieval in provenance, including matters of courtship and marital bonding, clerical misogyny, and the interpretation of "traditional" gender roles as a whole.[1]

The emergence of outstanding female figures in the church and the wider religious world surrounding it in the later Medieval Period was not the only factor contributing to a startling redefinition of relations between women and men at that time and since, but it was undoubtedly a crucial factor, perhaps even the major one.

The resulting compass of relationships between individual women and men is wide. It ranges from tender, supportive friendships such as those (among others) of Sts. Clare and Francis of Assisi; St. Dominic and a host of women, including the girls and women he plucked from prostitution to inaugurate his Order; Henry Suso and Elsbet Stagl; and Richard Rolle and Margaret Kirkby; to more vexed matters such as those between Abelard and Heloise; and eventually to severe, sometimes abusive relationships such as that between St. Elizabeth of Hungary and her spiritual director, Conrad von Marburg. The social tension between the genders was realized within the church especially in the decades-long struggles between male and female members of the Cistercian Order, the Premonstratensians, the Dominicans, and

---

[1] Robert Johnson's recent book, *The Fisher King and the Handless Maiden* (HarperSanFrancisco; 1993), testifies to the persistent influence of medieval romance on the contemporary literary and therapeutic imagination. Social themes have been traced ·in works such as Georges Duby, *The Knight, the Lady and the Priest: The Making of Modern Marriage in Medieval France*, trans. Barbara Bray (New York: Pantheon, 1983), and William H. McNeill, *Plagues and Peoples* (Garden City, NY: Doubleday, 1976). Barbara Tuchman's *A Distant Mirror: The Calamitous Fourteenth Century* (New York: Knopf, 1978) remains a well-known statement of the manifold political, economic, and military influence of the Middle Ages on the twentieth century.

others. In the later Middle Ages, the tendency to resolve such conflicts by violent and destructive actions on the part of both churchmen and statesmen became increasingly manifest, first against individual "pseudo-women" such as Marguerite Porete and St. Joan of Arc, then towards a countless host of victims of the witchcraft mania of the fifteenth and subsequent centuries.

The effort to define and redefine gender relationships in the Middle Ages demarcates less a Christian than a *European* enterprise which affected the court, the world of letters, commerce, the university, civic life, and not least of all the family, as demonstrated in the strained situations we glimpse in anecdotes from the lives of St. Catherine of Siena and Margery Kempe. But the most volatile zone of intersexual tension was undeniably the church. In that regard, the present essays are of particular significance because of the light they shed on matters of historical fact as well as of doctrinal influence and textual dependence, areas still overshadowed by the dark heritage of Christian misogyny.

Misogyny and Mysticism

Early in the Middle Ages, it was commonly accepted among both religious and secular writers that women as a whole were not only deficient in reason, but morally weak and therefore prone to sin, especially lapses of a sensual nature.[2] It is therefore hardly surprising to find that women were deprived of legal status except as property, and found themselves hedged in by restrictive moral and physical sanctions not applicable to males. Access to educational opportunities were barred to laywomen except those of noble birth. Careers in law, medicine, commerce, teaching, much less military service, were virtually nonexistent.

For any respectable woman, the available paths of personal development were either marriage or a life of consecrated virginity as a nun safely walled into a monastery. Widows, even queens such as St. Elizabeth of Hungary, could be turned out of home or castle at the whim of the dominant male authority. Eleanor of Aquitaine was imprisoned for fifteen years by her husband, Henry II.[3] In regard to

[2] "The classical idea of woman as defective male was augmented by the Middle Ages' view of her as moral cripple: if Eve had not disobeyed, we would all still be in the Garden of Eden. Disobedience was Eve's worst sin, but only one of many. Her defective reason was passed along, with the result that all her daughters were also more prone to vice." Frances Beer, *Women and Religious Experience in the Middle Ages* (Woodbridge, Suffolk and Rochester, NY: Boydell Pres), 1992), 22.

[3] See Desmond Seward, *Eleanor of Aquitaine: The Mother Queen* (New York: Dorset Press, 1978), 137–51. Eleanor had, of course, conspired against Henry and set his sons against him. It is not without significance, however, that she generously favored the great double monastery at Fontrevrault, which had been founded by Robert of Arbrissel as a haven for "all female victims of society, especially those who had been ill-treated by men." (Seward, 197–98.)

the church, which was often the most favorable environment for women of talent and ambition, even abbesses had few rights and little protection outside their own walls.

The roots of Christian misogyny are ancient, as Michael Sells observes.[4] Some of the sources which directly influenced medieval attitudes have been vividly adumbrated by Frances Beer in her recent book, *Women and Religious Experience in the Middle Ages*. As early as the second century, Tertullian (c. 160–c. 240) accused women of responsibility for the fall of Man, not just of men:

> Do you not know that you are Eve? . . .God's sentence still hangs over all your sex and his punishment weighs down upon you. . . . You are the one who opened the door to the devil, you are the one who first deserted the divine law. . . . All too easily you destroyed the image of God, man. Because of [you] . . . even the Son of God had to die.[5]

According to Clement of Alexandria, "every woman should be overwhelmed with shame at the thought that she is a woman."[6] Thus, for St. Jerome, "She who serves Christ will cease to be a woman and will be called a man."[7] Jerome's antagonism towards women is wholesale: "Lift the corner of the dress," he wrote, "and you will find the tip of the tail."[8]

While more temperate in his attitude and language, Augustine, too, took a dim view of women's intellectual and moral capabilities. He rested his case on the Pauline texts that warned, "If [women] want to learn anything, they should ask their husbands at home" (1 Cor. 14:35), for as "Christ is the head of every man, . . . a husband is the head of his wife" (1 Cor. 11:3). Women should not presume to teach, then. Augustine also endorsed the view that women are by nature weak—carnal, deficient in understanding, and unable to rule their own concupiscence.[9] St. John Chrysostom, the patriarch of Constantinople, was even more brief and pointed in this regard: "The woman taught once, and ruined all . . . The sex is weak and fickle. . . . The whole female race transgressed. . . ."[10]

[4] See Sells, note 27.

[5] Tertullian, 'The Apparel of Women,' trans. E. A. Quain, *The Fathers of the Church* (New York: n.p., 1959), 188. Cited, Beers, 3.

[6] Beers, 3.

[7] Beers, 3.

[8] Beers, 3. See Jane Barr, "The Influence of St. Jerome on Medieval Attitudes to Women," in *After Eve: Women, Theology, and the Christian Tradition*, ed. Janet Soskice (London: Collins-Marshall Pickering, 1990), 89–102.

[9] See Ritamary Bradley, *Julian's Way: A Practical Commentary on Julian of Norwich* (London: HarperCollins, 1992), 20–21. Her citations from Augustine are taken from his *Commentary on the Gospel of John*, Tractate 15, chap. 41–42.

[10] Beer, 21.

Similar passages from both Greek and Latin Fathers could be multiplied indefinitely. By the High Middle Ages, Andreas Cappellanus was thus able to articulate a cumulatively encompassing vision of female depravity:

> According to the nature of [her] sex . . . every woman is by nature a miser, . . . she is also envious and a slanderer of other women, greedy, a slave to her belly, inconstant, fickle in her speech, disobedient and impatient of restraint, spotted with the sin of pride . . . , a liar, a drunkard, a babbler, no keeper of secrets, too much given to wantonness, prone to every evil, and never loving any man in her heart.[11]

Similar arguments are produced in the *Ancrene Riwle* as a motive for a woman's becoming a recluse:

> It was commanded in the Old Law that a pit should always be covered; and if an animal fell into an uncovered pit, the man who had uncovered the pit had to pay the penalty. These are terrible words for the woman who shows herself to men's sight. . . . The pit is her fair face, and her white neck, and her light eye, and her hand. . . . She is guilty . . . and must pay for his soul on the Day of Judgment.[12]

Gottfried von Strassburg, in his secular romance, *Tristan*, echoes the view of woman's insatiable concupiscence: "Women do many things just because they are forbidden."[13] For Gottfried and other medieval writers, to the extent that a woman rises above her nature and overcomes such debasing tendencies, she has in effect ceased to be a woman, as Jerome and other early theologians had urged:

---

[11] Beer, 22–23, citing Andreas Cappellanus, *The Art of Courtly Love*, trans. J. J. Parry (New York: Frederick Unger, 1969), 201.

[12] *The Ancrene Riwle*, trans. M. B. Salu (London: n.p., 1959), 3. Cited by Beers, 3. *The Nun's Rule*, another English treatise for anchoresses, describes woman's condition in terms of Eve's being tempted by the forbidden fruit, especially of sexuality: "This apple, my dear sister, symbolizes all those things towards which desire and sinful delight turn. When you look upon a man, you are in Eve's case; you are looking at the apple. . . . [Eve] has many daughters who, following their mother, answer in the same way: 'But do you think . . . that I shall leap upon him because I look at him?' God knows, my dear sister, more surprising things have happened. Your mother, Eve, leapt after her eyes had leapt; from the eye to the apple, from the apple in paradise down to the earth, from earth to hell, where she remained in prison, four thousand years and more, together with her husband, and she condemned all her children to leap after her, to endless death." Beers, 4.

[13] Gottfried von Strassburg, *Tristan*, trans. A. T. Hatto (Harmondsworth: Penguin, 1960), 277. Cited by Beers, 4, along with several other contemporary passages from French literature of the period. The citation continues, "God knows, these same thistles and thorns are inborn in them! . . . In the first thing she ever did . . . [Eve] proved true to her nature and did what was forbidden! . . . She wanted none but that one thing in which she devoured her honour! Thus they are all daughters of Eve who are formed in Eve's image after her."

> When a woman grows in virtue despite her inherited instincts and gladly
> keeps her honour, reputation and person intact, she is only a woman in
> name, but in spirit she is a man! . . . When a woman lays aside her
> woman's nature and assumes the heart of a man, it is as if the fir dripped
> with honey, . . . a nettle bore roses above ground![14]

The logical outcome of such diatribes were works such as the *Malleus
Maleficarum*, the "Hammer of Witches."[15] Published in 1486 by two Dominican
friars from the southern Rhineland, it is surely the most vicious misogynist work of
the later Middle Ages, one which provided both justification and procedures for the
interrogation, torture, and execution of thousands of women (and men) on the
mere accusation of witchcraft.

It is against this infamous background that the women mystics of the earlier
Medieval Period appear in such striking contrast and provide an instructive parallel
for many women today. The place of Meister Eckhart as mystical *lebemeister* and
lesemeister in the midst of the flowering of women's spirituality in the thirteenth and
fourteenth centuries also assumes new significance in view of the accomplishments
and catastrophes being revealed by historical and textual discoveries regarding those
remarkable women.

Eckhart and His Sources: A Widening Circle

In reassessing the place of Meister Eckhart in German spirituality and literature,
the preceding essays affirm not only that Eckhart was far from being a
theological and philosophical aberration, but was a preacher and teacher closely
in touch with the dominant concerns of his world, preeminently the rising
spiritual aspirations of women.

As Frank Tobin and Maria Lichtmann (and elsewhere Oliver Davies[16]) have
shown, connections between Eckhart and the women mystics of the previous
century were noted very early in the present period of recovery first by Wilhelm
Preger and Heinrich Denifle and then by Herbert Grundmann and Josef Koch. But
the likelihood that direct influence might have been at work seems to have dawned
very slowly on the scholarly world. Only recently has the true extent to which
Eckhart was indebted to the women mystics of the preceding generation begun to
be revealed by critical textual comparison.

---

[14] *Tristan*, 278. Cited by Beers, 5.

[15] *Malleus Maleficarum* (Reprint, London: Hogarth Press, 1969).

[16] Oliver Davies, *Meister Eckhart: Mystical Theologian* (London: SPCK, 1991), esp. 76–77.

The studies presented in this volume significantly advance the textual integration of Eckhart's doctrine with that of Hadewijch of Antwerp, Mechthild of Magdeburg, and especially the French Beguine and martyr, Marguerite Porete. The importance of this last tragic figure for Eckhart studies has received increasing recognition since the discovery by Romana Guarnieri in 1946 that she was the author of *The Mirror of Simple Souls*. Only in the mid-1980s, however, Kurt Ruh, Edmund College, J. C. Marler, and other scholars began to argue that Eckhart composed his sermon *Beati pauperes spiritu* specifically with Porete's teachings in mind.[17] The possible influence of Beatrice of Nazareth and other Beguines on Eckhart has yet to be assessed.

Matters of Influence

Whatever else may be said about the sources and impact of the great Rhineland mystics of the thirteenth and fourteenth centuries, the originality and frequent profundity of their respective doctrines remains undeniably evident, a fact which can be eclipsed by the fascinating hunt among them for the elusive quarry, "influence." Despite the equally undeniable and inviting similarity of certain teachings and modes of expression, literary or even doctrinal *dependence* must still often be postulated and remains largely inferential, particularly with regard to the female predecessors of Meister Eckhart.[18] What flows into the watershed of Eckhart's sermons and treatises from Mechthild's or Marguerite Porete's books or the poetry of Hadewijch is less easily identified than what flows out of it into the sermons and writings of subsequent centuries, including the metaphor of flux itself.

Clearly, however, the dominant mystical currents of this spiritual flood-period coursed along the linguistic banks of the Rhine, from the high Swiss and middle high German Alps to the low and middle lowlands of the Brabant, Flanders, and Holland. That there were certain nodal intersections—whether chronological, ideological, or geographical—is also plain.[19] But how these elements of language

---

[17] Additional references and discussion regarding these developments can be found in Ellen Babinsky's introduction to her translation of *The Mirror of Simple Souls*, Classics of Western Spirituality Series (New York: Paulist Press, 1993), 5 and 49f.

[18] As Michael Sells aptly remarks in regard to the striking similarity between Eckhart's and Marguerite's works, "This affinity is not dependent upon any direct textual influence or upon any personal relationship between the two writers. The resonances between the two sets of writings would be just as profound in the unlikely event that Eckhart had never read or heard any of Porete's ideas." (note 72.)

[19] Several authors have referred to Oliver Davies' suggestion of a plausible "link" between Mechthild of Magdeburg and Eckhart in Dietrich of Apolda, a Dominican friar of Erfurt whose writings cite the Latin version of the *Flowing Light of the Godhead*. (Davies, *Meister Eckhart*, 60.)

and doctrine were connected and which way influence passed is not so self-evident. Did the second Hadewijch influence Eckhart or did Eckhart influence the second Hadewijch, as Saskia Murk-Jansen asks in her retrospective analysis of the dispute between A. C. Bouman and J. van Mierlo. Was the influence possibly even reciprocal? Could Eckhart's use of language have influenced Henry of Nördlingen's translation of *The Flowing Light of the Godhead* as much as Mechthild's language and doctrine contributed to Eckhart's style and content? Is it even possible that Eckhart's early teaching had some indirect "influence" on the development of Marguerite Porete's doctrine?

Even given the growing likelihood that significant passages in Eckhart's sermons and treatises contain specific references to the works of his mystical predecessors, overall, it still seems virtually axiomatic that *as a whole* the texts and teachings of Hadewijch of Antwerp, Mechthild of Magdeburg, Marguerite Porete (and Hildegard of Bingen, for good measure) are more different than alike with regard to each other and especially to Eckhart, as Frank Tobin underscores clearly in relation to Mechthild. Moreover, the acknowledged (and indeed fascinating) "parallels" among the women mystics do not pertain uniformly to the most salient features of Eckhart's doctrine.

Here, Oliver Davies' argument that in citing Hildegard's characteristic and delightful use of "greenness" (*viriditas*) as a spiritual metaphor, Eckhart intentionally altered its meaning, a twist which would have been obvious to anyone familiar with her writings, provides a useful model for looking at some of the images found in Eckhart and Mechthild, Hadewijch, and Marguerite Porete.[20]

Hadewijch and Eckhart

In 1991, Oliver Davies drew attention to important textual parallels between Eckhart and Hildegard of Bingen as well as Mechthild and Marguerite Porete while questioning the likelihood that the Saxon Eckhart would have been able to understand Hadewijch's Netherlands dialect.[21] Saskia Murk-Jansen's carefully

---

[20] Davies, *Meister Eckhart*, 57–59. The reversal of valence with regard to *viriditas* in Eckhart's development of desert imagery is also conveyed by Hildegard's use of "dryness" (*ariditas*), which characterizes the desert as a place of chaos and drought deprived of beauty and blessing rather than one of peace and stillness. The desert for Eckhart represents the final stage of the spiritual journey—union with God. In *Predigt* 48 he describes the soul's desire to "go into the simple ground, into the quiet desert in which distinction never gazed, not the Father, nor the Son, nor the Holy Spirit. . . ." True blessedness is thus found "in the soul's return to its divine ground" (Colledge-McGinn trans., 198).

[21] Davies, *Meister Eckhart*, 79, note 1.

nuanced study seems to have overcome that objection, and also reopened the case with regard to the possibility that reciprocal influence might have been at work with respect to the later poems *if* they were not actually by the hand of the thirteenth-century figure. Thus, however improbable at first glance, the "influence" on Eckhart of the little-known Dutch Beguine may have been profound. As Murk-Jansen and Paul Dietrich urge with persuasive force, the poems of the "later" Hadewijch clearly resonate with some of Eckhart's most distinctive themes.

Still, despite similarity, the existence of passages in the writings of Hadewijch, Beatrice of Nazareth, Mechthild of Magdeburg, Marguerite Porete, and even, as Michael Sells affirms, Al Junayd,[22] which "parallel" or "echo" phrases or themes in Eckhart's sermons and treatises are not sufficient by themselves to provide evidence of influence, whether direct or indirect. Mystics may not all come from the same country and speak the same language, but even if they do tend to draw water from the same wells, that need not imply that they use each others' cups.

Mechthild and Eckhart: Sin and Virtual Existence

Formally, the writings of Eckhart and Mechthild could scarcely be more dissimilar. For the most part, both their doctrine and their modes of expressing it are also very different. Mechthild's single book is a mélange of styles—allegory, legend, dialogue, poetry, prayers, visions and other revelations, commentary, and letters. Eckhart's many German and Latin works fall into four categories: sermons, treatises, commentaries on Scripture, and fragments of technical scholastic discussion. Mechthild fills her book with imagery. Fascinated with eschatology as well as the protocols of courtly love, she provides descriptive maps of purgatory, hell, along with demons and angels, suffering souls, Christ, Mary, and a variety of saints—all rare or absent in Eckhart. Her references to the Sacred Heart and the divinity of Mary are unique.[23]

Eckhart's work is lean and stark by comparison, his doctrine and style as apophatic as Mechthild's are kataphatic. Mechthild's book is also virtually devoid of the Meister's most characteristic themes: the birth of the Word in the soul, detachment, the reciprocal nothingness of God and creatures, essential identity with the Son, the equality of justice, the simplicity and purity of God and the soul, the obstacles to union with God, "breakthrough," and the return of all things to

---

[22] Sells, note 42.

[23] For examples of the latter, see *The Revelations of Mechthild of Magdeburg (1210 to 1297), or The Flowing Light of the Godhead*, trans. Lucy Menzies (London: Longmans Greens, 1953), 65 (hereafter: Menzies).

God—most of them tinged with the Christian Neo-Platonism associated with the school of Albert the Great.

Yet, there are areas of overlap—themes and images, even matters of verbal similarity between the two mystical writers which are sufficiently close to suggest influence.[24] One of these is the image of the desert, which Frank Tobin has subjected to linguistic scrutiny, along with the themes of the Trinity and universality.[25]

In regard to the desert theme, Frank Tobin has adequately revealed the scope of similarities and differences between the two German mystics. Suffice it to say that, as with the difference between Hildegard's and Eckhart's use of "greenness" and aridity, Eckhart alters the sense and reference of the metaphor as he inherited it from Mechthild. The difference lies largely in Eckhart's understanding of the mutual groundedness of God and the soul in the divine wilderness, the trackless void wherein lies no distinction of person or ontological differentiation between Creator and creature. For Eckhart, that desert is not the origin or the proving ground, nor even the soul, but the ultimate destination of all spiritual encounter.

Also of interest are certain themes, and their linguistic similarity, which apparently occasioned opposition to Mechthild and were formally attacked in Eckhart's work as heretical. Paramount among them is the acceptance of sinfulness as the condition for receiving God's mercy. Mechthild writes, "I would rather be clothed with hell and crowned by all devils than be without my sin."[26] Similarly, in the *Book of Divine Consolation*, Eckhart explains,

> . . . because in some way or other it is God's will that I should have sinned,
> I should not want not to have done so, for in this way God's will is done
> "on earth," that is, in misdeeds, "as it is in heaven," that is, in good deeds.
> Thus a man wishes to be deprived of God for God's own sake and for

[24] Menzies suggests as much on page xxvi, citing Dom Gall Morel, ed., *Das fliessende Licht der Gottheit (Einsiedeln MS 277)* (Regensburg, 1869); see also Menzies, 17, n. 1.

[25] In Umberto Eco's *roman à clef, The Name of the Rose* (New York: Harcourt Brace Jovanovich, 1983), Eckhart himself does not appear. However, his name is mentioned (unfavorably) by his ideological adversaries, the Spiritual Franciscans traveling to Rome in the train of their nominalist hero, William of Ockham, whose name is likewise mentioned (favorably), but who also fails to appear. Eckhart's influence is more sharply felt in the reflections of the narrator, the monk Adso, who in the beginning and end of his account describes his longing for the "silent desert where diversity is never seen, in the privacy where no one finds himself in his proper place. . . . the silent and uninhabited divinity where there is no work and no image" (501). The penultimate citation in Eco's novel, "*Got is ein lauter Nichts, ihn rührt Nun noch Hier,*" is from Angelus Silesius' seventeenth-century poetic paraphrase of Eckhart, but the phrases appear in several of the Meister's sermons, e.g., Pr. 59 and Pr. 69.)

[26] Menzies, Book VI, 1: 167–68.

God's own sake to be separated from God, and that alone is true
repentance for my sins.[27]

Eckhart's reason is that someone should be "so much of one will with God that he
wills everything that God wills, and in the fashion in which God wills it."
    Similarly, in his earlier *Talks of Instruction*, Eckhart had said:

> Yes, that man would indeed be established in God's will who would not
> wish that the sin into which he had fallen had never been committed, not
> because it was against God, but since, through that, you are obliged to
> greater love, and, through that, brought low and humbled. He should only
> wish that he had not acted against God.[28]

That there is a significant difference in their accounts is revealed in Mechthild's
qualification of her own statement:

> . . . there is no sin so small
> That it is not an eternal blot
> On our souls. Why? Because no sin
> Was ever so changed into holiness
> That it were not better
> Never to have been committed.[29]

She concludes in terms very foreign to Eckhart's approach:

> Therefore if we would stand well with God
> We must stand prayerfully before Him
> In fear.

    A second example of Eckhart's shifting the metaphorical significance of
common themes is found in the two mystics' description of the preexistence of the
ideas of creatures in the mind of God. Mechthild asks,

> Where was God before He created all things? He was in Himself and all
> things were present and open to Him as they are today. How was our Lord
> God set there? Everything was enclosed in God just as in a cell without
> lock or door. The lower part of the cell is a bottomless prison below every
> abyss. The upper part is a height above all other heights. The circum-
> ference of the cell is inconceivable. God had not yet become the creator;
> when He did create all things, the cell was opened up. God is complete in

---

[27] DW 5: 22, 5–8. 10, Colledge-McGinn trans., 216–17.
[28] Colledge-McGinn trans., 261–62.
[29] Menzies, Book VII, 27: 227.

Himself and will ever remain complete. When He became Creator, all creatures became manifest in themselves; man, in order to love, enjoy and know God and be obedient to Him; birds and beasts to know their own nature. . . .[30]

Eckhart's typical statements tend to "echo" the last sentence in particular:

God *becomes* when all creatures say "God"—then God comes to be.

When I subsisted in the ground, in the bottom, in the river and font of Godhead, no one asked me where I was going or what I was doing: there was no one to ask me. When I flowed forth, all creatures said "God." If anyone asked me, "Brother Eckhart, when did you leave your house?", then I was in there. That is how all creatures speak of God.[31]

Again,

While I yet stood in my first cause, I had no God and was my own cause. . . . I was free of God and all things. But when I left my free will behind and received my created being, *then* I had a God. For before there were creatures, God was not "God": He was That which He was. But when creatures came into existence and received their *created* being, then God was not "God" in Himself—He was "God" in creatures.[32]

Once again, the ground has been subtly altered, away from the sense of brooding confinement in a cell first to the surging, ebullient life of an underground river, then to an apparently ordinary house. Moreover, Eckhart expands the notion that before Creation, creatures were unmanifest to the startling and paradoxical view that before Creation, God was not God.[33]

The Case of Marguerite Porete

Considerable attention has been given in the present collection to the life and teaching of Marguerite Porete and the likelihood that Eckhart not only knew her

[30] Menzies, Book VI, 31: 195.

[31] Pr. 26, Walshe trans., No. 56, Vol. II, 81.

[32] Pr. 52, Walshe trans., No. 87, Vol. II, 271.

[33] Eckhart shares the theme of the virtual preexistence of creatures in God also with Beatrice of Nazareth, Hadewijch, and Marguerite Porete. But in each instance, there are variations that suggest differential development rather than simple borrowing. With Eckhart, "breaking-through" to union with God is not so much a reversion to a precreated state, characterized by a kind of metaphysical sleep, as the realization of a new way of being what one always was only now forever and fully "awake."

story and her doctrine, but to a considerable degree (just how considerable is still debatable) sympathized with her teaching.

Two areas of recent discussion warrant notice—the problem that embodiment posed for Porete and Eckhart, and the struggle towards "gender-parity" which affected not only them but other mystical aspirants of the time.

Embodiment

In contextualizing the variegated milieux in which Marguerite Porete and other medieval women mystics found themselves ranged against a phalanx of male persecutors and protectors, Amy Hollywood and Michael Sells emphasize the place of the body in the interpretation of both experience and doctrine. Redefining embodiment and bodily ways of knowing was a crucial element in the spirituality of the Beguines, and as such constituted metaphysical as well as practical grounds for tension with their male instructors, antagonists, counterparts (Richard Rolle and Henry Suso being exceptions), and biographers.

John Giles Milhaven has recently explored the ethical and epistemological implications of this factor in his important study, *Hadewijch and Her Sisters: Other Ways of Loving and Knowing*.[34] Milhaven couples "bodily knowing" with "loving mutuality" as joint themes characteristic of but not limited to Hadewijch and her circle. The experience and value of friendship, particularly spiritual friendship, between medieval women and men occupied the focus of other leading figures, from Aelred of Rievaulx to the Friends of God. And it is precisely the mutuality present (or absent) in these relationships that is the salient feature. The employment of language rich in bodily metaphors for knowing has, moreover, provided ample matter for critics then and now who remain committed to "traditional" interpretative criteria for evaluating the relationships among males and females with regard to knowing and loving: "male" representing reason, disembodied knowledge, and sufficiency, whereas female stands for emotion, feeling, impulsiveness, eros, and, of course, deficiency, echoes of which are present even in Porete as well as Eckhart.

Eckhart's attitude toward the body is thus an important area of exploration in regard to the complex relationship of his teaching with Beguine spirituality before his time as well as during and after it.

---

[34] John Giles Milhaven, *Hadewijch and Her Sisters* (Albany: State University of New York Press, 1993).

Eckhart and the Body

Without doubt, Eckhart taught consistently that one of the three obstacles to union with God was human corporeality.[35] And while Amy Hollywood accurately assesses the spirit of both Eckhart's and Marguerite Porete's effort "to subvert the association of women with the body, suffering, and Christ's suffering humanity" by means of apophasis, she also exaggerates in claiming that the Meister *rejected* "bodily and ecstatic forms of spirituality." I suggest, rather, as Frank Tobin notes in regard to visions and ecstasies,[36] that unlike Porete, Eckhart nowhere "vilifies" or disparages the body as "wretched" or "corrupt." He indeed establishes "the moral neutrality of the body," just as he accepts the inescapable reality of suffering without either denouncing it or endorsing it. Eckhart directs our attention *beyond* the body, time, suffering, and ecstatic imagination.

Hollywood does not exaggerate, on the other hand, in claiming that by "undercutting the place of asceticism, paramystical phenomena, and visionary experience in the religious life, Porete and Eckhart effectively undermine the main avenues of religious authority and expression open to women in their culture" (p. 112). This is especially true in the case of suffering pain as a means of attaining sanctification, a view which Eckhart tacitly repudiates.

The Quest for Parity

Marguerite Porete's silence at her trial has been interpreted in varying ways. Very likely, it conveyed, among other things, her protest at being judged by an all-male tribunal for whom her right to speak at all on matters theological was nonexistent to begin with. And this primarily because of her gender. Similar if less drastic actions were taken or at least threatened in the cases of Hildegard of Bingen and Mechthild of Magdeburg, and later of two Doctors of the Church, Sts. Catherine of Siena and Teresa of Avila.

The attempt to achieve equality among women and men was a vital element in the new religious movements of the Middle Ages, one which did not always end in tragedy or stalemate. In her analysis of the letters between the fourteenth-century

---

[35] For instance, in Pr. 12: "There are three things that prevent us from hearing the eternal Word. The first is corporeality, the second is multiplicity, the third is temporality. If a man had transcended these three things, he would dwell in eternity, he would dwell in the spirit, he would dwell in unity and in the desert—and there he would hear the eternal Word." (Walshe trans., No. 57, Vol. II, 83. See also Pr. 29.)

[36] Tobin, 45: "Eckhart nowhere condemns visions and ecstasies; rather, he pays them scant attention while, at the same time, emphasizing the astonishing union with God possible to souls based simply on their nature as his creatures."

Dominican nuns and their spiritual advisers, Debra Stoudt has pointed to "insights into the divergent attempts religious women made at asserting their own spiritual identity and offering the male confessors some advice and guidance of their own."[37] In the period immediately after Eckhart, she notes:

> It is Margaretha Ebner's single letter to Heinrich of Nördlingen that offers the greatest step toward spiritual partnership between two equals. . . . Heinrich's true accomplishment is the fostering of the mystical gifts given to others, particularly Margaretha. Margaretha responds to his nurturing of her spirit by revealing her own very personal feelings: her illness and her wish that Heinrich visit Medingen. From Henry's more numerous letters it is clear that he treasured their friendship highly. Based on epistolary evidence, it is between Margaretha and Heinrich that there is the most spiritual reciprocity.[38]

Other examples can be cited from Mechthild,[39] as well as from the life of Eckhart's disciple Henry Suso, whose spiritual friendship with Elsbet Stagl created some of the finest epistolary literature of the Middle Ages.[40]

How much Eckhart himself contributed to the sense of mutuality and equality among women and men, and especially in this regard the Beguines and Dominican nuns with their Dominican and other spiritual advisors, is difficult to assess. Eckhart's language exalts equality, particularly the identity of all human persons because of their common nature, which was redeemed and divinized by the Incarnation.[41]

---

[37] Debra Stoudt, "The Production and Preservation of Letters by Fourteenth-Century Dominican Nuns, " *Medieval Studies* 53 (1991): 325.

[38] Stoudt, 326.

[39] Beer observes in her regard, "Contemporary heterosexual models [of union with God] tended to be unequal; in marriage, the husband was dominant; in the courtly relationship the knight became the vassal, bowing down before his often aloof lady. But the lovers in Mechthild's experience are equal because they are of the same nature, and their longing for one another is fully mutual. With this affirmation of her essential participation, by nature, in the divine, Mechthild transcended the medieval misogynist view of women as "naturally" corrupt, and found the confidence to speak out—insisting on the legitimacy of her own voice and experience" (159).

[40] Such achievements of parity were not restricted to the Rhineland mystics, as Frances Beer relates of Margaret Kirkby and the fourteenth-century mystic, Richard Rolle: " . . . the bond of love between Margaret and Richard was one of mutual benefit: as she was helped along her spiritual path, so he was able to attain a degree of tenderness and generosity that on his own might not have been possible. For him, to love God perfectly was not so difficult as to love another soul well; in this respect, perhaps Margaret was the leader, and Richard the disciple" (Beer, 129).

[41] For an exploration of the development of this Christian Neo-Platonic theme in Eckhart, see Richard Woods, O.P., "I am the Son of God: Eckhart and Aquinas on the Incarnation," *Eckhart Review* (June 1992): 27–46.

On the other hand, as several authors have noted, Eckhart sometimes reverts to stereotypical notions of male supremacy in characterizing (for instance) the *ratio superior*, the highest intellect, as "the man of the soul," and so forth. But it likewise seems evident from the apocryphal literature associated with Eckhart, especially "Meister Eckhart's Daughter"[42] and "Schwester Katrei,"[43] that Eckhart was perceived, perhaps within his lifetime, as an advocate and practitioner of gender parity and reciprocity.

To the limited extent the medieval effort to establish parity between women and men can be said to have succeeded, its greatest triumphs occurred among the outstanding religious figures of the period. But with the exception of the Cistercian abbesses of the twelfth and thirteen centuries and the Friends of God in the Rhineland a century later, such successes were normally restricted to personal, even individual relationships—spiritual friendships in which the equality extolled by Mechthild and Eckhart was most closely approximated. But like the tradition of courtly love from which they drew much of their inspiration, the Platonic relationships between such holy friends did not long survive the "century born to woe." The execution of Joan of Arc in 1431 on charges of witchcraft and heresy presaged a reign of religious terror that blackened the skies of Europe for two centuries with the smoke of execution, a holocaust disproportionately female in composition. Only in the nineteenth century did civil and religious emancipation again rise to the fore of European consciousness. Not entirely by chance, the mid-nineteenth century also witnessed the scholarly rediscovery of the mystical literature of the Middle Ages.

If those two currents of liberation continued to flow in largely separate channels for another century, it is at least now evident in the growing confluence of our own era that the spirit of freedom is inseparable from the spirit of justice. Marguerite Porete's "Little Church" is gradually, painfully rediscovering the meaning and value of women in its journey towards wholeness.

Destabilizing Gender Disparity

Michael Sells has argued persuasively that both Porete and Eckhart sought to "undo" gender distinctions by a linguistic destablization of gender distinctions in regard to God. Whether this was consciously Eckhart's intention may be debated, and the Meister waffles occasionally in his political correctness. The evident fact that

---

[42] Walshe, Vol. III, 138–39.

[43] "The 'Sister Catherine' Treatise," trans. Elvira Borgstädt, *Meister Eckhart: Teacher and Preacher*, ed. Bernard McGinn, Classics of Western Spirituality Series (New York: Paulist Press, 1986), 347–87.

Eckhart intentionally reduced the erotic aspect of the Beguines' portrayals of union with God can, however, be cited in favor of "degendering" God.

More questionable is Sells' interpretetation of Eckhart's trinitarian theology in light of the double birth metaphor (the birth of the Word in the bosom of the Father and the birth of the Word in the soul of the just). Sells fails to differentiate precisely enough with regard to intricate, often reciprocal references, both implicit and explicit, to the (distinct) Persons of the Trinity and the (indistinct) *Gottheit* which unites them. In terms of divinity, the union of Trinitarian Persons is one of indistinction, insofar as it is not their common divinity which distinguishes the Persons, but their relations, as Eckhart would have assumed. Similarly, the culminating union of creature and Creator is a union of indistinction. But the unions are not the same, since they differ ontologically. (The opposite would be the case with respect to the hypostatic union, in which the two natures of Christ differ ontologically in the unity of a single Person.) Thus, the generation of the Word/Son pertains to the distinction of Persons. God does not *as God* generate/beget/give birth to the Word/Son, but *as Father*. Which is to say that the Word/Son is generated/begotten/born not *as God*, but *as Son*.[44]

Conclusion: Widening the Circle

In attempting to establish the provenance of Eckhart's fundamental themes and characteristic expressions in the writings of his predecessors, some danger exists of reducing a preacher and writer of brilliance, creativity, and true influence to the stature of a compiler of other people's ideas and phrases, in the main women and men of demonstrably lesser brilliance and linguistic mastery. But whatever else he was, Eckhart was no mere redactor or revisionist who polished the clumsier expressions of his mystical predecessors and rendered them more theologically palatable to ecclesiastical and scholastic tastes.

The present studies of Eckhart's use of themes and expressions current in his milieu illustrate, rather, how a preacher, theologian, and master of language transformed such themes, and by deepening and grounding them in the greater tradition of Christian mysticism related the spiritual quest of his generation to the

---

[44] Within the parameters of Christian theology, it is nevertheless correct (if paradoxical) to say that the Virgin Mary is the Mother of God, not because she is somehow the "ground" of divinity (the Godhead), but the mother of Jesus Christ, the Incarnate Word/Son of God who is truly both God and human. She is not, however, the Mother of God in the sense of "Mother of the Father" or "Mother of the Holy Spirit," nor is she "Mother of the Trinity." The title is Christological and pertains to the hypostatic union of natures in Christ by virtue of which Mary is the mother of the whole Christ—divine and human, head and members.

older and wider pursuit. That Eckhart ultimately failed to persuade his ecclesiastical critics that many of the suspect doctrines of mystics such as Hadewijch, Mechthild of Magdeburg, and the tragic Marguerite Porete were consonant with the ancient tradition of Christian apophaticism says more about the confusion of the times and the preoccupations of the Academy and the Chancery than it does of Eckhart's diminishing powers. His own fidelity to the church remained unshaken to the end. But Eckhart also knew the difference between ancient tradition and scholastic pettifoggery and thus never wavered in his conviction that neither in intention nor expression were the suspect propositions heretical, including those which which "echoed" or "paralleled" the condemned propositions of Marguerite Porete.

Some concluding reflections may be in order at this point. First, it is manifestly impossible any longer to fully understand or appreciate the mystical doctrine of Meister Eckhart without reference to the great women mystics who preceded him and to the influx of whose ideas he was directly or indirectly indebted—most notably Hildegard of Bingen, Hadewijch of Antwerp, Mechthild of Magdeburg, and Marguerite Porete. Eckhart's motives for incorporating Beguine teachings in particular into his teaching remain unclear. Undoubtedly, their currency among the many women religious entrusted to his care and preaching ministry demanded some attention. But the degree to which these ideas penetrated Eckhart's message thematically, especially the Poretian allusions in his *Predigt* 52, *Beati pauperes spiritu*, strongly suggests that this "prince of medieval mystics," the progenitor of German as a theological language, and master preacher, entertained much more than a superficial or tactical sympathy with the vision and aspirations of those remarkable women.

Second, the comparative study of Eckhart's writings and those of his female antecedents has made it clearer that Eckhart's metaphysical preoccupations were neither purely speculative nor original in the sense that they first appear with him. They are, in fact, traditional themes in Christian mystical theology with roots extending at least as far back as third-century Alexandria with Origen. But in several instances, their more immediate provenance must be located in the writings of the Beguine mystics.

Third, as a pastor, Eckhart addressed the concerns of his auditors in terms they were more or less familiar with, but here, according to our authors, he made a two-fold contribution. (1) He located these complex themes (e.g., spiritual poverty, the "spark of the soul," the ontological "nothingness" of God and the soul, the union of indistinction) within a wider context of Christian thought and praxis, including scriptural theology, thereby revealing their orthodox meaning and deeper signifi-cance. (2) He also transformed them into a comprehensive and coherent mystical doctrine, at least the outlines of which are still recognizable despite the fragmentary character of his German works in particular.

Fourth, the authors in this volume do not reduce the significant differences in approach and expression between Eckhart and the women mystics of the thirteenth-century Rhineland (including Marguerite Porete) to that of a fundamental divergence between male and female ways of knowing and loving, which would be simplistic and facile as well as anachronistic. It would also be wrong insofar as their more important (if fewer) similarities belie such a cleavage. Surely what contemporary psychologists refer to as "cognitive style," rooted in personality type and environmental factors rather than biology, plays at least as important a role in determining modes of mystical expression as do the canons and conventions of readership and venue in the academy, the convent chapel, and the street corner.

Fifth, the present contributors seem keenly aware, on the other hand (as are Carolyn Bynum Walker, John Giles Milhaven, and other scholars), that a significant difference in modes of discourse with regard to ways of knowing and loving estranged all these mystics, male and female, from the ecclesiastical and academic commissions which sat in judgment on them in their own day and since. However implicit the recognition, it seems evident that the Academy and the Curia understand that the tensions introduced into theological discourse by the innovative use of language by the Beguines and their supporters among the Rhineland mystics threatened to subvert the established order of the day. Changing words changes the world.

Finally, widening the circle of resources from which Eckhart drew to create his sermons to include the great women mystics of the preceding era in no way diminishes the luster of his originality. Rather, it augments the stature of his creativity, revealing his sensitivity to the crucial spiritual and indeed theological issues which these prophetic figures had raised to new levels of awareness and expression. It also further unveils Eckhart's mastery at weaving these themes often seamlessly into the fabric of his own teaching, sometimes transforming them in order better to expose their consonance with the age-old (and ever-new) mystical tradition he sought to interpret for his own times.[45]

---

[45] Although known from his own times by his academic title, and the only medieval figure to be so remembered forever, Eckhart's Christian name has not been forgotten, as Michael Sells suggests (27). Eckhart *was* his Christian name. (See Woods, *Eckhart's Way*, 23, n. 1.)

Select Bibliography in English

Beer, Frances. *Women and Religious Experience in the Middle Ages*. Woodbridge, Suffolk, and Rochester, New York: Boydell Press, 1992.

Bowie, Fiona, ed. and introduction, with Oliver Davies, trans. *Beguine Spirituality: Mystical Writings of Mechthild of Magdeburg, Beatrice of Nazareth, and Hadewijch of Brabant*. New York: Crossroad, 1990.

Bynum, Caroline Walker, Steven Harrell, and Paula Richman, eds. *Gender and Religion: On the Compexity of Symbols*. Boston: Beacon Press, 1986.

Bynum, Caroline Walker. *Holy Feast and Holy Fast: The Religious Significance of Food to Medieval Women*. Berkeley: University of California Press, 1987.

Colledge, Edmund, and J. C. Marler. "'Poverty of the Will': Ruusbroec, Eckhart and *The Mirror of Simple Souls*." In *Jan van Ruusbroec: The Sources, Content and Sequels of His Mysticism*. Leuven: University of Leuven Press, 1984: 14–47.

Davies, Oliver. *Meister Eckhart: Mystical Theologian*. London: SPCK, 1991.

De Ganck, Roger, trans. and annotation. *The Life of Beatrice of Nazareth, 1200–1268*. Kalamazoo: Cistercian Publications, 1991.

Dronke, Peter. *Women Writers of the Middle Ages: A Critical Study of Texts from Perpetua (d. 203) to Marquerite Porete (d. 1310)*. Cambridge: Cambridge University Press, 1984.

Hadewijch: The Complete Works. Translated by Mother Columba Hart. New York: Paulist Press, 1980.

Lerner, Robert E. *The Heresy of the Free Spirit in the Later Middle Ages*. Berkeley: University of California Press, 1972.

McDonnell, Ernest W. *The Beguines and Beghards in Medieval Culture: With special emphasis on the Belgian scene*. New Brunswick: Rutgers University Press, 1972.

McGinn, Bernard. "Love, Knowledge and *Unio mystica* in the Western Christian Tradition." In *Mystical Union and Monotheistic Faith*. Edited by Moshe Idel and Bernard McGinn. New York: Macmillan, 1989: 59–86.

McGinn, Bernard. *The Foundation of Mysticism: Origins to the Fifth Century*. New York: Crossroad, 1991.

Meister Eckhart: The Essential Sermons, Commentaries Treatises and Defense. Edited by Edmund Colledge and Bernard McGinn, New York: Paulist Press, 1985.

Meister Eckhart: Teacher and Preacher. Edited by Bernard McGinn with the collaboration of Frank Tobin and Elvira Borgstädt. Preface by Kenneth Northcott. New York: Paulist Press, 1987.

Meister Eckhart: Sermons and Treatises. Edited and translated by M. O'C. Walshe. 3 vols. Longmead, Shaftesbury, Dorset: Element Books, 1987.

Milhaven, John Giles. *Hadewijch and Her Sisters.* Albany: State University of New York Press, 1993.

Murk-Jansen, Saskia. *The Measure of Mystic Thought: A Study of Hadewijch's Mengeldichten.* Goppingen: Kummerle, 1991.

Petroff, Elizabeth Alvida, ed. *Medieval Women's Visionary Literature.* New York: Oxford University Press, 1986.

Porete, Marguerite. *The Mirror of Simple Souls.* Translation and introduction by Ellen Babinsky. Preface by Robert Lerner. New York: Paulist Press, 1993

Sells, Michael A. *Mystical Languages of Unsaying.* Chicago: University of Chicago Press, 1994.

Stoudt, Debra L. "The Production and Preservation of Letters by Fourteenth-Century Dominican Nuns." *Medieval Studies* 53 (1991): 309–26.

Tobin, Frank. *Meister Eckhart: Thought and Language.* Philadelphia: University of Pennsylvania Press, 1986.

The Revelations of Mechthild of Magdeburg (1210 to 1297), or The Flowing Light of the Godhead. Translated by Lucy Menzies. London: Longmans, Greens, 1953.

Weeks, Andrew. *German Mysticism from Hildegard of Bingen to Ludwig Wittgenstein: A Literary and Intellectual History.* Albany: State University of New York Press, 1993.

Woods, Richard, O.P. *Eckhart's Way.* Collegeville, Minn: Liturgical Press, 1986.

Zum Bruun, Emilie and Georgette Epiney-Burgard. *Women Mystics of Medieval Europe.* New York: Paragon House, 1989.